ESSAYS IN THE ECONOMICS
OF EXHAUSTIBLE RESOURCES

CONTRIBUTIONS
TO
ECONOMIC ANALYSIS

150

Honorary Editor
J. TINBERGEN

Editors
D. W. JORGENSON
J. WAELBROECK

NORTH-HOLLAND
AMSTERDAM · NEW YORK · OXFORD

ESSAYS IN THE ECONOMICS
OF
EXHAUSTIBLE RESOURCES

Edited by
M. C. KEMP and N. V. LONG

1984

NORTH-HOLLAND
AMSTERDAM · NEW YORK · OXFORD

ISBN 0 444 86791 0

Published by:
ELSEVIER SCIENCE PUBLISHERS B.V.
P.O. Box 1991
1000 BZ Amsterdam
The Netherlands

Sole distributors for the U.S.A. and Canada:
ELSEVIER SCIENCE PUBLISHING COMPANY INC.
52 Vanderbilt Avenue
New York, N.Y. 10017
U.S.A.

Library of Congress Cataloging in Publication Data

Main entry under title:

Essays in the economics of exhaustible resources.

(Contributions to economic analysis ; 150)
Includes indexes.
1. Natural resources--Addresses, essays, lectures.
2. Natural resources--Mathematical models--Addresses,
essays, lectures. I. Kemp, Murray C. II. Long, N. V.
III. Series.
HC13.2.E87 1984   333.7   84-6080
ISBN 0-444-86791-0

PRINTED IN THE NETHERLANDS

Introduction to the series

This series consists of a number of hitherto unpublished studies, which are introduced by the editors in the belief that they represent fresh contributions to economic science.

The term "economic analysis" as used in the title of the series has been adopted because it covers both the activities of the theoretical economist and the research worker.

Although the analytical methods used by the various contributors are not the same, they are nevertheless conditioned by the common origin of their studies, namely theoretical problems encountered in practical research. Since for this reason, business cycle research and national accounting, research work on behalf of economic policy, and problems of planning are the main sources of the subjects dealt with, they necessarily determine the manner of approach adopted by the authors. Their methods tend to be "practical" in the sense of not being too far remote from application to actual economic conditions. In addition they are quantitative rather than qualitative.

It is the hope of the editors that the publication of these studies will help to stimulate the exchange of scientific information and to reinforce international cooperation in the field of economics.

The Editors

Preface

This collection of essays is a sequel to our *Exhaustible Resources, Optimality, and Trade*, published by North-Holland in 1980. Since the appearance of the earlier collection, the economics of exhaustible resources has continued to be a prime focus of theoretical and empirical research. Like its predecessor, the present collection is a contribution to an ongoing process, not a stock-taking at the end of the process. However, we do include a brief essay on the current state of the art.

As with the earlier collection, the essays have been written by past and present members of the University of New South Wales and the Australian National University. However, not all of the writing was done at those institutions. During the winter of 1979–80 Kemp was a visitor at the Hebrew University of Jerusalem and the University of Tel-Aviv, and in March and April of 1982 he was a guest of Columbia University; and during the second half of 1982 Long was a visitor first at the University of Mannheim, then at the CORE, University of Louvain. We are deeply appreciative of the stimulating research environments in which we were able to work on those occasions.

Most of the essays are completely new. However, six of the shorter essays are revisions of papers which first appeared elsewhere. Thus, Essay 3 first appeared in the *Journal of International Economics* (1982), Essay 6 in A. Ulph and A. Ingham, eds., *Demand, Equilibria and Trade: Essays in Honour of Professor Ivor Pearce* (Macmillan, 1984), Essays 7 and 12 in W. Eichhorn et al., eds., *Economic Theory of Natural Resources* (Physica-Verlag, Würzburg, 1982), and Essays 9 and 10 in the *International Economic Review* (1983). To the proprietors of those publications we are grateful for permission to reprint.

Contents

PART 1

INTRODUCTION

The state of the art

MURRAY C. KEMP and NGO VAN LONG

1. Introduction

Since its beginnings, nearly two hundred years ago, the working or policy-oriented branches of economic theory have rested on the notion that primary or non-produced factors of production, which together with knowledge of methods of production are the ultimate sources of supply, yield their services in steady immutable streams, for ever. To this broad generalization the recognition that productivity can be raised, on the average, by schemes of crop rotation, and that land can be run down by over-use or improved by the application of fertilizers and by capital outlays on drainage, terracing, fencing, etc. is a minor exception – a small ripple on the surface of the classical pond.

The disruption of world raw-materials markets in the early 1970s drew attention to the inadequacy of standard theory; in particular, it focused attention on the failure of the theory to accommodate exhaustible natural resources, that is, primary factors of production which yield their services not in steady and immutable flows but in variable and controlled flows for just as long as the resource-stocks survive.

The omission is not a trivial one. Thus, in 1977 the value added by mining accounted for 3.5 percent of U.S. gross national product and in 1980 minerals and fuels accounted for 29 percent of the value of world commodity exports. (If the latter calculation had been in terms of value added the share would have been much higher.)

During the past decade there has been a sustained effort to reconstruct economic theory in the light of resource exhaustibility.[1] Most of the

---

[1] There were pioneers – one thinks of Gray (1914), Hotelling (1931), Scott (1955), and Herfindahl (1967) – but their work passed almost unnoticed when it appeared.

Essays in the Economics of Exhaustible Resources, edited by M. C. Kemp and N. V. Long
© *Elsevier Science Publishers B.V., 1984*

traditional policy-oriented branches of theory – notably the theory of price and distribution, the theory of international trade, the theory of public finance, and the economics of welfare – have been effected. In this brief introductory essay we offer an assessment of recent developments, under the four headings: survival, optimal exploitation, competitive market exploitation, and non-competitive market exploitation. We do not pretend that the review is comprehensive. Rather, we focus on what seem to us to have been the more significant developments and on what appear to be the major outstanding gaps. For more detailed expositions of current theory, the reader may turn to three recent symposia, edited by Siebert (1980), Kemp and Long (1980a) and Eichhorn et al. (1982), also the textbook of Dasgupta and Heal (1979); and for a comprehensive statement of the implications of the exhaustibility of resources for the theory of international trade he may consult Kemp and Long (1983).

2. Survival

If an exhaustible and non-renewable resource is itself essential to the production of an essential consumption-good, then the survival of any constant or growing population is in doubt. Of course, survival is assured if nature blesses the community with costless and sufficiently rapid resource-saving technical improvements. But belief in exogenous technical progress is an act of faith for which, nowadays, few economists are prepared. The question of survival then is whether it is possible, by means of investment in research and development or by means of investment in facilities for the production of resource-substitutes, to reduce reliance on the resource rapidly enough to avoid exhaustion of the stock without ever forcing consumption below the survival level.

Evidently the answer to the question depends on (i) the ease with which augmentable raw materials and durable equipment can be substituted for the resource, and on (ii) the ease with which resource-saving improvements in the technology for producing substitute raw materials can be achieved by means of expenditure on research and development. In his pioneering paper on the subject, Solow (1974) concentrated on the first of the two roads to survival. Specifically, he asked whether by the progressive substitution of the services of durable equipment for a resource-based raw material it is possible to place a positive bound under consumption and at the same time ensure that the resource-stock is never exhausted. He showed that if extraction of the resource is costless and if the elasticity of substitution between capital and the resource is constant, then a positive level of consumption can be maintained indefinitely if and only if *either* the elasticity of substitution is greater than one *or* the elasticity of substitution is equal to one and the elasticity of output with respect to capital exceeds the elasticity of output with respect to the resource. Shortly after, Suzuki (1976) explored the second road to survival. Specifically he asked whether it is possible by means of a program of research and development to generate resource-saving technical improvements fast enough to ensure survival in Solow's sense. Confining himself to the Cobb–Douglas case, Suzuki showed that survival is possible if and only if the elasticity of output with respect to cumulative investment in research and development exceeds the sum of the elasticities of output with respect to capital and the resource.

The papers of Solow and Suzuki are landmarks in the analysis of survival. However, they left several questions unasked and unanswered. For example, they were argued in terms of special constant-elasticity-of-substitution production functions, they neglected costs of extraction, and they dealt only with economies closed to international trade and investment. Some of the gaps in their analyses have been filled subsequently. Thus, Mitra (1978) and Buchholz (1982) have derived a necessary and sufficient condition for Solow–survival in a context of general concave production functions; Kemp and Long (1982a) have generalized Solow's condition by allowing for costly extraction; and Mitra et al. (1982) and Kemp and Long (1982b) have derived conditions for the survival of a small open economy which can obtain an essential resource only by trade, on steadily deteriorating terms, with other, relatively resource-rich countries.

The next two essays, which form Part II of the present volume, provide a fairly systematic account of recent developments as well as some modest extensions. Essay 2 is devoted to the problem of survival in a closed economy, Essay 3 to survival in a small open economy.

3. Optimal exploitation

Whether or not survival is assured, one can consider the problem of determining the optimal path of extraction. Indeed, it is this problem which, during the past decade, has been examined most thoroughly. We now have blueprints of the optimal path of extraction of a resource-stock in each of a great variety of circumstances – the resource essential or non-essential, flow substitutes available or unavailable, costs of extraction absent or present, with uncertainty (about the extent of the deposit or the duration of title to it, and about future prices and technology) or with complete certainty, with resource-renewability or without it, with international trade and investment or without them. The details are well known; we therefore content outselves with a brief and selective bibliography: Hotelling (1931), Gale (1967), Stiglitz (1974), Koopmans (1974), Kemp and Suzuki (1975), Long (1974, 1975), Kemp (1976, ch. 23), Gilbert (1979), Loury (1978), Mitra (1980), and Kasanen (1982).

However, almost always the question of optimality has been posed in the context of a single homogeneous resource-stock. In fact, of course, the typical exhaustible resource is available in deposits which vary enormously in quality, including accessibility. When the heterogeneity of deposits is recognized, the optimal path of extraction is seen to have not one but two characteristics: the *rate* of aggregate extraction and the *order* of extraction. Moreover, the path of the optimal rate of extraction depends on the variability of quality over deposits. Thus, to abstract from the heterogeneity of deposits is not merely to simplify the problem of determining the rate of extraction, it is to distort it.

There are exceptions to the general rule. Thus, Robson (1979) has considered the problem of ordering the exploitation of deposits with zero costs of extraction but possibly of unknown extent. He showed that if there are two deposits, one of known extent and the other of unknown size, then it is optimal to exhaust the deposit of unknown extent before turning to the other deposit. Moreover, long ago, Herfindahl (1967) examined the problem of ordering the exploitation of several deposits of known extent and with average costs of extraction constant with respect to the rate of extraction but varying from deposit to deposit. He demonstrated, on the basis of a partial-equilibrium analysis, that it is optimal to exploit the deposits in strict sequence, beginning with the lowest-cost. His finding later was confirmed by Solow and Wan (1976) on the basis of less restrictive assumptions. On the other hand, Kemp and Long (1980b) have shown that there are circumstances in which it is suboptimal to exploit in strict order.

Thus, the Herfindahl–Solow–Wan conclusion has a field of application but lacks complete generality. What is needed is a careful charting of the boundaries of that field. Essays 4–8, which comprise Part III of the volume, only partly meet that need; for example, they are confined to the case of complete certainty. However, they do register progress. Essay 4, which is confined to non-renewable resources, provides a unifying summary and generalization of earlier work, as well as several new findings. In Essay 5 the deposits are taken to be self-renewing. In Essays 6–8, on the other hand, it is assumed that there exists, or can be made to exist (by expenditure on research and development), a technology capable of producing (from non-exhaustible factors of production) a flow substitute for the resource. The problem of ordering there takes a slightly different form: It must be decided when to introduce the flow substitute or when to begin investing in the creation of a technology capable of producing the substitute.

4. Competitive market exploitation

Given the optimal plan for the exploitation of available resource-deposits, can that plan be effected by a system of free competitive markets? The question has been the subject of a desultory and inconclusive debate. It has been held by several authors, and denied by others, that there are properties of exhaustible resources which may make it impossible for competitive markets to sustain efficient extraction; indeed, it has been suggested that uncertainty about the extent of resource-stocks is incompatible with perfect competition. Specifically, it has been argued, by Hotelling (1931) and by Weinstein and Zeckhauser (1975), that, under conditions of perfect foresight, competitive extraction is necessarily efficient; but Heal (1980) has denied the proposition. Similarly, it has been argued, by Weinstein and Zeckhauser (1975), Heal (1975), and Hoel (1978, 1980), that if particular kinds of uncertainty prevail and if resource-extracting firms are averse to risk, then extraction will be inefficient; but Kemp and Long (1980a, ch. 5) have denied the claim, arguing that, given enough markets (in both flows and stocks), competitive extraction is necessarily efficient. Finally, it has been argued by Kemp and Long (1980a, ch. 4) that if resource-stocks are of uncertain extent, then rational behaviour by firms may be incompatible with perfect competition. In Essay 12 of the present volume an attempt is made to sort out and settle these issues.

It should be noted that the debate just alluded to has nothing to do with standard arguments for competitive inefficiency. Thus, throughout the debate it has been taken for granted that the competitive outcome may be inefficient if markets are incomplete, if price expectations are unreliable, if there are technical externalities or public intermediate goods, or if there are unavoidable moral hazards. Thus, whatever the final adjudication of the debate, there is bound to be a case for tax-subsidy or other interference with market processes. But the theory of tax incidence, even in competitive markets, is largely a static and partial-equilibrium theory and therefore is not immediately applicable to economies of the type studied in this volume. There is need of a new dynamic analysis of tax-subsidy incidence in economies combining capital accumulation and resource depletion. Essay 13 contains the elements of such a theory and, in particular, corrects a widespread misunderstanding concerning the desirability of allowing "true economic depreciation" as a tax deduction for mining firms.

5. Non-competitive market exploitation

Historically, the exploitation of important exhaustible resources (like tin, bauxite, and oil) has been under the intermittent control of international cartels. And the recent interest of governments in off-shore fishing and mining has inevitably injected an oligopolistic element into some markets. The modelling of oligopolistic markets for exhaustible resources is still in its infancy. (For a very brief survey of recent developments, see Kemp and Long (1983, sections 8–10).) Essays 10 and 11 are fair samples of the state of the art. Essay 10 models the oligopolistic market for a renewable resource, Essay 11 the market for a non-renewable resource.

References

Buchholz, W. (1982), On the possibility of economic growth with exhaustible resources, in: W. Eichhorn et al., eds. Economic Theory of Natural Resources (Physica-Verlag, Würzburg and Vienna) pp. 295–299.
Dasgupta, P. A. and G. M. Heal (1979), Economic theory and Exhaustible resources (James Nisbet, London).
Eichhorn,W., R. Henn, K. Neumann and R. W. Shephard, eds. (1982), Economic Theory of Natural Resources (Physica-Verlag, Würzburg and Vienna).
Gale, D. (1967), On optimal development in a multi-sector model, Review of Economic Studies 34, 1–18.
Gilbert, R. J. (1979), Optimal depletion of an uncertain stock, Review of Economic Studies 66, 47–57.
Gray, L. C. (1914), Rent under the assumption of exhaustibility, Quarterly Journal of Economics 28, 66–89.
Heal, G. (1975), Economic aspects of natural resource depletion, in: D. W. Pearce and J.

Rose, eds., The Economics of Natural Resource Depletion (Macmillan and Company, London) pp. 118–139.

Heal, G. (1980), Intertemporal allocation and intergenerational equity, in: H. Siebert, ed., Erschöpfbare Ressourcen (Arbeitsfagung des Vereins für Social politik, Mannheim 1979) (Duncker and Humbolt, Berlin) pp. 37–73.

Herfindahl, O. C. (1967), Depletion and economic theory, in: M. M. Gaffney, ed., Extractive Resources and Taxation (University of Wisconsin Press, Madison, Wisconsin) pp. 63–90.

Hoel, M. (1978), Resource extraction when a future substitute has an uncertain cost, Review of Economic studies 45, 637–644.

Hoel, M. (1980), Extraction of an Exhaustible Resource under Uncertainty (Verlag Anton Hain, Königstein).

Hotelling, H. (1931), The economics of exhaustible resources, Journal of Political Economy 38, 137–175.

Kasanen, E. (1982), Dilemmas with infinitesimal magnitudes: The case of the resource depletion problem, Journal of Economic Dynamics and Control 4, 295–301.

Kemp, M. C. (1976), Three Topics in the Theory of International Trade (North-Holland Publishing Company, Amsterdam).

Kemp, M. C. and N. V. Long (1980a), Exhaustible Resources, Optimality, and Trade (North-Holland Publishing Company, Amsterdam).

Kemp, M. C. and N. V. Long (1980b), On two folk theorems concerning the extraction of exhaustible resources, Econometrica 48, 663–673.

Kemp, M. C. and N. V. Long (1982a), A note on Solow's survival problem, Economics Letters 10, 381–384.

Kemp, M. C. and N. V. Long (1982b), Conditions for the survival of a small resource-importing economy, Journal of International Economics 13, 135–142.

Kemp, M. C. and N. V. Long (1983), The role of natural resources in trade models, in: R. W. Jones and P. B. Kenen, eds., Handbook of International Economics (North-Holland Publishing Company, Amsterdam).

Kemp, M. C. and H. Suzuki (1975), International trade with a wasting but possibly replenishable resource, International Economic Review 16, 712–732.

Koopmans, T. C. (1974), Proof for a case where discounting advances the doomsday, Review of Economic Studies, Symposium on the Economics of Exhaustible Resources, 117–120.

Long, N. V. (1974), International borrowing for resource extraction, International Economic Review 15, 168–183.

Long, N. V. (1975), The pattern of resource extraction under uncertainty about possible nationalization, Journal of Economic Theory 10, 42–53.

Loury, G. C. (1978), The optimal exploration of an unknown reserve, Review of Economic Studies 45, 621–636.

Mitra, T. (1978), On maintaining consumption levels and exhaustible resources, State University of New York at Stony Brook, Working Paper 198.

Mitra, T. (1980), On optimal depletion of exhaustible resources: Existence and characterization results, Econometrica 48, 1431–1450.

Mitra, T., M. Majumdar and D. Ray (1982), Feasible alternatives under deteriorating terms of trade, Journal of International Economics 13, 105–134.

Robson, A. (1979), Sequential exploitation of uncertain deposits of a depletable natural resource, Journal of Economic Theory 21, 88–110.

Scott, A. (1955), Natural Resources: The Economics of Conservation (University of Toronto Press, Toronto).

Siebert, H., ed. (1980), Ersochöpfbare Ressourcen (Arbeitsfagung des Vereins für Social-politik, Mannheim 1979) (Duncker and Humblot, Berlin).

Solow, R. M. (1974), Intergenerational equity and exhaustible resources, Review of

Economic Studies, Symposium on the Economics of Exhaustible Resources, 29–45.

Solow, R. M. and F. Y. Wan (1976), Extraction costs in the theory of exhaustible resources, Bell Journal of Economics 7, 359–370.

Stiglitz, J. E. (1974), Growth with exhaustible natural resources: Efficient and optimal growth paths, Review of Economic Studies, Symposium on the Economics of Exhaustible Resources, 123–137.

Suzuki, H. (1976), On the possibility of steadily growing *per capita* consumption in an economy with a wasting and non-replenishable resource, Review of Economic Studies 43, 527–535.

Weinstein, M. C. and R. J. Zeckhauser (1975), Optimal consumption of depletable natural resources, Quarterly Journal of Economics 89, 371–392.

PART II

THE PROBLEM OF SURVIVAL

The problem of survival: A closed economy

MURRAY C. KEMP, NGO VAN LONG and KAZUO SHIMOMURA

1. Introduction

Robert Solow (1974) posed the question: If production requires the input of a raw material derived from an exhaustible resource-stock, if the available stock is finite and non-augmentable, and if technical progress is absent, can a country with a stationary population survive in the sense of generating a consumption stream bounded above zero? Evidently the possibility of survival depends on the ease with which augmentable factors can be substituted for the non-augmentable raw material, and Solow proceeded to give precision to this intuitive notion. He showed that if extraction of the resource is costless and if the elasticity of substitution between capital and raw material is constant, then a positive level of consumption can be maintained if and only if either (i) the elasticity of substitution is greater than one or (ii) the elasticity of substitution is equal to one (that is, the production function is Cobb–Douglas) and the elasticity of output with respect to capital exceeds the elasticity of output with respect to the resource (that is, the capital exponent of the Cobb–Douglas production function exceeds the raw-material exponent).

That is an elegant answer to an interesting question. However, one may wonder how the answer stands up if Solow's specifications are relaxed, i.e. if the production function is not CES, if extraction of the resource is costly, if man-made technical improvements are possible, and if there is more than one essential raw material.

We take up each part of the puzzle in turn. In section 2 we re-examine Solow's question without the assumption of a constant elasticity of substitution. Given as background only very mild restrictions on the

Essays in the Economics of Exhaustible Resources, edited by M. C. Kemp and N. V. Long
© *Elsevier Science Publishers B.V., 1984*

production function (notably, non-increasing returns to scale in capital and the raw material alone, and indispensibility of the raw material), it is shown that consumption can be maintained at a positive level if and only if there is some positive level of output such that the area under the isoquant corresponding to that output, from the initial stock of capital to infinity, is finite. It is easy to verify that in the CES case this condition reduces to Solow's. It is shown also that, in the Cobb–Douglas case, if survival is feasible, then consumption can be made to grow without bound, at an exponential rate which approaches a positive constant. Next, in section 3, the analysis is extended to accommodate any number of essential raw materials, each derived from a finite and non-augmentable resource-stock. It is shown that the condition for survival derived in section 2 generalizes in a natural way. In section 4 we tack in a different direction. There allowance is made for the possibility that extraction of the resource is costly. It is shown that if the production function satisfies the very mild background assumptions of section 2 and if the extraction function satisfies even weaker assumptions, then the condition for survival remains unchanged. In section 5 we extend the analysis of section 2 in yet another direction, by introducing the possibility of man-made technical improvements. It is shown that, subject to some very weak restrictions on the "technical-progress function" and to some reinterpretation of terms, the condition derived in section 2 remains valid. Thus, that condition is revealed to be quite robust, relevant in a considerable variety of circumstances.

   We are not the first to have laboured in Solow's field. Several of the propositions set out below are already known in some form or other. Special mention must be made of the highly original papers of Suzuki (1976), Mitra (1978), and Buchholz (1982); detailed reference will be made to these and other papers as we proceed. Our purpose has been the pedagogic one of knitting together old and new propositions with the aid of common assumptions which are exceedingly weak but which yet retain enough teeth to allow brief and straightforward proofs.

2. More general production functions

We consider a very simple economy which, however, allows us to pose our question with a minimum of distracting complication.

   There is a single produced commodity which serves both as consumption good and as capital good. Net output y is a function of the capital stock k, the flow of raw material m, and the flow of labour l.

However, the population and labour force are constant, so we may write, simply:[1]

$$y = f(k, m).$$ (1)

It is assumed that

$$\partial f/\partial k \equiv f_k > 0, \qquad \partial f/\partial m \equiv f_m > 0, \quad \text{for all } (k, m) > 0,$$ (2a)

$$f(k, 0) = 0, \quad \text{for all } k \geq 0,$$ (2b)

$$\lambda f(k, m) \leq f(\lambda k, \lambda m), \quad \text{for all } (k, m) > 0 \text{ and all } \lambda \in [0, 1].$$ (2c)

Thus, the resource is assumed to be indispensable (eq. (2b)), and f is supposed to display non-increasing returns to scale in capital and the raw material alone, which is compatible with any kind of scale returns in all three inputs.[2] Given any attainable output y we can derive from (1) the associated isoquant, the equation to which is

$$m = I^f(k; y),$$ (3)

where it is understood, of course, that k and y take only those non-negative values for which there exists an m such that y can be produced.

We shall say that an allocation $\{k(t), m(t)\}$ is feasible if it satisfies

$$\dot{k}(t) = f(k(t), m(t)) - c(t),$$

$$\int_0^\infty m(t)\,dt < \infty,$$

$$k(t), m(t), c(t) \geq 0,$$ (4)

$$k(0) = k_0, \text{ given.}$$

Theorem 1.[3]   Given (2), the following are equivalent statements.

[1]Output is defined to be net of capital depreciation. Let depreciation be written $\delta(k, m)$. Gross output is then:

$$Y = f(k, m) + \delta(k, m) \equiv F(k, m).$$ (1')

[2]Reverting to footnote 1, if the gross-output function F displays non-increasing returns to scale and if the depreciation function δ displays non-decreasing returns (as is highly plausible), then the net-output function f must display non-increasing returns.

[3]Mitra (1978) provided the prototypical theorem. He restricted his formal analysis to the special case in which output is homogeneous of degree one in capital and the raw material alone, but remarked that the assumption of homogeneity is unnecessary. Unaware of Mitra's work, Buchholz (1982) proved a similar theorem. In the meantime, Cass and Mitra (1979) proved a very general proposition of which the present theorem is a special case. However the price of the Cass–Mitra generality is an extraordinarily complicated proof.

(i) There exists $(k_0, \bar{c}) > 0$ such that (4) is satisfied with $c(t) = \bar{c}$ for all $t \geq 0$.

(ii) There exists $(k^*, y^*) > 0$ such that $\int_{k^*}^{\infty} I^f(k; y^*)\, dk < \infty$.

Proof. Suppose that (ii) is satisfied and consider the allocation defined by

$$y^* = f(k(t), m(t)) \quad \text{or} \quad m(t) = I^f(k(t); y^*),$$

$$c(t) = (1 - s)y^*, \qquad 0 < s < 1, s \text{ constant},$$

$$\dot{k}(t) = sy^*,$$

$$k(0) = k^*.$$

For this allocation,

$$\int_0^{\infty} m(t)\, dt = \int_0^{\infty} I^f(k(t); y^*)\, dt$$

$$= [1/(sy^*)] \int_{k^*}^{\infty} I^f(k; y^*)\, dk,$$

which implies that the allocation is feasible.

Suppose that (i) is satisfied and denote a feasible allocation by $\{\hat{k}(t), \hat{m}(t)\}$. Without loss, we can take $d\hat{k}/dt$ to be non-negative for all $t \geq 0$; therefore, after an appropriate choice of unit, we can take $f(\hat{k}(t), \hat{m}(t))$ to be greater than one for all $t \geq 0$. From (2c), on the other hand,

$$1 \leq f\left(\frac{k}{f(k, m)}, \frac{m}{f(k, m)}\right) \equiv b(k, m) \tag{5}$$

or

$$m = y\, I^f(k/y; b(k, m)),$$

where $b(k, m) \geq 1$. Hence, for the feasible path $\{\hat{k}(t), \hat{m}(t), \hat{y}(t)\}$,

$$\infty > \int_0^{\infty} \hat{m}(t)\, dt$$

$$= \int_0^{\infty} \hat{y}(t)\, I^f(\hat{k}(t)/\hat{y}(t); b(\hat{k}(t), \hat{m}(t)))\, dt$$

$$\geq \int_0^{\infty} \hat{y}(t)\, I^f(\hat{k}(t); 1)\, dt \quad \text{(from (2a), (5) and } y(t) > 1)$$

$$= \int_{k_0}^{\infty} [\hat{y}(t)/(\hat{y}(t) - \bar{c})] I^f(k; 1) \, dk$$

$$\geq \int_{k_0}^{\infty} I^f(k; 1) \, dt. \qquad\qquad\qquad\qquad \text{Q.E.D.}$$

Remark. If $(k_0, \bar{c}) > 0$ satisfies (4) then, from (2c), so does $(\alpha k_0, \alpha \bar{c})$, $0 < \alpha \leq 1$. Thus, if survival is possible for some initial stock of capital, then it is possible for any positive initial stock.

The commonsense of theorem 1 has been provided by Mitra:

... if a positive consumption level is maintainable, then a positive output level should also be maintainable. Along the isoquant of this maintained output level, we must be producing an amount of output, which, after allowing for a positive maintained consumption level, allows for sufficient capital accumulation to offset the effect of a (rapidly) decreasing resource input, and produce on the same isoquant again. This suggests strongly that capital at time t ... must be growing at the rate of t. This in turn should mean that, since the total resource stock is finite, the area under this isoquant from the initial positive capital stock to infinity, must be finite .... (Mitra (1978, pp. 20–21); see also Buchholz (1982, p. 3).)

Example. In the Cobb–Douglas case on which Solow concentrated,

$$y = k^{\alpha} m^{\beta}, \qquad \alpha, \beta > 0, \qquad \alpha + \beta \leq 1,$$

so that the equation for an isoquant is

$$m = I^f(k; y) = k^{-\alpha/\beta} y^{1/\beta},$$

and, if $\alpha > \beta$,

$$\int_{k_0}^{\infty} I^f(k; y) \, dk = -k_0^{1-(\alpha/\beta)} y^{1/\beta}/(1 - (\alpha/\beta)) < \infty.$$

Now consider the feasible allocation

$$\bar{y} = k^{\alpha} m^{\beta}, \qquad \alpha > \beta > 0,$$

$$\bar{c} = (1 - s)\bar{y}, \qquad 0 < s < 1,$$

$$\dot{k} = s\bar{y},$$

$$k(0) = k_0, \text{ given.}$$

and define the function

$$\phi(\gamma) = \int_0^\infty \exp(\gamma t) \cdot m(t)\, dt.$$

By assumption, $\phi(0) < \infty$ whence, from the theory of Laplace transformations, there exists a positive γ^* such that $\phi(\gamma) < \infty$ for all $\gamma \in [0, \gamma^*)$. It follows that the consumption path

$$c = \bar{c} + k^\alpha (m \exp(\gamma t))^\beta - k^\alpha m^\beta$$
$$= \bar{c} + \bar{y}\,(\exp(\beta\gamma t) - 1 > \bar{c}$$

is feasible. But

$$\frac{\dot{c}}{c} = \frac{\beta\gamma\bar{y}\exp(\beta\gamma t)}{\bar{c} + \bar{y}\,(\exp(\gamma t) - 1)},$$

and this expression goes to $\beta\gamma$ as t goes to infinity. Thus, if the production function is Cobb–Douglas and if $\alpha > \beta$, then there is a feasible allocation such that the growth rate of consumption converges to a positive constant.[4]   Q.E.D.

3. Many deposits

Suppose that there is any number of raw materials, each essential to production and each obtained from a finite, non-renewable deposit. The production function is then

$$y = f(k, m_1, \ldots, m_n), \tag{6}$$

where

$$\partial f/\partial k \equiv f_k > 0, \qquad \partial f/\partial m_j \equiv f_j > 0, \quad \text{for all } (k, m_1, \ldots, m_n) > 0, \tag{7a}$$

$$f(k, 0, m_2, \ldots, m_n) = \cdots = f(k, m_1, \ldots, m_{n-1}, 0) = 0,$$
$$\text{for all } (k, m_1, \ldots, m_n) \geqq 0, \tag{7b}$$

$$\lambda f(k, m_1, \ldots, m_n) \leqq f(\lambda k, \lambda m_1, \ldots, \lambda m_n),$$
$$\text{for all } (k, m_1, \ldots, m_n) \geqq 0 \text{ and all } \lambda \in [0, 1]. \tag{7c}$$

---

[4]Buchholz (1982, theorem 2) showed that if the production function is Cobb–Douglas and homogeneous of degree one, and if survival is feasible, then consumption can grow as fast at t^p, where $p < (\alpha/\beta) - 1$.

Consider now the dual cost-minimizing and output-maximizing problems

(P) $\min\limits_{m_1,\ldots,m_n}$ $m \equiv \sum p_j m_j$

       s.t. $f(k, m_1, \ldots, m_n) \geqq \bar{y}$

and

(DP) $\max\limits_{m_1,\ldots,m_n}$ $y \equiv f(k, m_1, \ldots, m_n)$

       s.t. $\sum p_j m_j \leqq \bar{m},$

where p_j, $\bar{m}$, and $\bar{y}$ are positive constants. In view of (7b), corner solutions can be ruled out.

Solving the first-order conditions for (P), we obtain:

$$m_j = h_j(p_1, \ldots, p_n; k, \bar{y}) > 0, \qquad j = 1, \ldots, n,$$

whence, substituting into the objective function for (P):

$$m = \sum p_j h_j(p_1, \ldots, p_n; k; \bar{y})$$
$$\equiv I^f(p_1, \ldots, p_n; k; \bar{y}). \tag{8}$$

Similarly, solving the first-order conditions for (DP) we obtain:

$$m_i = H_i(p_1, \ldots, p_n; k; \bar{m}),$$

whence, substituting into the objective function for (DP):

$$y = f(k, H_1(p_1, \ldots, p_n; k, \bar{m}), \ldots, H_n(p_1, \ldots, p_n; k, \bar{m}))$$
$$\equiv F(p_1, \ldots, p_n; k; \bar{m}). \tag{9}$$

Eq. (8) describes the isoquant $y = \bar{y}$ of the reduced-form production function F defined by (9). Moreover, F has the same properties as f in section 2:

$$\partial F/\partial k \equiv F_k > 0, \qquad \partial F/\partial m \equiv F_m > 0, \quad \text{for all } (k, m) > 0, \tag{10a}$$

$$F(p_1, \ldots, p_n; k, 0) = 0, \quad \text{for all } k \geqq 0, \tag{10b}$$

$$\lambda F(p_1, \ldots, p_n; k, m) \leqq F(p_1, \ldots, p_n; \lambda k, \lambda m),$$

$$\text{for all } (k, m) \geqq 0 \text{ and all } \lambda \in [0, 1]. \tag{10c}$$

Hence, applying theorem 1, we have:

Lemma 1. Given (10), the following are equivalent statements.

(i) There exists $(k_0, \bar{c}) > 0$ and $(p_1, \ldots, p_n) > 0$ such that

$$\dot{k}(t) = F(p_1, \ldots, p_n; k(t), m(t)) - \bar{c}, \qquad k(0) = k_0,$$

$$k(t), m(t) \geqq 0, \quad \text{for all } t \geqq 0,$$

$$\int_0^\infty m(t)\, dt < \infty$$

(ii) There exists $(k^*, m^*) > 0$ and $(p_1, \ldots, p_n) > 0$ such that $\int_{k^*}^\infty I^f(p_1, \ldots, p_n; k; y^*)\, dk < \infty$.

Lemma 1 comes to life only when (i) is related to the definition of survival. Let us say that an allocation $\{k(t), m_1(t), \ldots, m_n(t)\}$ is feasible if it satisfies

$$\dot{k}(t) = f(k(t), m_1(t), \ldots, m_n(t)) - c(t),$$

$$k(0) = k_0, \text{ given,}$$

$$k(t), m_1(t), \ldots, m_n(t), c(t) \geqq 0, \quad \text{for all } t \geqq 0, \tag{11}$$

$$\int_0^\infty m_j(t)\, dt < \infty, \qquad j = 1, \ldots, n,$$

and let us suppose that for some $(k_0, \bar{c}) > 0$ there is a feasible allocation $\{k^*(t), m_1^*(t), \ldots, m_n^*(t)\}$. Then for each $t \geqq 0$ and for any positive constant $p_1, \ldots, p_n$, we can consider the problem:

(P')
$$\min_{m_1, \ldots, m_n} \quad m \equiv \sum p_j m_j$$
$$\text{s.t. } f(k^*(t), m_1^*(t), \ldots, m_n^*(t)) \leqq f(k^*(t), m_1, \ldots, m_n).$$

Denoting by $\{\tilde{m}_1(t), \ldots, \tilde{m}_n(t)\}$ the solution to (P'), we have:

$$\tilde{m}(t) \equiv \sum p_j \tilde{m}_j(t) \leqq \sum p_j m_j^*(t),$$

which implies (i) from lemma 1. On the other hand, if (i) of lemma 1 is established, then a feasible allocation exists; for, from the construction of F, there exist $m_j(t) = H_j(p_1, \ldots, p_n; k(t), m(t))$, the solutions to (DP) with $k = k(t)$ and $\bar{m} = m(t)$. Thus we arrive at:

Lemma 2. Given (10), the following are equivalent statements.

(i) There exist $(k_0, \bar{c}) > 0$ such that (11) is satisfied with $c(t) = \bar{c}$ for all $t \geqq 0$.
(ii) There exist $(k^*, y^*) > 0$ and $(p_1, \ldots, p_n) > 0$ such that $\int_0^\infty I^f(p_1, \ldots, p_n; k; y^*) \, dk < 0$.

Even lemma 2 is not quite satisfactory since it leaves open the possibility that survival is possible for some positive $(p_1, \ldots, p_n)$ but not for others. However, as is intuitively appealing, the finiteness of the integral is a property of the technology summarized by f and of (k^*, y^*), and is independent of the particular value assigned to $(p_1, \ldots, p_n)$. This is formally established in the following lemma.

Lemma 3. If for some $(k^*, y^*) > 0$ there exists $(p_1, \ldots, p_n) > 0$ such that

$$\int_{k^*}^\infty I^f(p_1, \ldots, p_n; k; y^*) \, dk < \infty, \tag{12}$$

then (12) holds for any $(p_1, \ldots, p_n) > 0$.

Proof. I^f is homogeneous of degree one in $(p_1, \ldots, p_n)$. For any $\mu > 0$, therefore,

$$\int_{k^*}^\infty I^f(\mu p_1, \ldots, \mu p_n; k; y^*) \, dk = \mu \int_{k^*}^\infty I^f(p_1, \ldots, p_n; k; y^*) \, dk < \infty.$$

Moreover, $\partial I^f / \partial p_i \geqq 0$. For any $(\tilde{p}_1, \ldots, \tilde{p}_n) > 0$, therefore, there exists $\mu > 0$ such that $(\mu p_1, \ldots, \mu p_n) > (\tilde{p}_1, \ldots, \tilde{p}_n)$ and

$$I^f(\tilde{p}_1, \ldots, \tilde{p}_n; k; y^*) \leqq I^f(\mu p_1, \ldots, \mu p_n; k; y^*).$$

Hence (12) holds for $(\tilde{p}_1, \ldots, \tilde{p}_n)$. Q.E.D.

Combining lemmas 2 and 3, we obtain:

Theorem 2. Given (10), the following are equivalent statements.
(i) There exists $(k_0, \bar{c}) > 0$ such that (11) is satisfied with $c(t) = \bar{c}$ for all $t \geqq 0$.
(ii) There exists $(k^*, y^*) > 0$ such that for any $(p_1, \ldots, p_n) > 0$:

$$\int_{k^*}^\infty I^f(p_1, \ldots, p_n; k; y^*) \, dk < \infty.$$

Example. In the Cobb–Douglas case with two deposits:

$$\ln y = \alpha \ln k + \beta_1 \ln m_1 + \beta_2 l_n m_2, \tag{13}$$

where $(\alpha, \beta_1, \beta_2) > 0$ and $\alpha + \beta_1 + \beta_2 \leqq 1$. The equation to the reduced-form isoquant is then:

$$(\beta_1 + \beta_2) \ln m = -\alpha \ln k + \ln y + \text{const.},$$

where $m = \min(p_1 m_1 + p_2 m_2)$ subject to (13). For the area under the isoquant to be finite, and for survival to be feasible, it is necessary and sufficient that $\alpha > \beta_1 + \beta_2$.   Q.E.D.

4. Costly extraction

Let us now take a step in another direction by acknowledging the possibility that extraction of the resource is costly, requiring inputs of both capital and labour. It will be assumed that the extracted raw material is not storable; however, that assumption has no bearing on the conclusions of this section.

Throughout the present section we shall write the output of the consumption good as:

$$y = g(k_1, m, l_1), \tag{14a}$$

and the rate of extraction as:

$$m = h(k_2, l_2), \tag{14b}$$

where k_1 is the amount of capital used in producing the consumption good, etc. and where

$$k_1 + k_2 \leqq k; \qquad l_1 + l_2 \leqq l.$$

Since storage is not possible, there is no harm in using the input symbol m to indicate the output of the raw material also. The functions g and h have properties similar to those assigned to f in section 2:

$$\partial g/\partial k_1 \equiv g_k > 0, \qquad \partial g/\partial m \equiv g_m > 0, \qquad \partial g/\partial l_1 \equiv g_l > 0,$$
$$\text{for all } (k_1, m, l_1) > 0, \tag{15a}$$

$$g(k_1, 0, l_1) = 0, \quad \text{for all } (k_1, l_1) \geqq 0, \tag{15b}$$

$$\lambda g(k_1, m, l_1) \leqq g(\lambda k_1, \lambda m, l_1),$$
$$\text{for all } (k_1, m, l_1) \geqq 0 \text{ and all } \lambda \in [0, 1], \tag{15c}$$

$$\partial h/\partial k_2 \equiv h_k > 0, \qquad \partial h/\partial l_2 \equiv h_l > 0, \quad \text{for all } (k_2, l_2) > 0. \tag{15d}$$

From (14a) we obtain the equation to the isoquant:

$$m = I^g(k_1; y, l_1),$$

where it is understood, of course, that k_1, y, and l_1 take only those non-negative values for which there exists an m such that y can be produced. Finally, we shall say that an allocation $\{k_1(t), k_2(t), l_1(t), l_2(t)\}$ is feasible if

$$\dot{k}_1(t) + \dot{k}_2(t) = g(k_1(t), m(t), l_1(t)) - c(t),$$

$$m(t) = h(k_2(t), l_2(t)),$$

$$\int_0^\infty m(t)\mathrm{d}t < \infty, \tag{16}$$

$$k_1(0) + k_2(0) = k_0, \text{ given},$$

$$k_1(t), k_2(t), m(t), c(t) \geqq 0.$$

Theorem 3.[5]   Given (15), the following are equivalent statements.
  (i) There exists $(k_0, \bar{c}) > 0$ such that (16) is satisfied with $c(t) = \bar{c}$ for all $t \geqq 0$.
  (ii) There exists $(k_1^*, y^*, l_1^*) > 0$ such that $\int_{k_1^*}^\infty I^g(k_1; y^*, l_1^*)\mathrm{d}k_1 < \infty$.

Proof.   Given (ii), consider the allocation defined by:

$$y^* = g(k_1, m, l_1^*) \quad \text{or} \quad m = I^g(k_1; y^*, l_1^*),$$

$$m \leqq h(k_2, l - l_1^*),$$

$$c = (1 - s)y^*, \qquad 0 < s < 1, \text{ } s \text{ constant},$$

$$\dot{k}_1 = bsy^*, \qquad k_1(0) = k_1^*, \qquad 0 < b < 1, \text{ } b \text{ constant},$$

$$\dot{k}_2 = (1 - b)sy^*,$$

where the initial value, $k_2(0)$, is determined by setting $t = 0$ in the first two equations. Since $\dot{k}_j(t) > 0$ for all $t \geqq 0$, $\dot{m}(t)$ is always negative and $\dot{h}$ is always positive. Hence, $m(t) < h(t)$ if $t > 0$, the allocation is feasible, and we arrive at (i).

  Given (i), denote a feasible allocation by $\{\hat{k}_1(t), \hat{k}_2(t), \hat{l}_1(t), \hat{l}_2(t), \hat{m}(t), \hat{y}(t)\}$. Without loss we can take $\mathrm{d}\hat{k}/\mathrm{d}t \equiv \mathrm{d}\hat{k}_1/\mathrm{d}t + \mathrm{d}\hat{k}_2/\mathrm{d}t$ to be non-negative for all $t \geqq 0$; therefore, after an appropriate choice of

---

[5] A Cobb–Douglas version of theorem 3 was established by Kemp and Long (1982).

commodity unit, we can take $f(\hat{k}_1(t), \hat{m}(t), \hat{l}_1(t))$ to be greater than one for all $t \geq 0$. From (15c), on the other hand:

$$1 \leq f\left(\frac{k_1}{f(k_1, m, l_1)}, \frac{m}{f(k_1, m, l_1)}, \frac{l_1}{f(k_1, m, l_1)}\right)$$

$$\equiv b(k_1, m, l_1),$$

or

$$m = yI^g\left(\frac{k_1}{y}; b(k_1, m, l_1), \frac{l_1}{y}\right),$$

where $b(k_1, m, l_1) \geq 1$. Hence, for the feasible path $\{\hat{k}_1(t), \hat{k}_2(t), \hat{l}_1(t), \hat{l}_2(t), \hat{m}(t), \hat{y}(t)\}$:

$$\infty > \int_0^\infty \hat{m}(t)\, dt$$

$$= \int_0^\infty \hat{y}(t) I^g(\hat{k}_1(t)/\hat{y}(t); b(\hat{k}_1(t), \hat{m}(t), \hat{l}_1(t)), \hat{l}_1(t)/\hat{y}(t))\, dt$$

$$> \int_0^\infty \hat{y}(t) I^g(\hat{k}_1(t); 1, l)\, dt$$

$$= \int_{k_0}^\infty [y(t)/y(t) - \bar{c})] I^g(\hat{k}_1; 1, l)\, d\hat{k}$$

$$> \int_{k_0}^\infty I^g(\hat{k}_1; 1, l)\, d\hat{k},$$

and we arrive at (ii).   Q.E.D.

Example.   In the Cobb–Douglas case:

$$y = k_1^\alpha m^\beta l\gamma, \qquad \alpha + \beta \leq 1,$$

$$m = k_2^\delta l_2^\varepsilon, \qquad \delta + \varepsilon \gtreqless 1,$$

and

$$I^g(k_1; y, l_1) = (yk_1^{-\alpha} l_1^{-\gamma})^{1/\beta}.$$

Hence

$$\int_{k_1^*}^{\infty} I^g(k_1; y^*, l_1^*)\, dk_1 = (y^* l_1^{*-\gamma})^{1/\beta} \int_{k_1^*}^{\infty} k_1^{-\alpha/\beta}\, dk_1$$

$$= (y^* l^{*-\gamma})^{1/\beta} \frac{\beta}{\beta - \alpha} [k_1^{(\beta-\alpha)/\beta}]_{k_1^*}^{\infty},$$

which, if and only if $\alpha > \beta$, is finite for all

$$(y^*, k_1^*, l_1^*) > 0. \qquad\qquad\qquad\qquad\qquad \text{Q.E.D.}$$

5. Technical progress

In section 2 we asked whether a country with a limited and unaugmentable stock of an essential resource can survive by substituting augmentable equipment for the resource. The entire ensuing investigation was conducted under the ground rule that the state of the art is invariant through time.

It will be apparent that the question asked in section 2 can be turned about, with the stock of capital invariant through time and the state of the art augmentable by investment in research and development. It will be apparent also that if the state of the art is a simple integral of such investment, then theorem 1, with k reinterpreted as the state of the art, remains relevant.

In fact, one can state a generalization of theorem 1. To achieve this extension one adds to the production function (1) the relationship

$$\dot{k} = q(y - c), \qquad y - c \geqq 0, \tag{17a}$$

where

$$q \in \mathscr{C}^1, \quad q'(y - c) > 0. \tag{17b}$$

(In Suzuki (1976) one finds the special constant-elasticity form $\dot{k} = (y - c)^\xi$, $0 < \xi < 1$, and in section 2 the even more special linear form $\dot{k} = y - c$.) With (4) generalized to include (17a), theorem 1 remains valid. The proof needs only minor modification, notably after the change in the variable of integration, where appeal is made to (17b).[6]

---

[6] A Cobb–Douglas version of the extended theorem 1, with investment in both equipment and ideas, was provided by Suzuki (1976).

References

Buchholz, W. (1982), On the possibility of economic growth with exhaustible resources, in: W. Eichhorn, R. Henn, K. Neumann and R. W. Shephard, eds., Economic Theory of Natural Resources (Physica-Verlag, Würzburg and Vienna) pp. 295–299.

Cass, D. and T. Mitra (1979), Persistence of economic growth despite exhaustion of natural resources, University of Pennsylvania, CARESS Working Paper 79-27.

Kemp, M. C. and N. V. Long (1982), A note on Solow's survival problem, Economics Letters 10, 381–384.

Mitra, T. (1978), On maintainable consumption levels and exhaustible resources, State University of New York at Stony Brook, Working Paper 198.

Solow, R. M. (1974), Intergenerational equity and exhaustible resources, Review of Economic Studies, Symposium on the Economics of Exhaustible Resources, 29–45.

Suzuki, H. (1976), On the possibility of steadily growing *per capita* consumption in an economy with a wasting and non-replenishable resource, Review of Economic Studies 43, 527–535.

The problem of survival: An open economy

MURRAY C. KEMP and NGO VAN LONG*

1. Introduction

Suppose that a small country is totally dependent upon its trading partners for an essential raw material derived from an exhaustible and non-renewable resource-stock. Suppose, further, that the net price (that is, price less average cost of extraction) of the raw material is rising exponentially. (Hotelling (1931) has shown that the net price of the raw material must behave in this way if the rest of the world is competitive and enjoys perfect myopic foresight.) Such a country will progressively economize in its use of the material by substituting for it the services of durable produced inputs or capital. Can the strategy of substitution succeed, in the restricted sense of imposing a positive lower bound on per capita consumption? Can it succeed in the sense of making possible ever-growing per capita consumption?

It will be shown that, for a Cobb–Douglas economy, a positive and growing level of per capita consumption is possible if and only if technical progress takes place at a sufficiently rapid rate, the required rate depending on the rate of growth of consumption. For a modest defence of the use of Cobb–Douglas production functions in the analysis of exhaustible resources, see Kemp and Long (1980, appendix).)

Questions similar to ours have been posed and answered in a splendid recent paper of Mitra, Majumdar and Ray (1982). However, their model of production is rather different from ours. On the one hand they work with general no-joint-products production functions and allow the terms

*The authors gratefully acknowledge the constructive comments of Carl Chiarella, Koji Okuguchi, and Makoto Tawada. An earlier version of the essay appeared in the *Journal of International Economics* 13 (1982) 135–142.

Essays in the Economics of Exhaustible Resources, edited by M. C. Kemp and N. V. Long
© *Elsevier Science Publishers B.V., 1984*

of trade to be non-exponential functions of time. On the other hand, they do not recognize labour as a factor of production and assume that production functions are homogeneous of degree one in capital and the raw material alone. Thus, a precise comparison of our conclusions with theirs is not possible.

2. Analysis

A small country produces a single commodity with the aid of capital, labour, and an imported raw material. The production function is of the Cobb–Douglas type. Thus:

$$y(t) = k(t)^{\alpha} r(t)^{\beta} l(t)^{\gamma} \exp(\beta \lambda t), \qquad 0 < \alpha, \beta, \gamma < 1; 1 - \alpha - \beta > 0, \quad (1)$$

where $y(t)$ is total output at time t, $k(t)$ is the stock of capital at time t, $r(t)$ is the input of the imported raw material at time t, $l(t)$ is the input of labour at time t, and λ is the constant rate of resource-saving technical progress. Thus, there are no restrictions on returns to scale with respect to all three factors jointly, but it is required that returns to scale with respect to capital and the raw material alone are declining. The labour force is assumed to be constant and, by choice of units, equated to one, so that (1) reduces to:

$$y(t) = k(t)^{\alpha} r(t)^{\beta} \exp(\beta \lambda t), \qquad 0 < \alpha, \beta < 1; 1 - \alpha - \beta > 0. \quad (2)$$

The produced commodity can be consumed, invested, or exported in exchange for the raw material. The net world price of the raw material, in terms of output, grows exponentially. Thus, if $p(t)$ is the gross price of the material and ε is the constant average cost of extraction,

$$p(t) - \varepsilon = [p(0) - \varepsilon] \exp(\delta t), \qquad \delta \text{ constant.}$$

However, the cost of extraction plays only a nuisance role in our analysis: none of the conclusions of the paper depends on the value assigned to ε; indeed, they remain unchanged if ε declines monotonically under the pressure of technical improvements in extraction. We therefore simplify at the outset by setting $\varepsilon = 0$ and writing

$$p(t) = p(0) \exp(\delta t), \qquad \delta \text{ constant.} \quad (3)$$

International trade is always balanced; moreover, imports of the raw material are immediately fed into the productive process. Thus:

$$y(t) = c(t) + \dot{k}(t) + p(t) r(t), \quad (4)$$

where $c(t)$ is the rate of consumption at time t.

If there is a feasible program which allows for survival (or survival-cum-growth) then there must be an efficient program with the same property. Hence, we may impose the efficiency condition that at each moment of time the marginal product of the raw material is equated to the price of the raw material:

$$\partial y(t)/\partial r(t) = \beta y(t)/r(t) = p(t). \tag{5}$$

Solving (2), (3), and (5) for $r(t)$:

$$r(t) = \left[\frac{p(0)}{\beta}\right]^{1/(\beta-1)} [k(t)]^{\alpha/(1-\beta)} \exp[(\beta\lambda - \delta)t/(1-\beta)]. \tag{6}$$

Substituting from (6) into (4), and recalling (2) and (3):

$$\dot{k}(t) = a[k(t)]^{\alpha/(1-\beta)} \exp(\theta t) - c(t), \tag{7}$$

where

$$\theta \equiv \beta(\lambda - \delta)/(1-\beta) \tag{8}$$

and

$$a \equiv (1-\beta)\left[\frac{p(0)}{\beta}\right]^{-\beta/(1-\beta)} > 0. \tag{9}$$

Finally, if attention is confined to positive exponential paths of consumption, we have:

$$c(t) = c(0) \exp(gt), \qquad c(0) > 0, \tag{10}$$

and (7) reduces to:

$$\dot{k}(t) = a[k(t)]^{\alpha/(1-\beta)} \exp(\theta t) - c(0) \exp(gt), \qquad c(0) > 0, \tag{11}$$

whence

$$\dot{k} = 0, \quad \text{iff } k(t) = \left[\frac{c(0)}{a}\right]^{(1-\beta)/\alpha} \exp[(g-\theta)(1-\beta)t/\alpha] > 0. \tag{12}$$

Eq. (11) will be the focus of our attention. In particular we must determine the conditions under which it has a positive solution with $g \geq 0$.

We begin by showing that such a solution does not exist if θ is negative.[1]

---

[1] Shimomura (1983) has shown that lemma 1 is valid without the restriction that the production function be Cobb–Douglas.

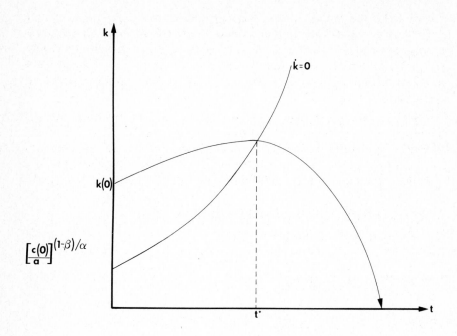

Figure 3.1 $g \geq 0 > \theta$

Lemma 1. If eq. (11) has a positive solution with $g \geqq 0$, then $\theta \geqq 0$. If eq. (11) has a positive solution with $g > 0$, then $\theta > 0$.

Proof. Suppose that

$$g \geqq 0 \geqq \theta, \quad \text{with at least one strict inequality.} \tag{13}$$

It will be shown that $k(t)$ must go to zero in finite time. The proof contains three steps.

First, we note, as an implication of (11) and of the assumption that $g > \theta$ (but independently of the sign of θ), that any trajectory which cuts the curve $\dot{k} = 0$ will hit the time axis in finite time (see fig. 3.1).

Next we note that the path of pure accumulation defined by

$$\dot{z}(t) = a[z(t)]^{\alpha/(1-\beta)} \exp(\theta t), \qquad z(0) = k(0), \tag{14}$$

provides an upper bound for $k(t)$.

Solving (14):

$$z(t) = \begin{cases} \left\{ \dfrac{1-\alpha-\beta}{1-\beta}\dfrac{a}{\theta}[\exp(\theta t)-1]+[k(0)]^{(1-\alpha-\beta)/(1-\beta)} \right\}^{(1-\beta)/(1-\alpha-\beta)} & \text{if } \theta \neq 0, \\[3mm] \left\{ \dfrac{1-\alpha-\beta}{1-\beta} at+[k(0)]^{(1-\alpha-\beta)/(1-\beta)} \right\}^{(1-\beta)/(1-\alpha-\beta)} & \text{if } \theta = 0. \end{cases}$$

$$(15)$$

From (12) and (14), bearing in mind (13), the locus $(z(t),t)$ intersects the locus $\dot{k}=0$ from above in finite time.

Pulling together the above pieces of information we see that any trajectory $\{k(t)\}$ beginning above the locus $\dot{k}=0$ must cut that locus and proceed to the time axis in finite time. Q.E.D.

Lemma 1 eliminates all but the following three cases: (a) $g = \theta \geq 0$, (b) $\theta > g \geq 0$, and (c) $g > \theta > 0$.

Lemma 2(a). If $g = \theta \geq 0$, then eq. (11) has a positive solution if and only if $c(0) \leq a[k(0)]^{\alpha/(1-\beta)}$.

Proof. Consider (11). If $c(0) > a[k(0)]^{\alpha/(1-\beta)}$, then $\dot{k}(t) < 0$ for all $t \geq 0$; indeed, $\dot{k}(t)$ goes to $-\infty$ as t goes to ∞, implying that $k(t) = 0$ in finite time. Hence, $c(0) > a[k(0)]^{\alpha/(1-\beta)}$ is infeasible. If, on the other hand, $c(0) \leq a[k(0)]^{\alpha/(1-\beta)}$, then $\dot{k}(t) \geq 0$. Hence, $c(0) \leq a[k(0)]^{\alpha/(1-\beta)}$ is feasible. Q.E.D.

Remark. From lemma 2(a), if $g = \theta \geq 0$, then the largest maintainable rate of consumption is $a[k(0)]^{\alpha/(1-\beta)}$. If consumption is maintained at that level, $k(t) = k(0)$ and, in view of (6), the rate of input of the raw material rises at the rate $(\beta\lambda - \delta)/(1 - \beta)$, which is negative if and only if $\theta > \delta$.

Lemma 2(b). If $\theta > g \geq 0$, then there exists $c^*(0)$, $c^*(0) > a[k(0)]^{\alpha/(1-\beta)}$, such that eq. (11) has a positive solution if and only if $c(0) \leq c^*(0)$.

Proof. Consider (11). If $c(0) \leq a[k(0)]^{\alpha/(1-\beta)}$, then $\dot{k}(t) > 0$ for all $t > 0$. If $c(0)$ exceeds $a[k(0)]^{\alpha/(1-\beta)}$ by a sufficiently small quantity, then $k(t)$ declines at first and later increases, with k always positive. If $c(0)$ exceeds $a[k(0)]^{\alpha/(1-\beta)}$ by a sufficiently large amount, then $k(t)$ will reach zero in finite time. There is a largest value of $c(0)$, say $c^*(0)$, such that $k(t)$

remains positive for all t. If that value is chosen, $k(t)$ declines asymptotically to zero (the upturn in $k(t)$ is at infinity).   Q.E.D.

Lemma 2(c).   If $g > \theta > 0$, then eq. (11) has a positive solution provided
that $c(0)$ is sufficiently small and $(1 - \beta)\theta/(1 - \alpha - \beta) > g$.

Proof.   From earlier reasoning (the first step in the proof of Lemma 1), a
program is feasible if and only if the path $\{k(t)\}$ lies everywhere above
the locus $\dot{k} = 0$, i.e. everywhere above the curve

$$\tilde{k}(t) = \left[\frac{c(0)}{a} \right]^{(1-\beta)/\alpha} \exp[(g - \theta)(1 - \beta)t/\alpha]. \tag{16}$$

Comparing (15) and (16), and bearing in mind that $g > \theta > 0$, we see
that if $c(0)$ is positive but sufficiently small and if

$$(1 - \beta)\theta/(1 - \alpha - \beta) > (g - \theta)(1 - \beta)/\alpha$$

or, equivalently,

$$g < (1 - \beta)\theta/(1 - \alpha - \beta), \tag{17}$$

then, for all $t \geq 0$, $z(t) \geq \tilde{k}(t)$.   Q.E.D.

Pulling together the salient features of lemmas 1 and 2, we have the
following:

Proposition.   Under the general assumptions of this section (stationary
population, Cobb–Douglas technology), a constant and positive level of
consumption can be maintained if and only if $\lambda - \delta \geq 0$, i.e. if and only if
the rate of exogenous resource-saving technical progress at least matches
the rate of deterioration of the terms of trade, and an exponentially
growing positive level of consumption is attainable if and only if
$(\lambda - \delta)/(1 - \alpha - \beta) > g/\beta$.

Remark 1.   Solow (1974) showed that a closed economy with a constant
population, a finite deposit of an essential, costlessly storable resource,
and a stationary, constant-returns Cobb–Douglas production function
can maintain a positive level of consumption if and only if the share of
capital exceeds the share of the resource, i.e. if and only if $\alpha > \beta$. And, of
course, even if Solow's condition is not met, survival is possible if there is
steady technical progress, at however modest a rate. In contrast, it has
emerged that for the survival of a small open economy with deteriorating

terms of trade, technical progress is always necessary, whether or not Solow's condition is met and whether or not returns to scale are constant, and that technical progress is sufficient only if it accrues at a rate which depends on the share of the resource and on the rate of decline of the terms of trade.

Remark 2. The condition for a constant and positive level of consumption is quite independent of the nature of returns to scale in capital and the resource. The intuitive explanation may be found in the fact that if $g = 0$, then output is constant and returns to scale never come into play. The conditions for a growing level of consumption, on the other hand, depend intimately on the nature of returns to scale: the larger is $\alpha + \beta$, the measure of returns to scale, the less severe the requirements placed on technical progress.

3. The possibility of storage

Throughout the argument of section 2 it was assumed that imports of the raw material are immediately used in production. The assumption would be inescapable if storage of the extracted resource were impossible. But in general extracted resources can be stored, at some cost. Does the possibility of storage make any difference to our conclusion that survival is impossible without technical progress? We proceed to sketch-argue that in the canonical case of exponential storage costs survival is impossible without technical progress.

Let a stock $R(t)$ of imported raw material be held and let the stock decay at the constant rate ε. Suppose, for the sake of the argument, that there is no technical progress, but that nevertheless there is an efficient trajectory $\{k^*(t), R^*(t), r^*(t)\}$ with $c(t) = c(0) > 0$. Along that trajectory the stock $R^*(t)$ must eventually decline. Let us suppose that it begins to decline at $t = T$. We pick up the evolution of the economy at T.

Consider two fictitious economies. The first is closed, with $k^{(1)}(T) = k^*(T) > 0$, $R^{(1)}(T) = R^*(T) > 0$, and $l^{(1)}(t) = l(t) = 1$ given and with the capacity to store the raw material subject to exponential decay; the second is open, with $k^{(2)}(T) = k^*(T) > 0$ and $l^{(2)}(T) = l(T) = 1$ given, able to trade at $p(0) \exp(\delta t)$ but unable to store the raw material. The economies share the production function (1). The first economy uses up its stock of raw material at the rate $-\dot{R}^*(t)$; the second economy imports the raw material at the rate $r^*(t)$. The first economy makes available goods for consumption at the rate $c^{(1)}(t) = \alpha^{(1)}(t)c(0)$, the second at the rate $c^{(2)}(t) = \alpha^{(2)}(t)c(0)$, where $\alpha^{(1)}(t) \equiv -\dot{R}^*(t)/(r^*(r) - \dot{R}^*(t))$, $\alpha^{(2)}(t) \equiv r^*(t)/(r^*(t) - R^*(t))$, and $\alpha^{(1)}(t) + \alpha^{(2)}(t) = 1$. Thus, collectively, the two fictitious economies yield consumption at the same rate as our small open economy. Moreover, from the concavity of the production function, $\dot{k}^{(i)}(t) > \dot{k}(t)$ and $k^{(i)}(t) > k(t)$ $(i = t, 2)$ for all $t > T$; and, of course, $R^{(1)}(t) = R^*(t)$ for $t > T$. It follows that if the program $\{k^*(t), R^*(t), r^*(t)\}$ is feasible, then so are the programs, just described, of the two fictitious economies and, a fortiori, so are those programs modified by the substitution of the positive constant $\bar{\alpha}^{(i)} \equiv \inf_t \alpha^{(i)}(t)$ for $\alpha^{(i)}(t)$. But it is known that such modified programs are infeasible: that the first is infeasible has been shown by Kemp and Long (1982), that the second is infeasible has been demonstrated in section 2. Hence, the trajectory $\{k^*(t), R^*(t), r^*(t)\}$ is infeasible and we arrive at a contradiction. Our small open economy cannot survive.

4. An alternative model

We have considered conditions for the survival of a small country which depends on foreign sources for an essential raw material. It was found in section 2 that survival is impossible if the rate of resource-saving technical progress is less than the rate of deterioration of the terms of trade. Suppose instead that the imported good is an essential consumption good. What then are the conditions of survival?

Sticking as close as possible to the formulation of section 2, we might write utility as

$$u(t) = y(t)^{\omega}r(t)^{\beta} \exp(\beta\lambda t), \qquad 0 < \omega, \beta < 1; \omega + \beta < 1,$$

and

$$y(t) = k(t)^{\mu}, \qquad 0 < \mu < 1, \tag{1*}$$

so that, substituting from the second equation into the first:

$$u(t) = k(t)^{\alpha}r(t)^{\beta} \exp(\beta\lambda t), \qquad 0 < \alpha \equiv \mu\omega < 1.$$

The analysis and conclusions of section 2 now apply, with $u(t)$ playing the role of $y(t)$.

Alternatively we might write

$$u(t) = y(t)^{\omega}r(t)^{\beta}$$

and

$$y(t) = k(t)^{\mu} \exp(\beta\lambda t/\omega),$$

so that, substituting from the second equation into the first, we again obtain (1*).

References

Hotelling, H. (1931), The economics of exhaustible resources, Journal of Political Economy 38, 137–175.

Kemp, M. C. and N. V. Long, eds., (1980), Exhaustible Resources, Optimality, and Trade (North-Holland Publishing Company, Amsterdam).

Kemp, M. C. and N. V. Long (1982), On the possibility of surviving when an essential natural resource depreciates through time, University of New South Wales.

Mitra, T., M. Majumdar and D. Ray (1982), Feasible alternatives under deteriorating terms of trade, Journal of International Economics 13, 105–134.

Shimomura, K. (1983), A note on the survival of a small economy, Kobe University.

Solow, R. M. (1974), Intergenerational equity and exhaustible resources, Review of Economic Studies, Symposium on the Economics of exhaustible resources, 39–45.

PART III

THE OPTIMAL ORDER OF EXPLOITATION

Towards a more general theory of the order of exploitation of non-renewable resource-deposits

MURRAY C. KEMP and NGO VAN LONG

1. Introduction

With just a handful of exceptions, the analysis of optimal resource depletion has proceeded on the radical assumption that the resource-stock is perfectly homogeneous in all respects. The relatively early work of Herfindahl (1967) is an outstanding exception. Herfindahl examined the preferred extraction profile of a competitive profit-maximizing firm with several deposits of an exhaustible resource, homogeneous in all respects except (constant) average cost of extraction. He showed what the firm will exploit its deposits in strict sequence, beginning with the lowest-cost. On the other hand, in a series of papers Kemp and Long (1980a, 1980b, 1980c, 1980d) have shown that there are circumstances in which it is suboptimal to exploit the deposits in the Herfindahl order. Thus, conclusions of Herfindahl type have a field of validity but lack complete generality. Our first purpose in the present essay, then, is to re-examine Herfindahl's question; in particular, we seek to delineate more sharply and completely than hitherto the boundaries of the field of application of Herfindahl's conclusions.

Herfindahl sought to relate the optimal order of extraction to the ranking of deposits in terms of extraction cost. With the benefit of hindsight, we can see that the question posed by Herfindahl is unnecessarily narrow. More generally, we can seek conditions on the parameters of the economy (among which constant average cost of extraction may or may not appear) which ensure that it is optimal to exploit the deposits in strict sequence, working just one at a time. Our second and more important objective, then, is to extend the analysis of

Essays in the Economics of Exhaustible Resources, edited by M. C. Kemp and N. V. Long
© *Elsevier Science Publishers B.V., 1984*

order as it has emerged to date by relating sequence to a much broader class of parameters.

The present essay is devoted to non-renewable resources. The question of order in a context of renewable resources is considered in essay 5 by Shimomura.

2. The simplest case: No fixed costs of extraction and no set-up costs

For the time being we ignore fixed costs of extraction, as well as set-up costs. In that respect we simply follow the existing literature.

2.1. *Assumptions and definitions*

Let there be n deposits of some resource. The rate of extraction from the kth deposit at time t is denoted by $Q_k(t)$, and the rate of depletion of the kth deposit is denoted by $E_k(t)$. Of course, $E_k(t) \geqq Q_k(t)$, the inequality allowing for costs of extraction and unavoidable wastage; more specific interpretations will be provided below. It is assumed that

$$Q_k = F_k(E_k),$$

where the function F_k is increasing and concave (possibly linear) and such that $F_k(0) = 0$. Let $\tilde{E}(t) \equiv (E_1(t), \ldots, E_n(t))$ be the vector of rates of depletion and let

$$U(t, \tilde{E}(t)) \equiv U(t, E_1(t), \ldots, E_n(t))$$

$$\equiv \tilde{U}(t, E_1(t), \ldots, E_n(t), Q_1(E_1(t)), \ldots, Q_n(E_n(t)))$$

denote the net social benefit derived from extraction of the resource. The social problem then is to find

$$\text{(P1)} \quad \max_{\{\tilde{E}(t)\}, T} \quad V \equiv \int_0^T D(t) U(t, \tilde{E}(t)) \, \mathrm{d}t, \qquad D(t) > 0,$$

$$\text{s.t.} \int_0^T E_k(t) \, \mathrm{d}t \leqq \bar{R}_k \qquad (k = 1, \ldots, n), \tag{1}$$

and $E_k(t) \geqq 0$, where $D(t)$ is a social discount function and $\bar{R}_k$ is the initial extent of the kth deposit. The maximizing values of $\tilde{E}(t)$ and T will be indicated by asterisks.

It will be useful to distinguish three mutually exclusive classes of net-benefit function.

Class 1. $U(t, \tilde{E})$ is strictly concave in $\tilde{E}$; that is, for all $\theta(0 < \theta < 1)$ and all $\tilde{E}^{(1)}$ and $\tilde{E}^{(2)}$ ($\tilde{E}^{(1)} \neq \tilde{E}^{(2)}$),

$$U(t, \theta\tilde{E}^{(1)} + (1 - \theta)\tilde{E}^{(2)}) > \theta U(t, \tilde{E}^{(1)}) + (1 - \theta)U(t, \tilde{E}^{(2)}).$$

Class 2. $U(t, \tilde{E})$ is the sum of two functions:

$$U(t, \tilde{E}) = U_1(t, \tilde{E}) + U_2(t, \tilde{E}),$$

where $U_1(t, \tilde{E})$ is concave (possibly strictly concave) in each E_k but not strictly concave in the vector $\tilde{E}$, and where $U_1(t, \tilde{E})$ is linear in the vector $\tilde{E}$ and such that, for all k, $\partial U_2/\partial E_k \neq 0$.

Class 3. $U(t, \tilde{E})$ is strictly concave in each E_k but not strictly concave in the vector $\tilde{E}$; moreover, $U(t, \tilde{E})$ does not belong to class 2.

It will be shown that if the net-benefit function is in class 1, then sequential extraction is suboptimal; that if the net-benefit function is in class 2 (and if some minor additional assumptions are made) then optimal extraction is necessarily sequential; and that if the net-benefit function is in class 3, then the optimal order of extraction may be a matter of indifference. (A formal definition of sequential extraction will be provided below.)

Each of the three classes of net-benefit function contains some interesting specimens, as we proceed to show.

Examples from class 1. Let $E(t) \equiv \sum E_k(t)$ and $Q(t) \equiv \sum Q_k(t)$. As our first example we offer:

(i) $U = R(t, E(t)) - w(t)\sum b_k(E_k(t))$,

where R is concave (possibly linear) in E and $b_k(E_k)$ is strictly convex and positive if E_k is positive. Identifying E_k with Q_k, so that $E = \sum E_k = \sum Q_k = Q$, we can interpret R as a total revenue function. Moreover, interpreting $w(t)$ as the wage rate and $b_k(E_k)$ as the amount of labour employed in exploiting the kth deposit, $w(t)\sum b_k(E_k)$ is revealed as a total cost function.

In our second example:

(ii) $U = R(t, Q(t)) - w(t)\sum m_k E_k(t)$,

where R is concave (possibly linear) in $Q(t) = \sum_k F_k(E_k)$, $F_k(E_k)$ is strictly concave, m_k is a positive constant, and $w(t)$ is positive. Here R may be interpreted as a total revenue function and m_k as the labour cost of extracting and processing material from the kth deposit. Retaining the interpretation of $w(t)$ as the wage rate, $w(t) \sum m_k E_k(t)$ becomes the total cost of extracting and processing. The strict concavity of F_k reflects diminishing returns in the processing activity.

Examples from class 2.   As our third example we have:

(iii) $U = R(t, E(t)) - w(t) \sum m_k E_k,$

where R is concave (possibly linear) in E and hence in each E_k, m_k is a positive constant and $w(t)$ is positive. Again, if E_k is identified with Q_k, then R may be interpreted as a total revenue function, and, of course, $w(t) \sum m_k E_k$ may be interpreted as a total cost function. Notice that R is not strictly concave in $\tilde{E}$.

Our fourth example is:

(iv) $U = p(t)E(t) - C(t, X(t)),$

where $p(t)$ is positive, m_k is a positive constant, and $X \equiv \sum m_k E_k$, and where C is a convex (possibly linear) function of X and hence of each E_k, with C positive if X is positive. If E_k is identified with Q_k, then pE may be interpreted as the revenue function (of, for example, a small country); moreover, X may be interpreted as the total labour required to extract $E_1, \ldots, E_n$ and C may be interpreted as the total cost function. The latter may be linear in X or, if the supply curve of labour is upward-sloping, strictly convex.

Examples from class 3.   Our next example is:

(v) $U = U(t, Y),$

where $Y \equiv A + E - \sum m_k E_k$, m_k is a constant proper fraction, and U is strictly concave in Y. By way of interpretation, we may consider a central planner with a fixed labour force A, able to extract oil from the kth deposit at an average cost of m_k units of labour, and able to produce a perfect substitute (perhaps solar energy) at an average cost of one unit of labour. On this interpretation, $A - \sum m_k E_k$ is the output of the oil-substitute and Y is the total output of energy from all sources.

Our final example is:

(vi) $U = U_1(t, Y - \gamma Z) + U_2(t, Z),$

where U_i is strictly concave in its second argument. By way of interpretation the new variable Z is the output of a third, non-energy good with constant average labour cost γ and $Y - \gamma Z$ is the total output of energy.

Some of the examples differ only slightly one from the other. (Compare examples (ii) and (iii).) However, those small differences are all important. We proceed to the demonstration after setting out some definitions. Let

$$S \equiv \{t : t \in [0, T], E(t) > 0\}, \tag{2}$$

let $\bar{G}$ be any connected subset of S, and let $G = (t_A, t_B)$, say, be the corresponding time interval.

Definition 2.1. An optimal path of extraction $\tilde{E}^*(t)$ is said to be *sequential* over the time interval G if, for all $t \in G$, $E^*(t) = \max\{E_1^*(t), \ldots, E_i^*(t), \ldots, E_n^*(t)\}$.

Definition 2.2. Extraction of the jth deposit is said to be *less costly* than extraction of kth deposit if:
  (a) the net-benefit function is as in examples (iii)–(vi), with $m_j < m_k$, *or*
  (b) the net-benefit function is as in example (i), with $b_j(y) < b_k(y)$ for all $y > 0$, *or*
  (c) the net-benefit function is as in example (ii), with $m_j < m_k$ and $F_j(y) > F_k(y)$ for all $y > 0$.

Definition 2.3. An optimal path of extraction $E^*(t)$ is said to be Herfindahl over the interval G if it is sequential over G and if, for any pair (j, k) such that the jth deposit is less costly than the kth,

$$\inf\{t \in G : E_k^*(t) > 0\} \geqq \sup\{t \in G : E_j^*(t) > 0\}. \tag{3}$$

Definition 2.4. An optimal path of extraction $\tilde{E}^*(t)$ is said to be anti-Herfindahl over the interval G if it is sequential over G and if, for any pair (j, k) such that the jth deposit is less costly than the kth,

$$\sup\{t \in G : E_k^*(t) > 0\} \leqq \inf\{t \in G : E_j^*(t) > 0\}. \tag{4}$$

We consider in turn the three classes of net-benefit function. As we have already noted, associated with each class are some agreeably strong propositions.

2.2.   *When net-benefit functions belong to class* 1

Proposition 2.1.   If the net-benefit function belongs to class 1, then no optimal path of extraction is sequential.

Proof.   It suffices to show that $\tilde{E}^*(t)$ is continuous over any G.

Let $\tilde{E}(t)$ be a feasible piecewise-continuous path of extraction with a jump discontinuity at $\tau \in G$. It will be shown that $\tilde{E}(t)$ is dominated by a feasible path which is continuous at τ. Given any sufficiently small $h > 0$:

(i) $E_k(t)$ is continuous over $(\tau - h, \tau)$ and $(\tau, \tau + h)$, and

(ii) the left-hand and right-hand limits of $E_k(t)$ exist at τ.

Let

$$E_k^- \equiv \lim_{t \to \tau^-} E_k(t) \equiv \lim_{h \to 0^+} E_k(\tau - h),$$

$$E_k^+ \equiv \lim_{t \to \tau^+} E_k(t) \equiv \lim_{h \to 0^+} E_k(\tau - h),$$

and let

$$\bar{E}_k(h) = \frac{1}{2h} \int_{\tau-h}^{\tau+h} E_k(t)\, dt.$$

Now consider the alternative extraction path

$$E_k^*(t) = \begin{cases} \bar{E}_k(h), & \text{if } t \in (\tau - h, \tau + h), \\ E_k(t), & \text{otherwise.} \end{cases}$$

For each deposit, total extraction is unchanged; hence $\tilde{E}^*(t)$ is feasible. Let

$$\gamma(h) \equiv \int_{\tau-h}^{\tau+h} D(t) U(t, \tilde{E}(t))\, dt - \int_{\tau-h}^{\tau+h} D(t) U(t, \tilde{E}^*(t))\, dt. \tag{5}$$

We seek to show that $\gamma(h) < 0$ for some sufficiently small and positive h.

Since $\gamma(0) = 0$, it suffices to show that $\gamma'(h) < 0$ for all h sufficiently small. This in turn is equivalent to showing that

$$\lim_{h \to 0^+} [\gamma(h) - \gamma(0)]/h < 0. \tag{6}$$

Let us re-write $\gamma(h)$ as:

$$\gamma(h) \equiv I_1(h) + I_2(h) - J_1(h) - J_2(h),$$

where

$$I_1(h) \equiv \int_{\tau-h}^{\tau} D(t) U(t, \tilde{E}(t))\, dt,$$

$$I_2(h) \equiv \int_\tau^{\tau+h} D(t) U(t, \tilde{E}(t)) \, dt,$$

$$J_1(h) \equiv \int_{\tau-h}^\tau D(t) U(t, \tilde{E}^*(t)) \, dt,$$

$$J_1(h) \equiv \int_\tau^{\tau+h} D(t) U(t, \tilde{E}^*(t)) \, dt,$$

Then:

$$\lim_{h \to 0^+} I_1(h)/2h = \tfrac{1}{2} D(\tau) U(\tau, \tilde{E}^-), \tag{7}$$

$$\lim_{h \to 0^+} I_2(h)/2h = \tfrac{1}{2} D(\tau) U(\tau, \tilde{E}^+), \tag{8}$$

$$\lim_{h \to 0^+} J_1(h)/2h = \tfrac{1}{2} D(\tau) U(\tau, \tfrac{1}{2}\tilde{E}^+ + \tfrac{1}{2}\tilde{E}^-)$$

$$= \lim_{h \to 0^+} J_2(h)/2h. \tag{9}$$

Since U is strictly concave in $\tilde{E}$ and since $\tilde{E}^+ \neq \tilde{E}^-$, inequality (6) follows from (7)–(9). Q.E.D.

A stronger result can be obtained if $U(t, \tilde{E})$ is of the form:

$$U(t, \tilde{E}) = R(t, E) - C(t, X), \tag{10}$$

where

$$X = \sum b_k(E_k) \tag{11}$$

and where $C_X \equiv \partial C/\partial X$ is positive and $b_k(E_k)$ is strictly convex and increasing.

Let us define

$$T_k \equiv \{t : E_k^*(t) > 0\}$$

and

$$S_j(k) \equiv \{t : E_j^*(t) > 0, E_k^*(t) = 0\}.$$

Proposition 2.2. If the net-benefit function satisfies (10) and (11), then for any pair (j, k) such that $b_j'(0) = b_k'(0)$ either $T_j \subseteq T_k$ or $T_k \subseteq T_j$.

Proof. We seek to show that either $S_j(k)$ is empty or $S_k(j)$ is empty.

Suppose that both $S_j(k)$ and $S_k(j)$ are non-empty. Then, for any $t_j \in S_j(k)$:

$$D(t_j)[R_E - C_X b_j'(E_j)] = \lambda_j, \tag{12}$$

$$D(t_j)[R_E - C_X b_k'(0)] \le \lambda_k, \tag{13}$$

where λ_j and λ_k are non-negative and constant Lagrange multipliers associated with the constraint (1). From (12) and (13):

$$\lambda_k - \lambda_j \ge D(t_j) C_X [b_j'(E_j) - b_k'(0)] > 0. \tag{14}$$

Similarly, for any $t_k \in S_k(j)$:

$$\lambda_j - \lambda_k \ge D(t_k) C_X [b_k'(E_k) - b_j'(0)] > 0. \tag{15}$$

But (14) and (15) are mutually inconsistent.   Q.E.D.

2.3.   *When net-benefit functions belong to class* 2

When attention is switched to functions in class 2 our conclusions undergo a radical change.

Proposition 2.3.   Suppose that:
   (a) $U(t) = R(t, E(t)) - w(t) \sum m_k E_k(t)$,   with $w(t) > 0$, $m_k \ge 0$ and $D(t)w(t)$ strictly increasing over the interval G, *or*
   (b) $U(t) = p(t)E(t) - C(t, X(t))$,   with $C_X > 0$, $X = \sum m_k E_k$, $m_k \ge 0$, and $D(t)p(t)$ positive and strictly increasing over G.
   Suppose, furthermore, that (P1) has a solution with $E_k(t)$ finite for all k. Then that solution is necessarily anti-Herfindahl over G.

Proof.   Without loss, consider any pair (j, k) such that $m_j < m_k$. The net-benefit function is of the form:

$$U(t, \tilde{E}) = R(t, E) - C(t, X), \tag{16}$$

where $X = \sum m_k E_k$. The Hamiltonian for (P1) is, therefore:

$$H = D(R - C) - \sum \lambda_k E_k,$$

where λ_k is the non-negative and constant Lagrange multiplier associated with the kth member of constraint (1).
   Let $E_j(t_j) > 0$ for some $t_j \in G$ and let $E_k(t_k) > 0$ for some $t_k \in G$. Then:

$$D(t_j)[R_E - m_j C_X(t_j, X)] - \lambda_j = 0, \tag{17}$$

$$D(t_j)[R_E - m_k C_X(t_j, X)] - \lambda_k \leqq 0, \tag{18}$$

$$D(t_k)[R_E - m_j C_X(t_k, X)] - \lambda_j \leqq 0, \tag{19}$$

$$D(t_k)[R_E - m_k C_X(t_k, X)] - \lambda_k = 0. \tag{20}$$

From (17) and (19):

$$D(t_j)[R_E(t_j, E) - m_j C_X(t_j, X)]$$
$$\geqq D(t_k)[R_E(t_k, E) - m_j C_X(t_k, X)], \tag{21}$$

and, from (18) and (20):

$$-D(t_j)[R_E(t_j, E) - m_k C_X(t_j, X)]$$
$$\geqq -D(t_k)[R_E(t_k, E) - m_k C_X(t_k, X)]. \tag{22}$$

Adding (21) and (22):

$$D(t_j)(m_k - m_j)C_X(t_j, X) \geqq D(t_k)(m_k - m_j)C_X(t_k, X), \tag{23}$$

which, since $m_k > m_j$, implies that:

$$D(t_j)C_X(t_j, X) \geqq D(t_k)C_X(t_k, X). \tag{24}$$

If the net-benefit function is of type (a), (24) reduces to:

$$D(t_j)w(t_j) \geqq D(t_k)w(t_k), \tag{25a}$$

which, if $D(t)w(t)$ is strictly increasing in t over G, implies that:

$$\inf\{t_j : E_j(t_j) > 0\} \geqq \sup\{t_k : E_k(t_k) > 0\}.$$

Suppose, alternatively, that the net-benefit function is of type (b). From (21):

$$D(t_j)R_E(t_j, E) - D(t_k)R_E(t_k, E)$$
$$\geqq D(t_j)m_j C_X(t_j, X) - D(t_k)m_j C_X(t_k, X). \tag{25b}$$

If $R_E = p(t)$, then from (24) and (25b):

$$D(t_j)p(t_j) \geqq D(t_k)p(t_k), \tag{26}$$

which, if $D(t)p(t)$ is strictly increasing in t over G, implies that:

$$\inf\{t_j : E_j(t_j) > 0\} \geqq \sup\{t_k : E_k(t_k) > 0\}. \qquad \text{Q.E.D.}$$

When the net-benefit function is of the form (16), something definite can be said about the structure of royalties.

Proposition 2.4. (Ricardian royalty structure). Suppose that the net-benefit function has the form (16). Then the shadow price of the less costly deposit is higher than that of the more costly deposit.

Proof. If $m_k > m_j$, then from (19) and (20):

$$\lambda_j - \lambda_k \geqq (m_k - m_j) C_X(t_k, X) D(t_k).$$

In particular, if deposits are ranked in order of increasing cost and if $k = j + 1$, then letting t_j and t_k approach the transition point τ in (17) and (20), respectively, we find that:

$$\lambda_j - \lambda_k = (m_k - m_j) C_X(\tau, X(\tau)) D(\tau). \qquad \text{Q.E.D.}$$

The following heuristic argument will expose the common sense of proposition 2.3(a). Suppose that $D(t)w(t)$ is *strictly increasing* over time, and consider a firm that plans to extract a lower-cost jth deposit at t_1 and a higher-cost kth deposit at $t_2 > t_1$. Then the present value of the firm's profit can be enhanced by extracting marginally more (less) of the higher-cost (lower-cost) deposit near t_1 and marginally less (more) near t_2, holding constant both the rate of aggregate extraction near t_1 and t_2 and the total extraction from each deposit. For the outcome of the perturbation is a reduction in the present value of the cost of extracting near t_2 of $D(t_2)w(t_2)(m_k - m_j) > 0$ and an increase in the present value of the cost of extracting near t_1 of $D(t_1)w(t_1)(m_k - m_j)$. Since $D(t)w(t)$ is higher near t_2, the firm achieves a net reduction of costs. To summarize: the most labour-intensive deposit will be exploited when the discounted wage rage is lowest.

Similar reasoning can be applied to part (b) of proposition 2.3. Suppose that $D(t)p(t)$ is increasing over the interval $(0, T)$. (One may imagine that after T a technological "breakthrough" places a ceiling on $p(t)$ which makes all extraction unprofitable.) And consider a firm which plans to extract a higher-cost kth deposit near $t_2 < T$ and a lower-cost jth deposit near $t_1 < t_2$. Then the present value of the firms's profit can be improved by extracting an additional amount δ_k from the higher-cost deposit near t_1, at the same time reducing by $\delta_j = \delta_k m_k / m_j$ extraction from the lower-cost deposit; and by reducing by δ_k units extraction from the higher-cost deposit near t_2, at the same time extracting an additional δ_j units from the lower-cost deposit. This perturbation of extraction leaves unchanged the cost of extraction both near t_1 and near t_2. Aggregate extraction near t_1 is reduced by $\delta_j - \delta_k$ which, since $m_k > m_j$, is positive; and aggregate extraction near t_2 is increased by the same amount. However, $D(t)p(t)$ is increasing over $[0, T]$; hence, the present value of sales increases.

An example of an anti-Herfindahl extraction path. Let there be two deposits, with $m_2 > m_1 > 0$. The price and wage rate are exogenous and such that

$$p(t^*) > m_2 w(t^*), \quad \text{for some } t^* > 0. \tag{27}$$

We seek to fill out the specification in such a way that there will exist an optimal extraction path such that the more costly deposit is extracted over $[0, t^*]$ and the less costly deposit over (t^*, T). Now we know that the following conditions are sufficient for the optimality of an anti-Herfindahl path:

(i) for $t \in [0, t^*)$:

$$[p(t) - m_2 w(t)]D(t) = [p(t^*) - m_2 w(t^*)]D(t^*), \tag{28}$$

$$[p(t) - m_1 w(t)]D(t) < [p(t^*) - m_1 w(t^*)]D(t^*); \tag{29}$$

(ii) for $t \in (t^*, T]$:

$$[p(t) - m_1 w(t)]D(t) = [p(t^*) - m_1 w(t^*)]D(t^*), \tag{30}$$

$$[p(t) - m_2 w(t)]D(t) < [p(t^*) - m_2 w(t^*)]D(t^*); \tag{31}$$

(iii) $p(t)$ and $w(t)$ are continuous functions.

We seek an example which will wear (27)–(31).

Consider the wage function:

$$w(t) = w(t^*) \exp[\alpha(t - t^*)], \quad \text{for all } t \geq 0, \tag{32}$$

and the price function defined by:

(a) for $t \leq t^*$:

$$D(t)p(t) = D(t^*)[p(t^*) - m_2 w(t^*)] + D(t)m_2 w(t^*) \exp[\alpha(t - t^*)]; \tag{33}$$

(b) for $t \geq t^*$:

$$D(t)p(t) = D(t^*)[p(t^*) - m_1 w(t^*)] + D(t)m_1 w(t^*) \exp[\alpha(t - t^*)]. \tag{34}$$

Clearly, if $-\dot{D}/D < \alpha$, then (28)–(31) are satisfied. Notice also that $p(t)$ is continuous, although

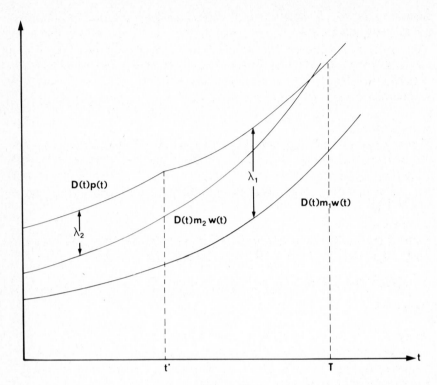

Figure 4.1

$$\frac{\mathrm{d}}{\mathrm{d}t}[D(t)p(t)]\bigg|_{t=t^{*-}} > \frac{\mathrm{d}}{\mathrm{d}t}[D(t)p(t)]\bigg|_{t=t^{*+}}. \qquad (35)$$

The relationship between $D(t)p(t)$ and $D(t)w(t)m_k$ $(k = 1, 2)$ is displayed in fig. 4.1. The vertical distance between $D(t)p(t)$ and $D(t)m_2 w(t)$ is equal to the positive constant λ_2 for all $t \leqq t^*$ and is less than λ_2 for all $t > t^*$. The vertical distance between $D(t)p(t)$ and $D(t)m_1 w(t)$ is equal to $\lambda_1 > 0$ for all $t \geqq t^*$ and is less than λ_1 for all $t < t^*$.

The price and wage paths depicted in fig. 4.1 may be identified with the competitive paths defined by the social planning problem

(P2) $\max \int\limits_0^T [R(E_1 + E_2) + (\bar{X} - m_1 E_1 - m_2 E_2) \exp(\alpha t)]D(t)\, \mathrm{d}t$

   s.t. $\int\limits_0^T E_k \mathrm{d}t = \bar{R}_k,$

where $m_1 E_1 + m_2 E_2$ is the labour used in extraction and $\bar{X} - m_1 E_1 - m_2 E_2$ is the labour employed in producing a second commodity ("corn"), the production function of which has the technical progress factor $\exp(\alpha t)$. (If $T = \infty$, (P2) has a solution provided that the "overtaking" criterion is applied.)

The following proposition is almost the converse of proposition 2.3.

Proposition 2.5.

(a) Suppose that $C(t, X) = w(t)X$, $X = \sum m_k E_k$, and that the kth deposit is more costly than the jth. Then an anti-Herfindahl path is optimal only if

$$D(t_k) w(t_k) \leqq D(t_j) w(t_j), \qquad t_k < t_j, \tag{36}$$

where $t_j \in T_j$ and $t_k \in T_k$.

(b) Suppose that $R(t, E(t)) = p(t)E(t)$ and that the kth deposit is more costly than the jth. Then an anti-Herfindahl path is optimal only if

$$D(t_k) p(t_k) \leqq D(t_j) p(t_j), \qquad t_k < t_j, \tag{37}$$

where $t_j \in T_j$ and $t_k \in T_k$.

Proof.

(a) If (36) is not satisfied, then the firm's profit can be increased by switching extraction from the kth deposit to the jth at time t_k, maintaining total extraction at all t.

(b) The proof is similar but, this time, total cost is kept unchanged at all t. Q.E.D.

Figure 4.2 displays a price–wage configuration which is consistent with an anti-Herfindahl order of exploitation. For $t \leqq t^*$, the distance between $D(t)p(t)$ and $D(t)m_2 w(t)$ is λ_2, a positive constant; for $t > t^*$, the distance is less than λ_2. Similarly, the distance between $D(t)p(t)$ and $D(t)m_1 w(t)$ is λ_1 for $t \geqq t^*$ and less than λ_1 for $t < t^*$. Fig. 4.2 is much the same as fig. 4.1; however, in fig. 4.2 it is not required that $D(t)w(t)$ be non-decreasing.

We turn to cases in which the Herfindahl order of exploitation is optimal. It is now easy to prove the following pair of propositions, which are the counterparts of propositions 2.3 and 2.5.

Proposition 2.6. Suppose that:

(a) $U(t) = R(t, E(t)) - w(t)\sum m_k E_k(t)$, with $w(t) > 0$, $m_k > 0$, and

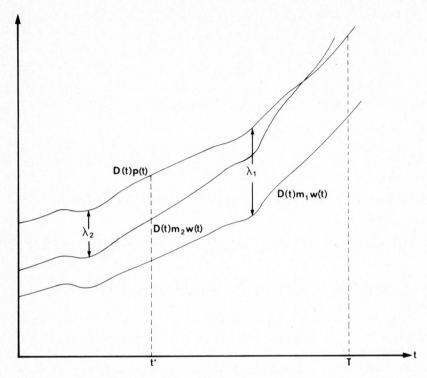

Figure 4.2

$D(t)w(t)$ strictly decreasing in t over the interval G, *or*

(b) $U(t) = p(t)E(t) - C(t, X(t))$, with $C_X > 0$, $X = \sum m_k E_k$, $m_k \geqq 0$, and $D(t)p(t)$ positive and strictly decreasing over G. Suppose, furthermore, that (P1) has a solution with $E_k(t)$ finite for all k. Then that solution is necessarily Herfindahl over G.

Proposition 2.7.

(a) Suppose that $C(t, X) = w(t)X$, $X = \sum m_k E_k$, and that the kth deposit is more costly than the jth. Then a Herfindahl path is optimal only if

$$D(t_k)w(t_k) \leqq D(t_j)w(t_j), \qquad t_k > t_j, \tag{38}$$

where $t_j \in T_j$ and $t_k \in T_k$.

(b) Suppose that $R(t, E(t)) = p(t)E(t)$ and that the kth deposit is more costly than the jth. Then a Herfindahl path is optimal only if

$$D(t_k)p(t_k) \lessgtr D(t_j)p(t_j), \qquad t_k > t_j, \tag{39}$$

where $t_j \in T_j$ and $t_k \in T_k$.

In the central propositions of this section, propositions 2.3 and 2.6, it is postulated that there exists an optimal path of extraction with finite $E(t)$ for all t. We now demonstrate that in the linear case, in which

$$R(t, E(t)) = p(t)E(t) \tag{40a}$$

and

$$C(t, X(t)) = w(t)\sum m_k E_k(t), \tag{40b}$$

the assumption is not trivial. If (40a) and (40b) hold, the integral to be maximized is:

$$\int_0^T D(t)p(t)[E(t) - (w(t)/p(t))\sum m_k E_k(t)]\,\mathrm{d}t. \tag{41}$$

Proposition 2.8. Suppose that the integrand is linear, as in (40a) and (40b).

(i) If $D(t)p(t)$ is an increasing function of time and the ratio $w(t)/p(t)$ is a non-increasing function of time, then it is optimal to postpone all extraction until the last moment, and suboptimal to do otherwise.

(ii) If $D(t)p(t)$ is a decreasing function of time and the ratio $w(t)/p(t)$ is a non-decreasing function of time, then it is optimal to exhaust all profitable deposits at the first instant, and suboptimal to do otherwise.

(iii) If $D(t)p(t)$ is a constant function of time, then it is optimal to concentrate all extraction at the first or last moment according as $w(t)/p(t)$ is an increasing or decreasing function of time, respectively, and it is suboptimal to do otherwise.

(iv) If $D(t)p(t)$ and $w(t)/p(t)$ are both constant functions, then the order of exploitation of profitable deposits is a matter of indifference.

Proof. Each part of the proposition follows directly from the integral (41). Of course the constructed example of an anti-Herfindahl optimal trajectory falls into none of the categories of proposition 2.8.   Q.E.D.

2.4. *When net-benefit functions belong to class* 3

Attention will be confined to net-benefit functions of the type defined in examples (v) and (vi) of section 2.1. The examples are here duplicated for convenience of reference:

(v) $\begin{cases} U = U(t, Y(t)), \qquad Y = A + E - \sum m_k E_k, \qquad 0 < m_k < 1. \\ U \text{ increasing and strictly concave in } Y. \end{cases}$

(vi) $\begin{cases} U = U_1(t, Y(t) - \gamma Z(t)) + U_2(t, Z(t)). \\ U_i \text{ increasing and strictly concave in its second argument} \\ (i = 1, 2). \end{cases}$

It will be recalled that in example (v) Y may be interpreted as the rate of production of energy from all sources and $A - \sum m_k E_k$ as the rate of production of solar energy; and that in example (vi) Z may be interpreted as the rate of production of a non-energy good and $Y - \gamma Z$ as the rate of production of energy from all sources.

Proposition 2.9.   If the net-benefit function is of type (v) and if along an optimal trajectory $A - \sum m_k E_k$ (the output of solar energy) is positive, then the order of exploitation of the deposits is within bounds a matter of indifference.

Proof.   Suppose that along the optimal trajectory $A - \sum m_k E_k$ is positive. Without loss, let I_i be an interval over which E_i is positive and I_j an interval over with E_j is positive; and let I_i and I_j be of equal length. Now let $(1 - m_i)E_i$ increase by ε and $(1 - m_j)E_j$ decrease by ε over I_j. The perturbation leaves unchanged the total output of energy, $A + \sum(1 - m_k)E_k$; but it changes the composition of output, thereby raising the rate of output of solar energy by $\varepsilon(m_j - m_i)/(1 - m_i)(1 - m_j)$ and depressing the rate of extraction of oil by the same amount. The perturbation is made feasible by a matching change in which $(1 - m_i)E_i$ is reduced by ε and $(1 - m_j)E_j$ raised by ε over I_i and which again leaves the total output of energy unchanged. Thus, the double perturbation leaves $U(t, Y)$ unchanged.   Q.E.D.

We proceed to show that proposition 2.9 is not empty, that there exist cases in which the optimal $A - \sum m_k E_k$ is positive for all t.

Proposition 2.10.   If

$$U(t, Y) = Y^\alpha + \phi(t), \qquad \phi(t) \geqq 0, \qquad 0 < \alpha < 1,$$

if $D(t) = \exp(-rt)$, r a positive constant, and if A is sufficiently large in relation to the m_k's, then along an optimal path $A - \sum m_k E_k$ is positive.

Proof. Since $\phi(t) \geqq 0$, the optimal T is infinite. Let us define

$$x_k \equiv (1 - m_k)E_k,$$

$$x \equiv \sum x_k,$$

$$\lambda \equiv \lambda_k / (1 - m_k).$$

A path $x(t)$ is optimal only if it satisfies:

$$D(t)U_Y(t, A + x(t)) = \lambda, \quad \text{for } t < t^*, \tag{42}$$

$$D(t)U_Y(t, A) \leqq \lambda, \qquad \text{for } t \geqq t^*, \tag{43}$$

$$\int_0^{t^*} x(t)\,dt = \sum \bar{R}_k / (1 - m_k) \equiv \bar{R}. \tag{44}$$

When $U = Y^\alpha + \phi(t)$ and $D(t) = \exp(-rt)$, $r > 0$, then (42) and (43) reduce to:

$$x(t) = [(\lambda/\alpha)\exp(rt)]^{1/(\alpha-1)} - A, \quad \text{for } t < t^*, \tag{42'}$$

$$x(t) = 0, \qquad \text{for } t \geqq t^*. \tag{43'}$$

Here λ and t^* are jointly determined by

$$[(\lambda/\alpha)\exp(rt^*)]^{1/(\alpha-1)} - A = 0 \tag{45}$$

and

$$(\lambda/\alpha)^{1/(\alpha-1)}[(\alpha-1)/r][\exp(rt/(\alpha-1))]_0^{t^*} - At^* = \bar{R}. \tag{46}$$

Simplifying (46) with the aid of (45), we obtain:

$$(\lambda/\alpha)^{1/(\alpha-1)} = [r/(1-\alpha)][At^* + \bar{R}] + A, \tag{47}$$

which can be inserted into (45) to yield:

$$F(t^*) \equiv \{[r/(1-\alpha)][At^* + \bar{R}] + A\}\exp[rt^*/(\alpha-1)] - A = 0. \tag{48}$$

Since $F(0) > 0$ and $F(\infty) < 0$, there exists $t^* > 0$ such that (48) is satisfied. Indeed, t^* is unique; for, when $F(t^*) = 0$:

$$F'(t^*) = [Ar/(\alpha-1)][1 - \exp(rt^*/(\alpha-1))] < 0.$$

Now let $m^* = \max\{m_k\}$. Then

$$\sum m_k E_k \leqq m^* \sum E_k = m^* \sum E_k (1 - m_k)/(1 - m_k)$$

$$\leqq [m^*/(1 - m^*)]\sum E_k(1 - m_k)$$

$$= [m^*/(1 - m^*)]x$$

$$\leqq [m^*/(1 - m^*)]x(0).$$

Hence, $A - \sum m_k E_k$ is positive provided that $m^*/(1 - m^*)$ is sufficiently small.   Q.E.D.

Remark concerning proposition 2.10.   In the example of proposition 2.10, solar energy is produced in positive amounts for *all* t. To achieve that result, the net-benefit function was severely restricted. However, to demonstrate merely that it may be optimal to simultaneously produce solar and non-solar energy for *some* t, much less restrictive examples suffice. Thus, if $U = U(Y)$ and $U(Y)$ is a strictly concave function, then from the proof of proposition 2.1 the optimal path $Y^*(t)$ must be continuous. And if $Y^*(t)$ is continuous, then it is optimal to simultaneously produce both types of energy and, from proposition 2.9, the order of extraction is, within limits, a matter of indifference.

Companion to proposition 2.9 we have:

Proposition 2.11.   If the net-benefit function is of type (vi) and if along an optimal trajectory $A - \sum m_k E_k - \gamma Z$ (the output of solar energy) is positive, then the order of exploitation of the deposit is within bounds a matter of indifference.

Proof.   The proof is similar to that of proposition 2.9.

And companion to proposition 2.10 we have:

Proposition 2.12.   If

$$U = (Y - \gamma Z)^\alpha + Z^\alpha,$$

if $D(t) = \exp(-rt)$, r a positive constant, and if A is sufficiently large in relation to the m_k's, then along an optimal path $A - \sum m_k E_k - \gamma Z$ is positive.

Proof.   The proof is similar to that of proposition 2.10.

Propositions 2.9 and 2.11 run counter to the intuitive principle that, if the rate of discount is positive, it is better to incur costs later than earlier. We therefore pause to explain in common-sense terms why that principle admits of exceptions in a context of exhaustible resources. As is clear from (42), the discounted net benefit from the resource must be the same at all points of time as long as not all profitable deposits are exhausted. If the entire labour force were devoted to extraction, it might be impossible to satisfy that condition, for net benefit might decline too rapidly. Thus, it might be optimal to produce the substitute before all deposits of the natural resource are exhausted. (This is so even if all deposits have the same cost so that, effectively, there is only one deposit.) Suppose that there are at least two unexhausted deposits with different costs, and that it is optimal to produce the substitute. Then, over some interval of time, it is possible to switch labour from an active relatively low-cost deposit to a relatively high-cost deposit, thus reducing the average efficiency of labour in mining, at the same time cutting back production of the resource-substitute, in which labour is less efficient again, on balance leaving both the total output of energy and the average efficiency of labour unchanged. Now let the switch be reversed during a second interval of time. Evidently the double switch leaves unchanged both the flow of net benefit and the accumulated output from each mine. It follows that if the initial pattern of extraction and substitute production is optimal, then so is the perturbed pattern. Thus, it is not suboptimal to incur higher extraction costs earlier rather than later if by doing so it is possible to defer even higher costs of producing the resource-substitute.

Implicit in propositions 2.9 and 2.11 is the assumption that the resource must be consumed or sold as it is extracted. Suppose, alternatively, that the extracted resource can be costlessly converted into a productive asset ("capital"). If the asset can produce a resource-substitute then, as Solow and Wan (1976) and Lewis (1982) have shown, the conclusions of propositions 2.9 and 2.11 must be modified. In particular, if the asset can produce a *perfect* resource-substitute, then the conclusions must be abandoned. (The conclusions may be preserved if only an inferior substitute can be produced.) Thus, let us denote by $K(t)$ the capital stock and by

$$S(t) = F(K(t)) \qquad (F' > 0, F'' \leqq 0)$$

the production function for the perfect substitute. Given a net-benefit function of type (v) the total consumption of energy is then:

$$S(t) + A + \sum E_k(t) - \sum m_k E_k(t) - I(t),$$

where $I(t)$ is the rate of gross investment,

$$I(t) = \dot{K}(t) + \beta K(t),$$

and β is the non-negative constant rate of depreciation.

Proposition 2.13. Given the above specifications, if $F'(K) > \beta$, then the optimal path of extraction is Herfindahl; moreover, along the optimal path $A - \sum m_k E_k = 0$ until all deposits with $m_k < 1$ are exhausted.

Proof. Without loss of generality, let $m_j < m_k$ for some j and k and let there be two intervals of time (t_1, t_2) and (t_3, t_4), $t_3 \geqq t_2$, such that, for some $\varepsilon > 0$, $E_k(t) > \varepsilon$ over the first interval and $E_j(t) > \varepsilon$ over the second interval. Now let εm_k units of labour be switched from the kth to the jth deposit during the first interval, and let the switch be reversed during the second interval. During the first interval, extraction from the kth deposit falls by ε and extraction from the second deposit rises by $\varepsilon(m_k/m_j) > \varepsilon$. If the additional output is invested, with consumption kept unchanged at all times, then since $F'(K) > \beta$, the additional capital will more than compensate for the reduction in aggregate extraction during the second interval.   Q.E.D.

3. Set-up costs and flow fixed costs[1]

3.1. *Concepts*

Set-up costs are costs which must be incurred once, before extraction can begin. They may be incurred at a point of time or over a finite interval of time; they may or may not be specific to a single deposit of a resource; and they may or may not depend on the proposed path of extraction (in particular, on the maximum rate of extraction). In a context of mineral extraction, one thinks of exploration, clearing of the overburden, and construction of access roads and loading facilities. Here it is assumed that set-up costs are specific to the individual deposits of a resource but are independent of the planned path of extraction and of time and therefore are not choice variables. Suppose that the planner wishes to begin extracting from the kth deposit at time t_k, and let S_k be the value at t_k of the set-up costs. As already noted, S_k may be a momentary outlay or the value at t_k of expenditures $I_k(t)$ over an interval $(t_k - h_k, t_k)$:

$$S_k = \int_{t_k - h_k}^{t_k} I_k(t) \exp[r(t_k - t)] \, dt.$$

[1]This section draws on Hartwick et al. (1980) and Kemp and Long (1980d).

Flow fixed costs, on the other hand, are incurred whenever extraction takes place but are independent of the rate of extraction. They may or may not be specific to individual deposits and may or may not depend on time. Here it is assumed that they are specific to individual deposits and independent of time.

3.2. *Some general results*

The analysis of this section is intrinsically more complicated than that of section 2. To ease the burden on the reader, we proceed by stages, first proving some general propositions before descending to specific forms of the net-benefit function. From the outset, however, the net-benefit function is assumed to be continuously differentiable and to take the form

$$U(t, \tilde{E}) \equiv B(t, E) - \sum v_k E_k - \sum \delta(E_k) f_k, \tag{49}$$

where B is increasing and strictly concave in E, v_k and f_k are non-negative constants, and

$$\delta(E_k) = \begin{cases} 0, & \text{if } E_k = 0, \\ 1, & \text{if } E_k > 0. \end{cases}$$

Evidently B may be interpreted as the gross benefit derived from total extraction, v_k as the constant average variable cost of extracting from the kth deposit, and f_k as the flow fixed cost of extracting from the kth deposit.

The task of the planner is to find

$$\text{(P3)} \quad \max_{t_k, \{E_k(t)\} 0} \int_{}^{\infty} D(t) U(t, \tilde{E}) \, dt - \sum D(t_k) S_k$$

$$\text{s.t.} \int_0^{\infty} E_k(t) \, dt \leq \bar{R}_k, \tag{50}$$

$$E_k(t) \begin{cases} = 0, & \text{if } t \leq t_k \\ \geq 0, & \text{if } t > t_k, \end{cases} \tag{51}$$

where $E_k(t)$ is a piecewise-continuous function. We proceed to establish properties of the optimal path $\tilde{E}^*(t)$.

The first property is obvious.

Proposition 3.1. If $f_k > 0$ for all k or if $v_j \neq v_k$ for all j and k $(j \neq k)$, then along any optimal path, deposits are worked sequentially, i.e.

$$E(t) \equiv \sum E_k(t) = \max\{E_1(t), \ldots, E_n(t)\}. \tag{52}$$

Let us denote by $t_{jk}^{(i)}$ the point of time at which, for the ith time, extraction is switched from the jth deposit to the kth so that, for all sufficiently small positive h:

$$E_j(t_{jk}^{(i)} - h) > 0, \qquad E_j(t_{jk}^{(i)} + h) = 0,$$
$$E_k(t_{jk}^{(i)} - h) = 0, \qquad E_j(t_{jk}^{(i)} + h) > 0.$$

Points $t_{jk}^{(i)}$ will be called *transition points* and points t_k *set-up* points.

We turn our attention to the behaviour of $E^*(t)$ at the transition point $t_{jk}^{(i)}$. For the time being it will be assumed that the transition point is not also a set-up point, i.e. that $t_{jk}^{(i)} \neq t_k$.

Suppose then that an optimal path exists. Let $t_{jk}^{(i)} \equiv \alpha^*$ be a point of transition from the jth deposit to the kth; let $(\alpha^* - h_j, \alpha^*)$ be an interval of time over which only the jth deposit is extracted and $(\alpha^*, \alpha^* + h_k)$ an interval over which only the kth deposit is extracted; and let

$$A_j \equiv \int_{\alpha^* - h_j}^{\alpha^*} E^*_j(t) \, dt; \qquad A_k \equiv \int_{\alpha^*}^{\alpha^* + h_k} E^*_k(t) \, dt.$$

From the Principle of Optimality, $E_j^*(t)$, $E_k^*(t)$, and α^* must be a solution of:

$$\text{(P4)} \quad \max_{\alpha, \{E_j(t), E_k(t)\}} \int_{\alpha - h_j}^{\alpha} D(t) U(t, E_j(t)) \, dt + \int_{\alpha}^{\alpha + h_k} D(t) U(t, E_k(t)) \, dt$$

$$\text{s.t.} \int_{\alpha - h_j}^{\alpha} E_j(t) \, dt \leq A_j, \tag{53}$$

$$\int_{\alpha}^{\alpha + h_k} E_k(t) \, dt \leq A_k. \tag{54}$$

Defining:

$$\text{(P5)} \quad W_k \equiv \max_{\{E_k(t)\}} \int_{\alpha}^{\alpha + h_k} D(t) U(t, E_k(t)) \, dt, \tag{55}$$

where the maximization is subject to (54), we may re-state (P4) in the equivalent form:

$$\text{(P6)} \quad \max_{\alpha, \{E_j(t)\}} \int_{\alpha - h_j}^{\alpha} D(t) U(t, E_j(t)) \, dt + W_k$$

subject to (53). Let the Hamiltonian of (P5) be:

$$H_k(t) \equiv D(t) U(t, E_k(t)) - \lambda_k E_k(t), \tag{56}$$

where λ_k is the constant multiplier associated with (54); and let the Hamiltonian of (P6) be:

$$H_j(t) \equiv D(t) U(t, E_j(t)) - \lambda_j E_j(t), \tag{56'}$$

where λ_j is the multiplier associated with (53). Then the transversality condition associated with the optimal choice of α in (P6) is:

$$\lim_{t \to \alpha^{*-}} H_j(t) \equiv H_j(\alpha^{*-}) = \partial W_k / \partial \alpha. \tag{57}$$

But it is well known that:

$$\partial W_k / \partial \alpha = H_k(\alpha^{*+}) \equiv \lim_{t \to \alpha^{*+}} H_k(t).$$

Thus we arrive at:

Lemma 3.1. $H_j(\alpha^{*-}) = H_k(\alpha^{*+})$ if α^* is a point of transition from the jth deposit to the kth and $\alpha^* \neq t^*_k$.

For the final step in our argument we need a familiar definition.

Definition 3.1. The consumers' surplus at time t, t not a transition point, is:

$$J(t) \equiv B(t, E(t)) - B_E(t, E(t)) E(t).$$

Suppose, for simplicity of exposition only, that $E_j^*(t) > 0$ for all $t \in (\alpha^* - h_j, \alpha^*)$ and that $E_k^*(t) > 0$ for all $t \in (\alpha^*, \alpha^* + h_k)$. Then, since for all $t \in (\alpha^* - h_j, \alpha^*)$ the Hamiltonian $H_j(t)$ is maximized with respect to E_j:

$$\lambda_j = D(t)(B_E - v_j) \tag{58}$$

and

$$H_j(t) = D(t)[J(t) - f_j]. \tag{59}$$

The following proposition follows immediately from (59) and lemma 3.1.

Proposition 3.2. If α^* is a point of transition from the jth deposit to the kth and if α^* is not the set-up point for the kth deposit ($\alpha^* \neq t_k^*$), then:

$$\left[\lim_{t \to \alpha^{*-}} J(t) \right] - \left[\lim_{t \to \alpha^{*+}} J(t) \right] = f_j - f_k, \tag{60}$$

i.e. the jump in consumers' surplus just compensates for the jump in flow fixed cost.

Both lemma 3.1 and proposition 3.2 can be generalized to accommodate the possibility that the transition point is also a set-up point. If $\alpha = t_k$, then clearly (P4) and (P6) must take the modified forms:

(P4') $\displaystyle \max_{\alpha,\{E_j(t),E_k(t)\}} \int_{a-h_j}^{\alpha} D(t)U(t, E_j(t))\,\mathrm{d}t$

$\displaystyle + \int_{\alpha}^{\alpha+h_k} D(t)U(t, E_k(t))\,\mathrm{d}t - D(\alpha)S_k$

and

(P6') $\displaystyle \max_{\alpha,\{E_j(t)\}} \int_{\alpha-h_j}^{\alpha} D(t)U(t, E_j(t)\,\mathrm{d}t + W_k - D(\alpha)S_k,$

respectively, and condition (57) becomes:

$$H_j(\alpha^{*-}) = (\partial W_k/\partial\alpha) - \dot{D}(\alpha^*)S_k. \tag{57'}$$

The required generalizations are then:

Lemma 3.1'. $H(\alpha^{*-}) = H(\alpha^{*+}) - \dot{D}(\alpha^*)S_k$ if α^* is a point of transition from the jth deposit to the kth and $\alpha^* = t_k^*$.

Proposition 3.2'.   If α^* is a point of transition from the jth deposit to the kth and if it is also the set-up point for the kth deposit, then:

$$\left[\lim_{t\to\alpha^{*-}} J(t)\right] - \left[\lim_{t\to\alpha^{*+}} J(t)\right] = f_j - f_k + [\dot{D}(\alpha)/D(\alpha)]S_k, \tag{60'}$$

i.e. the jump in consumers' surplus equals the jump in flow fixed costs plus the interest cost on the set-up capital expenditure.

3.3.   *The order of exploitation when average variable costs and flow fixed costs, but not necessarily set-up costs, are uniform across deposits*

We now set our general results to work in tracing the implications of non-uniformity of set-up costs and non-uniformity of deposit size. To avoid muddling the analysis, both average variable costs and flow fixed costs are constrained to be the same everywhere; that is, $v_k = v$ and $f_k = f$ for all k. All remaining assumptions from section 3.2 are retained.

Proposition 3.3.   Under the maintained assumptions of this section,

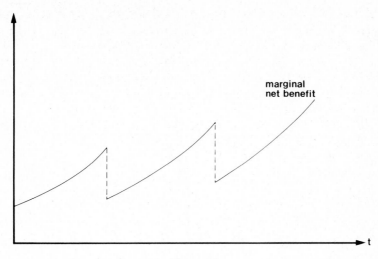

Figure 4.3

marginal net benefit $B_E - v$ follows a saw-tooth pattern, with downward jumps at set-up points.

Proof. Since B is a strictly concave function of E, the consumers' surplus is increasing in E. From proposition 3.2' and the uniformity of fixed costs, the consumers' surplus, and therefore E, jumps up at set-up points. Again from the strict concavity of B, each upward jump of E corresponds to a downward jump of B_E. From (58), between transitions $B_E - v$ rises at the rate of interest. Q.E.D.

Figure 4.3 illustrates the path of marginal net benefit when the rate of interest is constant.

Proposition 3.3 tells us nothing about the order of extraction. Let us define the set-up cost per unit of the resource $S_k / \bar{R}_k$. It might be thought that, if the rate of interest is positive, the deposits should be worked in strict sequence, beginning with the deposit with the lowest set-up cost per unit. Unfortunately this is not so, even under our restrictive maintained assumptions. However, there are two special cases in which, quite clearly, it is so.

Proposition 3.4. If the rate of interest is positive and if either (a) set-up costs are uniform across deposits ($S_k = S$ for all k) or (b) deposits are of equal size ($\bar{R}_k = \bar{R}$ for all k), then the deposits should be worked in strict sequence, beginning with the deposit with the lowest set-up cost per unit. The parallel with Herfindahl's theorem will be apparent.

Proposition 3.4 has an interesting corollary. Suppose that the deposits are of equal size R and bear equal set-up costs S, but that the set-up costs are payable not just once for each deposit but recurrently, once for each R' (or part thereof) of resource extracted. Then each deposit can be viewed as a collection of $m + 1$ subdeposits, all but one of size R', the remaining deposit of size $\bar{R} - mR'$. The total initial endowment can then be viewed as consisting of mn subdeposits each of size R' and n subdeposits each of size $\bar{R} - mR' < R'$. Applying proposition 3.4, it is optimal to extract the mn larger subdeposits before turning to the n smaller subdeposits. Fussier versions of the corollary can be obtained by allowing deposits to differ in size $\bar{R}_k$ or in set-up cost S_k or in frequency $1/R'_k$.

Proposition 3.4 has disposed of the easy cases in which deposits differ only in size *or* set-up cost. Clearly, if size and set-up cost are inversely related, the larger deposits bearing the lower costs, then matters remain very simple: deposits should be worked in strict sequence, beginning with the largest. Complications arise when size and set-up cost are directly related, with larger deposits bearing higher costs. Let us concentrate on that case. In particular, let us assume that the relationship of set-up cost to size is one of strict proportionality, so that set-up cost per unit $S_k/\bar{R}_k$ is the same for all k. Even in this case the optimal policy is far from obvious. Thus, suppose that there are just two deposits, with $S_1/\bar{R}_1 = S_2/\bar{R}_2$ and $R_2 = \mu\bar{R}_1$, $\mu \geqq 1$. If the smaller deposit is worked first and exhausted at time T_1, then the present value of set-up costs is:

$$\zeta_1 \equiv S_1 + D(T_1)\mu S_1, \tag{61}$$

and if the same consumption path is obtained by first working the larger second deposit, exhausted at $T_2 > T_1$, then the present value of set-up costs is

$$\zeta_2 \equiv \mu S_1 + D(T_2)S_1, \tag{62}$$

In general, $\zeta_2 - \zeta_1$ may be of either sign. This is so even when $D(t) = \exp(-rt)$, r a positive constant. In that case:

$$\zeta_2 - \zeta_1 = S_1(\mu - 1) + S_1[\exp(-rT_2) - \mu \exp(-rT_1)], \tag{63}$$

with the first term on the right-hand side positive, the second negative.

Each sequence yields a lower cumulative set-up cost and interest burden for part of the period of extraction and, without additional information, it is impossible to determine the balance. The additional information might concern the values of the parameters S_k, v, f, and $\bar{R}_k$, or it might concern the form of $B(t, E)$ or $D(t)$. Here we concentrate on the latter type of information.

Proposition 3.5. Let $B = \ln E$ and $D(t) = \exp(-rt)$, r a positive constant. Then it is optimal to exhaust the smaller deposit first if $\mu - 1$ is a sufficiently small positive number and if rS_1 is sufficiently large.

Proof. Suppose that the smaller deposit is worked first, so that $E(t) = E_1(t)$ for $t < T_1$ and $E(t) = E_2(t)$ for $t > T_1$, and let

$$E_1^- \equiv \lim_{t \to T_1^-} E(t); \qquad E_2^+ \equiv \lim_{t \to T_1^+} E(t).$$

During the interval $(0, T_1)$, marginal net benefit rises at the rate of interest:

$$[1/E(t)] \exp(-rt) = [1/E_1^-] \exp(-rT_1). \tag{64}$$

Thus, for $t < T_1$:

$$E(t) = E_1^- \exp(rT_1 - rt) \tag{65}$$

and

$$\int_0^{T_1} E(t) \, dt = E_1^-[\exp(rT_1) - 1]/r = \bar{R}_1,$$

so that

$$\exp(rT_1) = 1 + (r\bar{R}_1/E_1^-). \tag{66}$$

For $t > T_1$, on the other hand:

$$E(t) = E_2^+ \exp(rT_1 - rt). \tag{67}$$

Thus:

$$\int_{T_1}^{\infty} E(t) \, dt = E_2^+ \exp(rT_1) \int_{T_1}^{\infty} \exp(-rt) \, dt$$

$$= E_2^+/r = \bar{R}_2 = \mu \bar{R}_1. \tag{68}$$

At the point of transition from the smaller to the bigger deposit:

$$J(T^-) = J(T^+) - r\mu S_1.$$

Hence

$$\ln E_1^- = \ln E_2^+ - r\mu S_1 \tag{69a}$$

or

$$E_1^- = E_2^+ \exp(-r\mu S_1). \tag{69b}$$

From (68) and (69b):

$$E_1^- = r\mu \bar{R}_1 \exp(-r\mu S_1), \tag{70}$$

and from (66) and (70):

$$\exp(rT_1) = 1 + \mu^{-1} \exp(r\mu S_1) > 1$$

or

$$T_1 = \frac{1}{r} \ln[1 + \mu^{-1} \exp(r\mu S_1)]. \tag{71}$$

The net discounted utility is:

$$V_1 = \int_0^{T_1} (\ln E_1) \exp(-rt) \, dt + \int_{T_1}^{\infty} (\ln E_2)$$
$$\times \exp(-rt) \, dt - S_1 - \mu S_1 \exp(-rT_1). \tag{72}$$

The first integral is:

$$\int_0^{T_1} \ln(E_1^- \exp(rT_1 - rt)) \exp(-rt) \, dt$$

$$= \int_0^{T_1} [(\ln E_1^-) + rT_1 - rt] \exp(-rt) \, dt$$

$$= \left[\frac{1 - \exp(-rT_1)}{r} \right] (rT_1 + \ln E_1^- - 1) + T_1 \exp(-rT_1).$$

The second integral is:

$$\int_{T_1}^{\infty} [(\ln E_2^+) + rT_1 - rt] \exp(-rt) \, dt$$

$$= \frac{\exp(-rT_1)}{r} (rT_1 + \ln E_2^+ - 1) - T_1 \exp(-rT_1).$$

Hence:

$$V_1 = (rT_1 + \ln E_1^- - 1)/r + \exp(-rT_1)(\ln E_2^+ - \ln E_1^-)/r - S_1 - \mu S_1$$
$$\times \exp(-rT_1), \tag{73}$$

or, simplifying with the aid of (69a):

$$V_1 = (rT_1 + \ln E_1^- - 1)/r - S_1,$$

or, simplifying further by applying (70) and (71):

$$V_1 = (1/r)\{\ln[r\mu\bar{R}_1 + r\mu\bar{R}_1 \exp(r\mu\bar{R}_1)] - 1\} - (1 + \mu)S_1. \tag{74}$$

Suppose, alternatively, that the larger second deposit is exhausted first. Let us define:

$$E_2^- \equiv \lim_{t \to T_2^-} E(t); \qquad E_1^+ \equiv \lim_{t \to T_2^+} E(t).$$

Then, by now-familiar reasoning:

$$E_2^-[\exp(rT_2) - 1]/r = \mu\bar{R}_1,$$
$$\exp(rT_2) = 1 + (r\mu\bar{R}_1/E_2^-). \tag{66'}$$
$$E_1^+/r = \bar{R}_1, \tag{68'}$$

and

$$\ln E_2^- = \ln E_1^+ - rS_1, \tag{69a'}$$
$$E_2^- = E_1^+ \exp(-rS_1) \tag{69b'}$$
$$E_2^- = r\bar{R}_1 \exp(-rS_1) \tag{70'}$$
$$\exp(rT_2) = 1 + \mu \exp(rS_1),$$
$$T_2 = (1/r)\ln[1 + \mu \exp(rS_1)], \tag{71'}$$
$$V_2 = (rT_2 + \ln E_2^- - 1)/r + \exp(-rT_2)(\ln E_1^+ - \ln E_2^-)/r - \mu S_1 - S_1$$
$$\times \exp(-rT_2), \tag{73'}$$
$$V_2 = (1/r)\{\ln[r\bar{R}_1 + \mu r\bar{R}_1 \exp(rS_1)] - 1\} - (1 + \mu)S_1. \tag{74'}$$

From (74) and (74'):

$$\Delta \equiv V_2 - V_1 = (1/r)\{\ln[r\bar{R}_1 + \mu r\bar{R}_1 \exp(rS_1)]$$
$$- \ln[r\mu\bar{R}_1 + r_1\bar{R}_1 \exp(r\mu S_1)]. \tag{75}$$

Now $\Delta = 0$ if $\mu = 1$. Therefore if we can show that

$$\left.\frac{\partial \Delta}{\partial \mu}\right|_{\mu=1} > 0, \tag{76}$$

then we can conclude that the larger second deposit should be exploited first provided that $\bar{R}_2 - \bar{R}_1$ is sufficiently small. Similarly, if we can show that

$$\left.\frac{\partial \Delta}{\partial \mu}\right|_{\mu=1} < 0, \tag{77}$$

then we can conclude that the smaller first deposit should be exploited first provided that $\bar{R}_2 - \bar{R}_1$ is sufficiently small. Let $x = rS_1$ so that, from (75):

$$r\Delta = \ln\left(\frac{1 + \mu \exp(x)}{\mu + \exp(\mu x)}\right) \equiv \ln y, \tag{78}$$

and, differentiating:

$$\frac{\mathrm{d}(r\Delta)}{\mathrm{d}\mu} = \frac{1}{y}\left\{\frac{(1 - \mu x)\exp(\mu x + x) - 1 - x\exp(\mu x)}{(\mu + \exp(\mu x))^2}\right\} \tag{79}$$

Evaluated at $\mu = 1$, $\mathrm{d}(r\Delta)/\mathrm{d}\mu$ is negative if and only if the expression

$$(1 - x)\exp(2x) - 1 - x\exp(x) \tag{80}$$

is negative. Clearly (80) is negative if $x \geq 1$. Hence (77) holds for $x \geq 1$.

3.4. The order of exploitation when average variable costs and set-up costs, but not necessarily flow fixed costs, are uniform across deposits

We now turn our attention to the implications of non-uniformity of flow fixed costs. In the interests of clarity, both average variable costs and set-up costs are constrained to be the same everywhere; indeed, we may as well neglect them altogether, setting $v_k = 0 = S_k$ for all k, so that the average cost of extraction from the kth deposit is simply $f_k/E_k(t)$.

Suppose that there are just two deposits and that $f_2 > f_1 > 0$. Then it might seem that it is always optimal to exhaust the first or low-cost deposit before passing to the second, thus putting off the higher fixed cost as long as possible. However, applying Hotelling's rule piecemeal, along an optimal path the marginal net benefit from extraction must rise exponentially at the market rate of interest; and, if the utility function is strictly concave, this implies that between transitions the rate of extraction must decline. It follows that the strategy of first exhausting the low-cost deposit not only postpones the higher fixed cost but may increase the interval of time over which the higher cost is sustained. Thus, it becomes necessary to weigh the advantage of delaying the point of time at which the higher fixed cost is first incurred against the advantage of reducing the interval over which it is incurred. This suggests that, for some utility functions, it may be suboptimal to exhaust the low-cost deposit before working the high-cost deposit. It suggests also that there may exist utility functions such that the order of extraction is a matter of indifference, implying that repeated switching back and forth between two deposits may be optimal. (Since $f_1 > 0$ and $f_2 > 0$, it is never optimal to work the two deposits simultaneously.) We proceed to establish two propositions which confirm these possibilities.

Proposition 3.6. Let $n = 2$, $v_k = 0 = S_k$ for all k, $B = \ln E$, and $D(t) = \exp(-rt)$, r a positive constant. Then the order of extraction is a matter of indifference.

Proof. Consider the set of programs in which the jth deposit is exhausted before the kth deposit is touched. Let T be the transition point. The planner must solve the problem:

$$(\text{P7}) \quad \max_{T,\{E_j(t)\}} \int_0^T [\ln(E_j(t)) - f_j] \exp(-rt)\, dt + V_k(\bar{R}_k) \exp(-rT)$$

$$\text{s.t.} \int_0^T E_j(t)\, dt \le \bar{R}_j$$

$$E_j(t) \ge 0, \qquad \bar{R}_j, \text{ given,}$$

where $V_k(\bar{R}_k)$ is the value of the problem:

$$(\text{P8}) \quad \max_{\{E_k(t)\}} \int_0^\infty [\ln(E_k(t)) - f_k] \exp(-rt)\, dt$$

$$\text{s.t.} \int_0^\infty E_k(t)\, dt \le \bar{R}_k$$

$$E_k(t) \geqq 0, \qquad \bar{R}_k, \text{ given.}$$

Let $V_{jk}(\bar{R}_j, \bar{R}_k)$ be the value of (P7). From the first-order conditions for (P8), or from Hotelling's rule:

$$E_k^*(t) = E_k^*(T^{*+}) \exp[-r(t - T^*)], \qquad t \geqq T^*,$$

$$E_k(T^{*+}) = r\bar{R}_k.$$

Hence:

$$V_k(\bar{R}_k) = \int_{T^*}^{\infty} [\ln(r\bar{R}_k) - r(t - T^*) - f_k] \exp[-r(t - T^*)] \, dt$$

$$= [\ln(r\bar{R}_k) - f_k - 1]/r. \tag{81}$$

Now from lemma 3.1 and the fact (proved by Kemp and Long (1982) that $H(T^{*+}) = rV_k(\bar{R}_k)$:

$$\ln E_j(T^{*-}) - f_j - 1 = \ln(r\bar{R}_k) - f_k - 1,$$

whence

$$E_j(T^{*-}) = r\bar{R}_k \exp(f_j - f_k). \tag{82}$$

Again appealing to Hotelling's rule:

$$E_j(t) = E_j(T^{*-}) \exp[-r(t - T^*)], \qquad t \in [0, T^*). \tag{83}$$

Hence:

$$\bar{R}_j = \int_0^{T^*} E_j(t) \, dt$$

$$= \int_0^{T^*} r\bar{R}_k[\exp(f_j - f_k)][\exp(-r(t - T^*))] \, dt$$

$$= \bar{R}_k \exp(f_j - f_k)[\exp(rT^*) - 1],$$

and

$$T^* = (1/r) \ln[1 + (R_j/R_k) \exp(f_k - f_j)]. \tag{84}$$

Substituting (82)–(84) into the maximand of (P7):

$$V_{jk}(\bar{R}_j, \bar{R}_k) = \{\ln(r\bar{R}_k) - f_k - 1 + \ln[1 + (\bar{R}_j/\bar{R}_k) \exp(f_k - f_j)]\}/r. \tag{85}$$

Consider now the set of programmes in which the kth deposit is exhausted before extraction of the jth begins. Permuting subscripts in (85):

$$V_{kj}(\bar{R}_j, \bar{R}_k) = \{\ln(r\bar{R}_j) - f_j - 1 + \ln[1 + (\bar{R}_k/\bar{R}_j) \exp(f_j - f_k)]\}/r. \quad (85')$$

It is easy to verify that $\exp(V_{jk}) = \exp(V_{kj})$, implying that the order of extraction is a matter of indifference.

Our second proposition shows that it may be suboptimal to exhaust the low-cost deposit before working the high-cost deposit.

Proposition 3.7. Let $n = 2$, $v_k = 0 = S_k$, and $f_k > 0$ for all k, $B = E^\alpha + A(1 > \alpha > 0, A \gtreqless 0)$ and $D(t) = \exp(-rt)$, r a positive constant. If X_1 or X_2 is sufficiently small, where

$$X_k \equiv (1 - \alpha)^{(1-\alpha)/\alpha} r\bar{R}_k,$$

then it is suboptimal to exhaust the relatively low-cost deposit before exploiting the relatively high-cost deposit.

Proof. Consider the set of programs for which the jth deposit is exhausted before extraction of the kth deposit is begun. Let T_1^* be the switchpoint and T_2^* the point at which all extraction ceases. We begin by showing that T_2^* is finite. Insert the new-benefit functions into (P7) and (P8), obtaining (say) (P9) and (P10). If T_2^* were infinite, then from the first-order conditions for (P10) and from the form of B:

$$E_k^*(t) = E_k(T_1^{*+}) \exp[-r(t - T_1^*)/(1 - \alpha)], \quad \text{for } t \geq T_1^*. \quad (86)$$

Substituting from (86) into the first constraint of (P10) and solving:

$$E_k^*(T_1^{*+}) = r\bar{R}_k/(1 - \alpha).$$

It then follows that the value of the optimal program for (P10) would be:

$$\int_{T_1}^{\infty} \exp[-r(t - T_1)][(E_k(t))^\alpha + A - f_k] \, dt$$

$$= [(1 - \alpha)^{1-\alpha}(r\bar{R}_k)^\alpha - (f_k - A)]/r. \quad (87)$$

If, on the other hand, T_2 is finite, then from the transversality condition $H(T_2^{*-}) = B(0)$ and the continuity of $H(t)$ over $[T_1^*, T_2^*]$:

$$\lim_{t \to T_2^{*-}} [B(E_k) - f_k - (B')E_k] = B(0),$$

so that, for the present example:

$$A + (1 - \alpha)[E_k(T_2^{*-})]^\alpha - f_k = A$$

and

$$E_k(T_2^{*-}) = [f_k/(1-\alpha)]^{1/\alpha} \equiv \bar{E}_k. \tag{88}$$

However, from Hotelling's rule and the form of B:

$$E_k^*(t) = \bar{E}_k \exp[-r(t - T_2^*)/(1-\alpha)]. \tag{89}$$

From (88) and (89) and the first constraint of (P10) it then follows that:

$$T_2^* - T_1^* = \frac{1-\alpha}{r} \ln\left[\frac{rR_k(1-\alpha)^{1/\alpha}}{(1-\alpha)f_k^{1/\alpha}} + 1\right]. \tag{90}$$

The value of the optimal program with T_2^* finite is, therefore:

$$\frac{f_k}{r}\left\{\left[\frac{rR_k(1-\alpha)^{1/\alpha}}{(1-\alpha)f_k^{1/\alpha}} + 1\right]^\alpha - 1\right\} + \frac{A}{r}$$

$$= \{[(1-\alpha)^{(1-\alpha)/\alpha}r\bar{R}_k + f_k^{1/\alpha}]^\alpha - (f_k - A)\}/r, \tag{91}$$

which, since $f_k > 0$, is greater than (87).

Proceeding, we have, from the lemma 3.1 and the form of B:

$$A + (1-\alpha)[E_j^*(T_1^{*-})]^\alpha - f_j = A + (1-\alpha)[E_k^*(T_1^{*+})]^\alpha - f_k. \tag{92}$$

Substituting from (88) and (89) into (92):

$$(1-\alpha)[E_j^*(T_1^{*-})]^\alpha - f_j = (1-\alpha)(\bar{E}_k)^\alpha \exp(\alpha r(T_2^* - T_1^*)/(1-\alpha)) - f_k.$$

On the other hand:

$$E_j^*(t) = E_j^*(0) \exp[-rt/(1-\alpha)], \quad \text{for } t \in (0, T_1^*),$$

which, with the first constraint of (P10), yields:

$$E_j^*(t) = \frac{r\bar{R}_j}{1-\alpha} \cdot \frac{\exp[-rt/(1-\alpha)]}{1 - \exp[-rT_1^*/(1-\alpha)]}, \quad \text{for } t \in [0, T_1^*). \tag{93}$$

Substituting from (87), (89) and (93) into (92), we find that:

$$(1-\alpha)\left[\frac{r\bar{R}_j}{1-\alpha}\right]^\alpha \left[\frac{\exp(-rT_1^*/(1-\alpha))}{1 - \exp(-rT_1^*/(1-\alpha))}\right]^\alpha - f_j$$

$$= [r\bar{R}_k(1-\alpha)^{(1-\alpha)/\alpha} + f_k^{1/\alpha}]^\alpha - f_k,$$

whence

$$T_1^* - \frac{1-\alpha}{r} \ln\left[\frac{X_j + Y}{Y}\right], \tag{94}$$

where

$$X_j \equiv (1-\alpha)^{1/\alpha} r\bar{R}_j/(1-\alpha),$$

$$Y \equiv [((1-\alpha)^{(1-\alpha)/\alpha} r\bar{R}_k + f_k^{1/\alpha})^\alpha - (f_k - f_j)]^{1/\alpha}.$$

Pooling (89), (92), and (93):

$$V_{jk}(\bar{R}_j, \bar{R}_k) = \{[X_j + ((X_k + f_k^{1/\alpha})^\alpha + (f_j - f_k))^{1/\alpha}]^\alpha + A - f_j\}/r. \tag{95}$$

$V_{kj}(\bar{R}_j, \bar{R}_k)$ can be found by permuting subscripts in (95) and the difference between the two program values computed from:

$$[V_{jk}(\bar{R}_j, \bar{R}_k) - V_{kj}(\bar{R}_j, \bar{R}_k)]r$$
$$= (f_k - f_j) + [X_j + ((X_k + f_k^{1/\alpha})^\alpha + (f_j - f_k))^{1/\alpha}]^\alpha$$
$$- [X_k + ((X_j + f_j^{1/\alpha})^\alpha + (f_k - f_j))^{1/\alpha}]^\alpha$$
$$\equiv G(X_j, X_k),$$

where, of course,

$$X_k \equiv (1-\alpha)^{1/\alpha} r\bar{R}_k/(1-\alpha).$$

Evidently, $G = 0$ if $X_j = 0$ or $X_k = 0$. Moreover:

$$\left.\frac{\partial G}{\partial X_j}\right|_{X_j=0, X_k>0} = \alpha[(X_k + f_k^{1/\alpha})^\alpha + (f_j - f_k)]^{(\alpha-1)/\alpha}$$
$$- (X_k + f_k^{1/\alpha})^{\alpha-1}(f_k/f_j)^{(1-\alpha)/\alpha},$$

and this is negative if $f_j < f_k$. For, suppose that it is non-negative. Then:

$$(X_k + f_k^{1/\alpha})^\alpha + (f_j - f_k) \le (X_k + f_k^{1/\alpha})^\alpha (f_j/f_k),$$

whence

$$f_j - f_k \le (X_k + f_k^{1/\alpha})^\alpha (f_j - f_k)/f_k.$$

But this is not possible, for

$$(X_k + f_k^{1/\alpha})^\alpha / f_k > 1.$$

Similarly:

$$\left.\frac{\partial G}{\partial X_k}\right|_{X_j>0, X_k=0} < 0,$$

if $f_j < f_k$. Thus, $G(X_j, X_k) < 0$ if $f_j < f_k$ and X_j or X_k is sufficiently small;

that is, if X_j or X_k is sufficiently small, then it is suboptimal to exhaust the relatively low-cost deposit before exploiting the relatively high-cost deposit.

4. Final remarks

This has been a long and, in places, tedious excursion. Undoubtedly better ways of organizing the material will be found. And our interpretations of the mathematics are far from comprehensive. For example, in section 2, variations across deposits of average variable costs of extraction often can be re-interpreted as variations in the quality (for some purpose) of the extracted resource; that is to say, the same mathematical formulation can be interpreted as applying both to resources heterogeneous below ground but homogeneous above (the interpretation provided in section 2) and to resources homogeneous below ground but heterogeneous above.

References

Hartwick, J. M., M. C. Kemp and N. V. Long (1980), Set-up costs and the theory of exhaustible resources, University of New South Wales.

Herfindahl, O. C. (1976), Depletion and economic theory, in: M. M. Gaffney, ed., Extractive Resources and Taxation (University of Wisconsin Press, Madison, Wisconsin) pp. 63–90.

Kemp, M. C. and N. V. Long (1980a), On two folk theorems concerning the extraction of exhaustible resources, Econometrica 48, 663–673.

Kemp, M. C. and N. V. Long (1980b), On the optimal order of exploitation of deposits of an exhaustible resource: The case of certainty, in: H Siebert, ed., Erschöpfbare Ressourcen (Arbeitstagung des Vereins für Socialpolitik, Mannheim 1979) (Duncker and Humblot, Berlin) pp. 301–317.

Kemp, M. C. and N. V. Long (1980c), Exhaustible Resources, Optimality, and Trade, Essays 3 and 12 (North-Holland Publishing Company, Amsterdam).

Kemp, M. C. and N. V. Long (1980d), The optimal order of exploitation of resource deposits: the case of heterogeneous fixed costs, University of New South Wales.

Kemp, M. C. and N. V. Long (1982), On the evaluation of social income in a dynamic economy: Variations on a Samuelsonian theme, in: G. R. Feiwel, ed., Samuelson and Neoclassical Economics (Kluwer–Nijhoff Publishing, Boston) pp. 185–189.

Lewis, T. R. (1982), Sufficient conditions for extracting least cost resource first, Econometrica 50, 1081–1083.

Shimomura, K. (1982), On the optimal order of exploitation of deposits of a renewable resource, Doctoral thesis, University of New South Wales.

Sinn, H-W. (1981), The theory of exhaustible resources, Zeitschrift für Nationalökonomie 41, 183–192.

Solow, R. M. and F. Y. Wan (1976), Extraction costs in the theory of exhaustible resources, Bell Journal of Economics 7, 359–370.

The optimal order of exploitation of deposits of a renewable resource

KAZUO SHIMOMURA*

1. Introduction

Let there be several deposits of an exhaustible resource. The deposits differ in extraction cost and possibly in their initial extent. How should the deposits be extracted? Herfindahl (1967) showed that the deposits should be extracted in strict sequence, beginning with the lowest cost, with each deposit completely exhausted before extraction of the next begins. Since the appearance of Herfindahl's paper his conclusions have been shown to hold in much broader contexts (Solow and Wan (1976)) but to lack complete generality (Kemp and Long (1980a, 1980b, 1980c)).

Common to all earlier discussions is the assumption that the resource is non-renewable. In this essay we reconsider Herfindahl's problem in a context of renewable resources. We assume that there are two deposits from both of which society can extract the resource. The deposits differ both in initial extent and in extraction cost. Society seeks to maximize the present value of the utility derived from consumption of the resource.

As will be shown in subsequent sections, it is suboptimal to exhaust one deposit before tackling the next unless the rate of time preference is extremely high compared with "marginal reproductivity". However, one can still ask which deposit to exploit first, which second, and so on. Furthermore, there are interesting questions which do not make sense in

*This essay is based on my Ph.D. thesis (Shimomura (1982)) submitted to the University of New South Wales. I am indebted to Professor Murray C. Kemp for valuable comments and suggestions.

Essays in the Economics of Exhaustible Resources, edited by *M. C. Kemp and N. V. Long*
© *Elsevier Science Publishers B.V., 1984*

the absence of renewability: Should each deposit be guided to a constant (steady-state) value? If so, should its motions be monotone? Might temporary overshooting of the steady state be required? The answers are collected in the following sections.

In section 2 we formulate our social optimum problem. The problem involves two state variables; accordingly, the detailed analysis is rather complicated. Sections 3 and 4 are, therefore, devoted to some preliminary and especially tedious arguments. At least on a first reading, those sections may be skimmed. In section 5 we solve our problem. Section 6 contains a summary of our conclusions as well as a few concluding remarks.

2. Assumptions and formulation

There are two deposits of an exhaustible but renewable resource. After extraction, the resource is consumable but perishable, which implies that the rates of extraction and consumption are the same. There is a second perishable and consumable resource, say leisure, which is available in a steady flow. Leisure can be used also in extracting the renewable resource.

Social utility is a function of both the rate of consumption of the resource and the rate of consumption of leisure. We assume that it is strictly concave with respect to the latter. That is to say,

$$\text{(social utility)} = \bar{u}[c] + al, \tag{1}$$

where c is the rate of resource consumption, l is the rate of leisure consumption, a is a positive constant, and $\bar{u}[c]$ is strictly concave and such that:

$$\lim_{c \to 0} \frac{d\bar{u}}{dc} = +\infty, \qquad \frac{d\bar{u}}{dc} > 0, \quad \text{for any } c \geqq 0. \tag{2}$$

Evidently c is the rate of extraction from the two deposits combined; that is, $c = c_1 + c_2$. In what follows we assume that the deposits differ in their "labour productivity", that is,

$$\bar{v}_1 < \bar{v}_2, \tag{3}$$

where $1/\bar{v}_i$ is the constant "labour productivity" in extraction from the ith deposit. If the maximum socially available rate of leisure is constant, say $\bar{l}$, then

$$l = \bar{l} - \tilde{v}_1 c_1 - \tilde{v}_2 c_2. \tag{4}$$

Substituting from (4) into (1), we have:

$$(\text{social utility}) = u[c_1 + c_2] - v_1 c_1 - v_2 c_2, \tag{1'}$$

where $u[\cdot] \equiv \tilde{u}[\ ] + al$ and $v_i \equiv a\tilde{v}_i$, $v_1 < v_2$.

The same reproduction function prevails for each deposit. Denote it by

$$\frac{dS_i}{dt} \equiv \dot{S}_i = g[S_i], \tag{5}$$

where $S_i(t)$ is the amount of the resource in the ith deposit at time t. $g[\cdot]$ has the following properties:

$$g[0] = 0, \tag{6}$$

$$+\infty \geqq \frac{dg[S_i]}{dS_i}\bigg|_{S_i=0} > 0, \tag{7}$$

$$\frac{d^2 g[S_i]}{dS_i^2} < 0, \quad \text{for any } S_i \geqq 0, \tag{8}$$

there is $S_A(>0)$ such that $\dfrac{dg[S_i]}{dS_i}\bigg|_{S_i=S_A} = 0. \tag{9}$

From (8) and (9) there is $S_c(>S_A)$ such that $g[S_c] = 0$. Fig. 5.1 is the graph of the reproduction function.

Society seeks to maximize social utility

$$\int_0^\infty \exp[-\rho t]\{u[\textstyle\sum c_i] - \textstyle\sum v_i c_i\}\, dt, \tag{10}$$

where ρ is the positive constant rate of time preference, subject to

$$\dot{S}_i = g[S_i] - c_i, \qquad S_i(0) \text{ given, } i = 1, 2. \tag{11}$$

The Hamiltonian for this maximum problem is:

$$H \equiv u[\textstyle\sum c_i] - \textstyle\sum v_i c_i + \textstyle\sum \lambda_i\{g[S_i] - c_i\}. \tag{12}$$

Define $\mu_i \equiv \lambda_i + v_i$ and $\phi \equiv u'^{-1}$. We then have the following necessary conditions for optimality:

if $\mu_j < \mu_i$, then $c_j = \phi[\mu_j]$ and $c_i = 0$, \tag{13}

if $\mu_j = \mu_i$, then $c_i + c_j = \phi[\mu_i] = \phi[\mu_j]$, \tag{14}

$$\dot{\mu}_i = (\mu_i - v_i)\{\rho - g'[S_i]\}, \tag{15}$$

$$\dot{S}_i = g[S_i] - c_i. \tag{16}$$

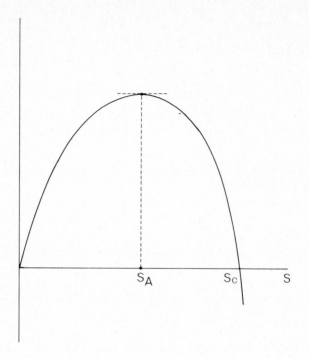

Figure 5.1

3. Some preliminary results

In the present section we state two propositions which will be useful in the subsequent argument; one places a restriction on the choice of the co-state variables μ_i and the other provides a sufficient condition for the existence of a steady state.

Lemma 1. Along the Pontryagin trajectory, if there exists $t^0 \geqq 0$ such that $\mu_i(t^0) > v_i(<v_j)$, then $\mu_i(t) > v_i(<v_j)$ for all $t \geqq 0$.

Proof. Denote the Pontryagin trajectory by $\{\mu_i^*(t), S_i^*(t)\}$, $i = 1, 2$, and suppose that there exists $t^* < +\infty$ such that $\mu_i^*(t^*) = v_i$. Then both $\mu_i^*(t)$ and $\mu_i(t) \equiv v_i$ are solutions to the differential equation

$$\dot{x} = (x - v_i)\{\rho - g'[S_i^*(t)]\},\tag{17}$$

with the initial condition $x(t^*) = v_i$, which contradicts the uniqueness of the solution to a differential equation with given initial condition. Q.E.D.

Corollary. Along the Pontryagin trajectory, if there is $t^0 \geqq 0$ such that $\mu_i(t^0) = v_i$, $i = 1, 2$, then $\mu_i(t) = v_i$ for all $t \geqq 0$.

Lemma 2. The Pontryagin trajectory is suboptimal if there is $t^0 > 0$ such that, along the trajectory, either

(i) $\mu_2(t^0) \geqq v_2 > v_1 \geqq \mu_1(t^0)$

or

(ii) $\mu_2(t^0) < v_2$ and $\mu_1(t^0) < v_1$.

Proof. Suppose (i) is established. Then, from lemma 1, for any $t \geqq 0$, $\mu_2(t) > \mu_1(t)$, which implies that the second deposit is never extracted. Obviously, such a feasible trajectory is suboptimal.

Suppose (ii) is established. Defining $\mu(t) \equiv \min\{\mu_1(t), \mu_2(t)\}$, which must be smaller than v_1, we have $\phi[\mu(t)] > \phi[v_1]$. Therefore

$$u[\phi[v_1]] - v_1 \phi[v_1] > u[\phi[\mu(t)]] - v_1 c_1 - v_2 c_2 \tag{18}$$

for any element of the set $\{(c_1, c_2) | c_1 \geqq 0, c_2 \geqq 0, \sum c_i = \phi[\mu(t)]\}$. Now let us consider the allocation $\{S_i^0(t), c_i^0(t)\}$ defined by:

$$c_1^0(t) + c_2^0(t) = \phi[v_1], \qquad c_i^0(t) \leqq c_i(t), \tag{19}$$

$$\dot{S}_i^0 = g[S_i^0] - c_i^0, \qquad i = 1, 2. \tag{20}$$

The allocation is obviously feasible and, from the inequality (18), total utility is greater than along the Pontryagin trajectory. Q.E.D.

Thus, we arrive at the first proposition.

Proposition 1. Along the optimal trajectory, for any $t \geqq 0$ either

(i) $\mu_i(t) \geqq v_i$, $\qquad i = 1, 2$,

or

(ii) $\mu_i(t) \geqq v_1$ and $\mu_2(t) \leqq v_2$,

where $\sum |\mu_i(t) - v_i| > 0$.

Let us consider now whether the Pontryagin trajectories contain an interior steady state. In this connection, the crucial relationship is that between v_i and $u'[2g[S_e]]$, where S_e is the solution to $\rho = g'[S]$. In what follows it is assumed that S_e exists and is positive. (S_e exists and is positive if and only if $\rho < g'[0]$.) For reasons which will be given below, it is assumed also that

$$2g'[S_e] > v_2 > v_1. \tag{21}$$

Proposition 2. Given (21), the steady state uniquely exists; at the steady state

$$S_1 = S_2 = S_e; \qquad \mu_1 = \mu_2 = \mu_e; \qquad c_1 = c_2 = g[S_e]. \tag{22}$$

Proof. In order that $\dot{\mu}_1 = \dot{\mu}_2 = 0$, it is necessary that at least one of the following statements be true.

(i) $\mu_i = v_i, \qquad i = 1, 2,$

(ii) $\mu_i = v_1$ and $S_2 = S_e,$

(iii) $S_1 = S_e$ and $\mu_2 = v_2,$

(iv) $S_1 = S_2 = S_e.$

Considering (21), it is obvious that a steady state satisfying (22) does exist as an optimal trajectory. It remains only to establish uniqueness. Let us inspect (i), (ii), and (iii) in turn. First, (i) implies that $\mu_1 < \mu_2$ at the steady state, which is suboptimal from proposition 1. Second, (ii) implies that $\mu_2 = v_1$ or $g[S_2] - \phi[\mu_2] = g[S_e] - \phi[v_1] = 0$ $(= \dot{S}_2)$, which contradicts (20). (Remember that ϕ has been defined as u'^{-1}.) By a similar argument, (iii) contradicts (21).   Q.E.D.

What can be said for assumption (21)? Evidently it is not the only possible ranking of v_1, v_2, and $u'[2g[S_e]]$. Thus we have, as additional possibilities:

$$v_2 = u'[2g[S_e]] > v_1, \tag{23}$$

$$v_2 > u'[2g[S_e]] > v_1, \tag{24}$$

$$v_2 > v_1 = u'[2g[S_e]], \tag{25}$$

$$v_2 > v_1 > u'[2g[S_e]]. \tag{26}$$

However, none of these rankings is as interesting as (21). Literally, (21) says that when consumption is at the maximum sustainable rate, with marginal reproductivity equal in each deposit to the rate of time preference, then the marginal utility of consumption is greater than the average cost of extraction in the higher-cost deposit; in other words, the resource is not plentiful and there are positive shadow prices. Under any of the rankings (22)–(25) the resource ultimately ceases to be scarce.

4. The stable locus

If there exists only one deposit it is easily verified that there exists a unique locus on the phase diagram such that if the initial condition is chosen on that locus, then the Pontryagin trajectory converges to the steady state and therefore is optimal. What we show in this section is that there may be a stable locus even in the context of multiple state variables.

Let us begin by examining the relationship between S_1, S_2, μ_1, and μ_2 under the assumption that the two deposits are worked simultaneously. For the simultaneous working of both deposits to continue, not only must μ_1 be equal to μ_2, but also $\dot{\mu}_1$ must be equal to $\dot{\mu}_2$. Therefore, from (15):

$$(\mu - v_1)\{\rho - g'[S_1]\} = (\mu - v_2)\{\rho - g'[S_2]\}. \tag{27}$$

Just for convenience, in what follows we rewrite $\rho - g'[S_i]$ as $z[S_i]$. From (8) and the definition of S_e, $z[\cdot]$ has the properties:

$$z' \equiv \frac{d}{dS} z > 0, \tag{28}$$

$$z[S] \gtreqless 0, \quad \text{according as } S \gtreqless S_e. \tag{29}$$

Furthermore, we shall assume that z' is a positive constant (as it is if $g[S] = \alpha S[\beta - S]$, where α and β are positive constants). Then (27) can be rewritten as:

$$\dot{\mu} = (\mu - v_1)z[S_1] = (\mu - v_2)z[S_2]. \tag{27'}$$

Totally differentiating the second equation with respect to time, we obtain:

$$(\mu - v_1)\dot{S}_1 - (\mu - v_2)\dot{S}_2 = \frac{1}{z'}(\mu - v_1)z[S_1](z[S_2] - z[S_1]). \tag{30}$$

On the other hand, from (14) and (16):

$$\dot{S}_1 + \dot{S}_2 = g[S_1] + g[S_2] - \phi[\mu]. \tag{31}$$

Solving (30) and (31) with respect to $\dot{S}_1$ and $\dot{S}_2$, we have:

$$\dot{S}_1 = \frac{(\mu - v_1)}{2\mu - (v_1 + v_2)}$$

$$\times \left\{ (g[S_1] + g[S_2] - \phi[\mu]) + \frac{z[S_2]}{z'}(z[S_2] - z[S_1]) \right\}. \tag{32}$$

The first equation of (27') and (32) can be regarded as a system of differential equations in (μ, S_1). (Notice that S_2 is a function of (μ, S_1) by the second equation of (27').) It is easily shown that (μ_e, S_e), defined in the previous section, is the steady state of this system. Evaluating the matrix

$$M \equiv \begin{bmatrix} \dfrac{\partial \dot{S}_1}{\partial S_1} & \dfrac{\partial \dot{S}_1}{\partial \mu} \\[2ex] \dfrac{\partial \dot{\mu}}{\partial S_1} & \dfrac{\partial \dot{\mu}}{\partial \mu} \end{bmatrix} \tag{33}$$

at (μ_e, S_e), we see that there is a unique locus in the phase diagram (μ, S_1) such that if the initial condition $(\mu(0), S_1(0))$ is on it, then the system converges to (μ_e, S_e). Let us call it the stable locus. We proceed to examine the properties of the locus.

Lemma 3. In a neighbourhood of (μ_e, S_e) the stable locus is downward-sloping (as in fig. 5.2).

Proof. A mathematical theorem ensures that the slope of the stable locus is equal to that of the characteristic vector associated with the negative characteristic root of

$$\sigma[\lambda] \equiv \det[\lambda I - M]\big|_e = 0. \tag{34}$$

(Pontryagin (1962, ch. 5, theorem 22).) Letting the negative root be λ^*, we have:

$$\frac{\dot{\mu}}{\dot{S}_1}\bigg|_e = \frac{\partial \dot{\mu}/\partial S_1\big|_e}{\lambda^* - (\partial \dot{\mu}/\partial \mu)\big|_e} = \frac{(\mu_e - v_1)z'}{\lambda^*}. \tag{35}$$

Thus, at least in a neighbourhood of (μ_e, S_e), the stable locus is the solution to the differential equation:

$$\frac{d\mu}{dS_1} = \frac{z'(\mu - v_1)(z[S_1] + z[S_2])}{z'(g[S_1] + g[S_2] - \phi(\mu)) + z[S_2](z[S_2] - z[S_1])} < 0, \tag{36}$$

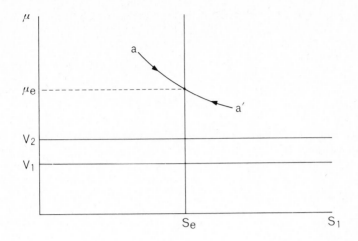

aa′ : the stable locus

Figure 5.2

with the initial condition (μ_e, S_e). Q.E.D.

Next let us inspect the global properties of the stable locus. Is it always downward-sloping on the phase diagram? In answering this question we make use of two lemmata.

Lemma 4. The stable locus is downward-sloping when $S_1 > S_e$.

Proof. Suppose that the stable locus has an upward-sloping portion, as is in fig. 5.3. Then we can consider the trajectory which starts at A, passes through B, jumps down from C to A, and then repeats the pattern. Compare that trajectory with the optimal trajectory $ABCD$. After C, μ is always smaller on the cyclical trajectory than on the optimal trajectory, which implies that, at any time after C has been passed, the rate of consumption associated with the optimal trajectory is greater than that associated with the optimal trajectory, a contradiction. Q.E.D.

Next, let us examine whether the stable locus is downward-sloping when $S_1 < S_e$. Consider the system composed of (27′) and

$$g[S_1] + g[S_2] - \phi[\mu] = 0. \tag{37}$$

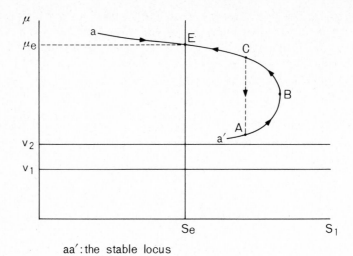

aa′: the stable locus

Figure 5.3

From this system, we obtain the relationship between μ and S_1, which in what follows is called the locus $g - \phi$. Since

$$\frac{z[S_2]}{z'}(z[S_2] - z[S_1]) > 0, \quad \text{for any } S_1 = S_e, \tag{38}$$

the locus $g - \phi$ is always to the north-east of the locus $\dot{S}_1 = 0$ in the phase diagram.

Lemma 5. The stable locus is to the north-east of the locus $g - \phi$.

Proof. The slope of the locus $g - \phi$ is:

$$\frac{d\mu}{dS_1}\bigg|_{g-\phi} = \frac{z'\{(\mu - v_2)(\rho - z[S_1]) + (\mu - v_1)(\rho - z[S_2])\}}{(\mu - v_2)\phi'[\mu] + (\rho - z[S_2] - z[S_1])}, \tag{39}$$

so that:

$$\frac{d\mu}{dS_1} - \frac{d\mu}{dS_1}\bigg|_{g-\phi} = \frac{(\mu - v_1)(\mu - v_2)(z_1[S_1] + z_2(S_2])\phi'[\mu]}{\text{(the denominator of (36)}}$$

$$\frac{+ z[S_1]z[S_2](v_1 - v_2)(z[S_2] - z[S_1])}{\times \text{(the denominator of (39))}}$$

$$< 0, \quad \text{for } S_1 < S_e. \tag{40}$$

Now suppose that in a neighbourhood of the steady state E the stable locus can be depicted as in fig. 5.4. Then there must be a locus like BC which follows (36), contradicting (40). Therefore in a neighbourhood of E the stable locus must be as in fig. 5.5. From (40), then, it is impossible that the stable locus intersects the locus $g - \phi$ (as in fig. 5.6 when $S_1 < S_e$). Q.E.D.

It follows that the stable locus cannot intersect the locus $\dot{S}_1 = 0$ either. Now we can prove our proposition regarding the shape of the stable locus.

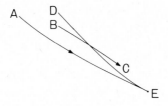

AE: the stable locus
DE: the locus g-ϕ

Figure 5.4

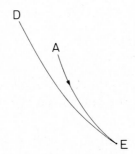

AE: the stable locus
DE: the locus g-ϕ

Figure 5.5

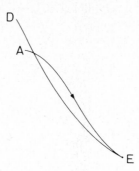

AE : the stable locus
DE : the locus g-ϕ

Figure 5.6

Proposition 3.
(i) The stable locus is downward-sloping in the plane (μ, S_1).
(ii) On the stable locus,

$$g[S_1] + g[S_2] - \phi[\mu] \gtreqless 0, \quad \text{according as } S_1 \gtreqless S_e. \tag{41}$$

(iii) Moreover, on the stable locus:

$$\lim_{S_1 \to 0} \mu = +\infty, \tag{42}$$

$$\lim_{S_1 \to 0} \mu = v_2. \tag{43}$$

(See fig. 5.7.)

Proof. (i) and (ii) are obvious from the previous lemmata. Let us prove (42) and (43). First suppose that $\lim_{S_1 \to 0} \mu = \mu^* < +\infty$ on the stable locus. Then, from (36):

$$\lim_{S_1 \to 0} \frac{d\mu}{dS_1} = -\frac{2(\mu^* - v_1)z[0]}{\phi[\mu^*]}, \tag{44}$$

contradicting (i). Next suppose that $\lim_{S_1 \to \infty} \mu = \mu^{**} > v_2$. Then $\lim_{S_1 \to 0}(\mu - (d\mu/dS_1)S_1)$ must be equal to μ^{**} on the stable locus (see fig. 5.8). From (36):

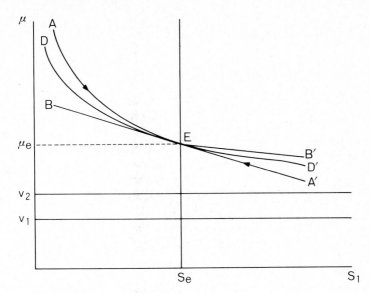

AEA′: the stable locus
DED′: the locus g-ϕ
BEB′: the locus $\dot{S}_1 = 0$

Figure 5.7

$$\frac{d\mu}{dS_1} \times S_1 = \frac{\left(1 + \dfrac{\mu - v_1}{\mu - v_2}\right)(\mu - v_1)S_1}{\left(\dfrac{g[S_1]}{z[S_1]} + \dfrac{g[S_2]}{z[S_1]} + \dfrac{\phi[\mu]}{z[S_1]}\right) + \dfrac{z[S_1](\mu - v_1)}{z'(\mu - v_2)}\left(\dfrac{\mu - v_1}{\mu - v_2} - 1\right)}. \quad (45)$$

Considering (27), it is obvious, under the supposition that $\lim_{S_1 \to \infty} \mu = \mu^{**} > v_2$, that S_2, $z[S_1]$, and $z[S_2]$ go to positive infinity when S_1 goes to positive infinity. Thus, resorting to l'Hôpital's rule:

$$\lim_{S_1 \to \infty} \frac{g[S_1]}{z[S_1]} = \lim_{S_1 \to \infty} \frac{\rho - z[S_1]}{z'} = \frac{\rho}{z'} - \lim_{S_1 \to \infty} \frac{z[S_1]}{z'}, \quad (46)$$

$$\lim_{S_1 \to \infty} \frac{g[S_2]}{z[S_1]} = \lim_{S_1 \to \infty} \frac{(\mu - v_1)}{(\mu - v_2)} \cdot \frac{g[S_2]}{z[S_2]}$$

$$= \frac{(\mu^{**} - v_1)}{(\mu^{**} - v_2)} \lim_{S_2 \to \infty} \frac{\rho - z[S_2]}{z'}$$

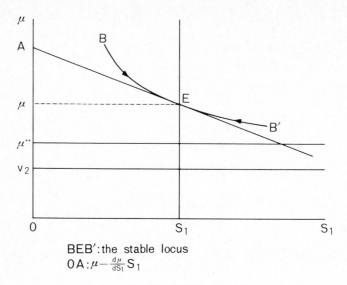

BEB′: the stable locus
$0A: \mu - \frac{d\mu}{dS_1} S_1$

Figure 5.8

$$= \frac{(\mu^{**} - v_1)}{(\mu^{**} - v_2)} \left(\frac{\rho}{z'} - \frac{(\mu^{**} - v_1)}{(\mu^{**} - v_2)} \lim_{S_1 \to \infty} \frac{z[S_2]}{z'} \right). \tag{47}$$

Therefore:

$$\lim_{S_1 \to \infty} \frac{d\mu}{dS_1} S_1 = -(\mu^{**} - v_1) z' \lim_{S_1 \to \infty} \frac{S_1}{z[S_1]}. \tag{48}$$

Appealing to l'Hôpital's rule again:

$$\lim_{S_1 \to \infty} \frac{d\mu}{dS} S_1 = -(\mu^{**} - v_1). \tag{49}$$

Therefore, on the stable locus:

$$\lim_{S_1 \to \infty} \left(\mu - \frac{d\mu}{dS_1} S_1 \right) = v_1 > 0, \tag{50}$$

a contradiction.   Q.E.D.

5. The optimal trajectory

We turn now to our main business, namely that of tracing the optimal trajectory. In the previous section we have learned that the stable locus,

$$\mu = \mu[S_1; \mu, S_e], \tag{51}$$

is the solution to the differential equalion (36) with the initial condition (μ_e, S_e) and that

$$\mu' \equiv \frac{d\mu}{dS_1} < 0. \tag{52}$$

Denoting by $S_2 = G[S_1]$ the relationship between S_1 and S_2 which satisfies (27') and (51), we have:

$$G' \equiv \frac{dG}{dS_1} = \frac{\mu - v_1}{\mu - v_2} + \frac{(v_1 - v_2)}{z'(\mu - v_2)^2} z[S_1]\mu' > 0. \tag{53}$$

The graph $S_2 = G[S_1]$ divides the (S_1, S_2) plane as in fig. 5.9. If the initial point $(S_1(0), S_2(0))$ is on *HED* then, setting $\mu_1(0) = \mu_2(0) = \mu[S_1(0); \mu_e, S_e]$, the Pontryagin trajectory converges to the steady state and, therefore, is optimal.

Suppose, however, that the initial point is not on *HED*. For example, suppose that the initial stocks are represented by point M in fig. 5.9 and

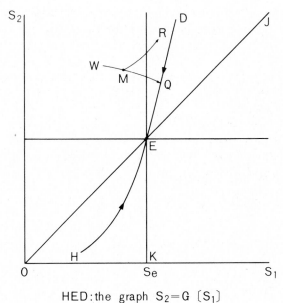

HED: the graph $S_2 = G [S_1]$

Figure 5.9

the Pontryagin trajectory which starts form M can be depicted as MQ. If at Q $\mu_1 = \mu_2 = \mu[S_1^Q; \mu_e, S_e]$, where S_1^Q is the S_1-coordinate of Q, then the Pontryagin trajectory MQE must be optimal, because it converges to the steady state E.

Lemma 6.   If the type of Pontryagin trajectory MQE exists for given initial stocks, then it is uniquely optimal with respect to the initial stocks.

Proof.   Suppose that there exists another optimal trajectory starting from the initial point M, and depicted as MR in fig. 5.9. Then:

$$(\mu_1(0), \mu_2(0))|_{MQ} \neq (\mu_1(0), \mu_2(0))|_{MR}. \tag{54}$$

For, otherwise, MR would coincide with MQ. Suppose, furthermore, that the trajectory MQ can be extended back to W. Regarding W as the (new) initial point, $WMQE$ is also an optimal trajectory. Now compare the optimal trajectory $WMQE$ with the following trajectory:
   (i) from W to M, it coincides with the optimal trajectory $WMQE$;
   (ii) at M (μ_1, μ_2) jumps to $(\mu_1(0), \mu_2(0))|_{MR}$;
   (iii) after M, it coincides with MR.
This trajectory is suboptimal because of the discontinuity of the co-state variables at M. However, society can obtain the same amount of utility from it as from the optimal trajectory $WMQE$, a contradiction.   Q.E.D.

Therefore, if we can show that this type of Pontryagin trajectory exists for any initial stocks, then our optimum problem is completely solved, at least for case (20).

   Let us concentrate for the time being on a neighbourhood of the stable locus HED of fig. 5.9. And suppose that there exists a Pontryagin trajectory of type MQE. Just before the Pontryagin trajectory reaches the stable locus HED, say at $t = 0$, it has slope:

$$\frac{dS_2}{dS_1} = \frac{g[S_2]}{g[S_1] - \phi[\mu_1]} \quad \text{or} \quad \frac{g[S_2] - \phi[\mu_2]}{g[S_1]}. \tag{55}$$

On the other hand, from (52) and (53), we have:

$$g' = \frac{z[S_2](g[S_1] + g[S_2] - \phi[\mu]) - \dfrac{1}{z}z[S_1]z[S_2](z[S_2] - z[S_1])}{z[S_1](g[S_1] + g[S_2] - \phi[\mu]) + \dfrac{1}{z}z[S_1]z[S_2](z[S_2] - z[S_1])}. \tag{53'}$$

Substracting (53′) from

$$\lim_{t \to 0} \frac{dS_2}{dS_1}\bigg|_{(55)},$$

we obtain:

$$\frac{(\sum g - \phi)\{g[S_2]z[S_1] - (g[S_1] - \phi[\mu])z[S_2] + \frac{1}{z'}z[S_1]z[S_2](z[S_2] - z[S_1])\}}{z[S_1](g[S_1] - \phi[\mu])\{(\sum g - \phi) + \frac{1}{z'}z[S_2](z[S_2] - z[S_1])\}},$$

(56)

when

$$\frac{dS_2}{dS_1}\bigg|_{(55)} = \frac{g[S_2]}{g[S_1] - \phi[\mu_1]},$$

and

$$\frac{(\sum g - \phi)\{(g[S_2] - \phi[\mu])z[S_1] - g[S_1]z[S_2] + \frac{1}{z'}z[S_1]z[S_2](z[S_2] - s[S_1])\}}{z[S_1]g[S_1]\{(\sum g - \phi) + \frac{1}{z'}z[S_2](z[S_2] - z[S_1])\}},$$

(57)

when

$$\frac{dS_2}{dS_1}\bigg|_{(55)} = \frac{g[S_2] - \phi[\mu_2]}{g[S_1]}.$$

Considering (32) and proposition 1, we have:

$$\frac{(\sum g - \phi)}{z[S_1]\{(\sum g - \phi) - \frac{1}{z'}z[S_2](z[S_2] - z[S_1])\}} \gtreqless 0, \quad \text{according as } S_1 \gtreqless S_e.$$

(58)

Lemma 7. Along any optimal trajectory which approaches the stable locus *HED* from the left-hand side (the right-hand side), μ_1 is greater (smaller) than μ_2 just before the optimal trajectory reaches the stable locus *HED*.

Proof. By Taylor's expansion, we have:

$$\mu_1(t) - \mu_2(t) = \frac{t^2}{2!}[\ddot{\mu}_2(0) - \ddot{\mu}_2(0)]$$

$$= \frac{-t^2 z'(\mu - v_2)}{2z[S_1]} \left\{ z[S_1] \lim_{t \to 0} \dot{S}_2 - z[S_2] \lim_{t \to 0} \dot{S}_1 \right.$$

$$\left. + \frac{1}{z'} z[S_1] z[S_2](z[S_2] - z[S_1]) \right\}, \tag{59}$$

where t is negative and in a small neighbourhood of zero. Now, suppose that along an optimal trajectory approaching the stable locus *HED* from the left-hand side (the right-hand side) μ_1 is smaller (greater) than μ_2 just before the optimal trajectory reaches the stable locus. Then $\mu_1(t) < (>) \mu_2(t)$ which, in view of (49), implies that

$$z[S_1] g[S_2] - z[S_2](g[S_1] - \phi[\mu]) + \frac{1}{z'} z[S_1] z[S_2](z[S_2] - z[S_1]) \geqslant 0$$

according as $S_1 \gtrless S_e$ if $\mu_1(t) < \mu_2(t)$, \tag{60}

$$z[S_1](g[S_2] - \phi[\mu]) - z[S_2] g[S_1] + \frac{1}{z'} z[S_1] z[S_2](z[S_2] - z[S_1]) \geqslant 0,$$

according as $S_1 \gtrless S_e$ if $\mu_1(t) > \mu_2(t)$ \tag{61}

We make use of (60) and (61), with (56)–(58), to establish the following propositions.

(i) For an optimal trajectory approaching a portion *HE* of the stable locus,

$$\lim_{t \to 0} \frac{dS_2}{dS_1} - G' \gtrless 0, \quad \text{according as } g[S_1] - \phi[\mu] \gtrless 0,$$

if it approaches from the left-hand side of *NE*; \tag{62}

$$\lim_{t \to 0} \frac{dS_2}{dS_1} - G' \gtrless 0,$$

if it approaches from the right-hand side of *HE*. \tag{63}

(ii) For an optimal trajectory approaching a portion *ED* of the stable locus,

$$\lim_{t \to 0} \frac{dS_2}{dS_1} - G' \gtrless 0, \quad \text{according as } g[S_1] - \phi[\mu] \gtrless 0,$$

if it approaches from the left-hand side of ED;   (64)

$$\lim_{t \to 0} \frac{dS_2}{dS_1} - G' \gtreqless 0, \quad \text{according as } g[S_1] \gtreqless 0,$$

if it approaches from the right-hand side of ED (65)

Consider (62). In terms of fig. 5.10, there are three possibilities for the optimal trajectory: A_1B, A_2B, and A_3B. Obviously, A_2B and A_3B are impossible for each of them implies that $\dot{S}_2 = g[S_2] < 0$. A_1B is also impossible, for it implies that $\dot{S}_1 = g[S_1] - \phi[\mu_1] > 0$ in a neighbourhood of B and therefore, from (62), that:

$$\lim_{t \to 0} \frac{dS_2}{dS_1} > G'. \tag{66}$$

However, the slope of A_1B in fig. 5.10 is obviously different from (66). Now consider (63). In terms of fig. 5.10, there are three possibilities for the optimal trajectory: D_1C, D_2C, and D_3C. Obviously, D_2C and D_3C are impossible, for each of them implies that $\dot{S}_1 = \dot{g}[S_1] < 0$. D_1C is also impossible, for it implies that $\lim_{t \to 0}(dS_2/dS_1) > G$, contradicting (63). Turning our attention to (64) we see that, in terms of fig. 5.11, there are three possibilities for the optimal trajectory: I_1F, I_2F, and I_3F. I_1F and I_2F are impossible, for each of them implies that $\dot{S}_1 = g[S_1] - \phi[\mu_1] > 0$ in a neighbourhood of F and therefore, from (64), that:

$$\lim_{t \to 0} \frac{dS_2}{dS_1} > G'. \tag{67}$$

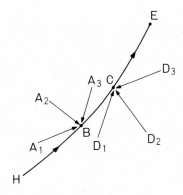

Figure 5.10

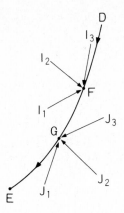

Figure 5.11

However, the slopes of I_1F and I_2F in fig. 5.11 are obviously different from (67). I_3F is also impossible, for it implies that $\dot{S}_1 = g[S_1] - \phi[\mu_1] < 0$ in a neighbourhood of F and therefore, from (64), that:

$$\lim_{t \to 0} \frac{dS_2}{dS_1} < G'. \tag{68}$$

However, the slope of I_2F in fig. 5.11 is obviously different from (68). Finally, consider (65). In terms of fig. 5.11, there are three possibilities for the optimal trajectory: J_1G, J_2G, and J_3G. J_1G is impossible, for it implies that $\dot{S}_1 = g[S_1] > 0$ and therefore, from (65), that:

$$\lim_{t \to 0} \frac{dS_2}{dS_1} < G'. \tag{69}$$

However, the slope of J_1G in fig. 5.11 is obviously different from (69). Similarily, J_2G and J_3G are impossible.   Q.E.D.

Next let us concentrate on the regions OEK and CEJ in fig. 5.9. It is possible that, for trajectories in those regions, there exists $t^0 < 0$ such that $\mu_1(t^0) = \mu_2(t^0)$? To check this possibility, we introduce the following function of (S_1, S_2), $S_1 \neq S_2$:

$$\bar{\mu}[S_1, S_2] \equiv \frac{v_1 z[S_1] - v_2 z[S_2]}{z[S_1] - z[S_2]}. \tag{70}$$

Consider fig. 5.12. One can imagine two winding stairs around a pole which stands at (S_e, S_e). Obviously, the stable locus is on this surface and

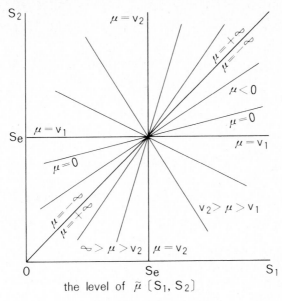

the level of $\tilde{\mu}\,[S_1, S_2]$

Figure 5.12

any level curve of it is expressed as a straight line passing through (S_e, S_e). Consider the level curve $\mu_e = \tilde{\mu}[S_e, S_e]$. We easily understand that this curve is tangent to the stable locus at $S_1 = S_e$ and lies to the right-hand side of that locus at $S_1 \neq S_e$ (see fig. 5.13).

Lemma 8. For any $\mu \in (\mu_e, \infty)\{\in(v_2, \mu_e)\}$, the level curve $\tilde{\mu} = \tilde{\mu}[S_1, S_2]$ intersects the stable locus only once. At the intersection, G' is smaller (greater) than the slope of the level curve.

Proof. The first part of this lemma is obvious from proposition 3. Consider the second part. Since

$$\left.\frac{\mathrm{d}S_2}{\mathrm{d}S_1}\right|_{\tilde{\mu}=\tilde{\mu}[S_1, S_2]} = \frac{\tilde{\mu} - v_1}{\tilde{\mu} - v_2}, \tag{71}$$

(53) implies that at the intersection:

$$G' = \left.\frac{\mathrm{d}S_2}{\mathrm{d}S_1}\right|_{\tilde{\mu}=\tilde{\mu}[S_1, S_2]} + \frac{(v_1 - v_2)z[S_1]\mu'}{z'(\mu - v_2)^2} \gtreqqless \left.\frac{\mathrm{d}S_2}{\mathrm{d}S_1}\right|_{\tilde{\mu}=\tilde{\mu}[S_1, S_2]},$$

according as $S_1 \gtreqqless S_e$. \tag{72}

Q.E.D.

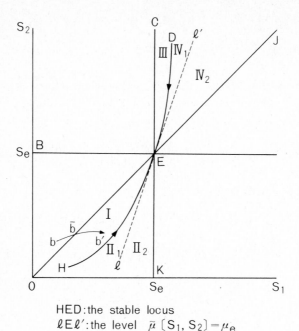

HED: the stable locus
$\ell E \ell'$: the level $\tilde{\mu}\,[S_1, S_2] = \mu_e$

Figure 5.13

Now consider the function of S_1:

$$x[S_1]\big|_{\tilde{\mu}} \equiv g[S_2]z[S_1] - (g[S_1] - \phi[\bar{\mu}])z[S_2]$$

$$+ \frac{1}{z'}z[S_1]z[S_2](z[S_2] - z[S_1]) \tag{73}$$

and

$$y[S_1]\big|_{\tilde{\mu}} \equiv (g[S_2] - \phi[\bar{\mu}])z[S_1] - g[S_1]z[S_2]$$

$$+ \frac{1}{z'}z[S_1]z[S_2](z[S_2] - z[S_1]), \tag{74}$$

where S_2 is determined by $\bar{\mu} = \bar{\mu}[S_1, S_2]$, $\bar{\mu}$ is constant. Obviously, $x[S_e]\big|_{\tilde{\mu}} = y[S_e]\big|_{\tilde{\mu}} = 0$ for any $\bar{\mu} = v_2$. Differentiating (73) and (74), we obtain:

$$\frac{dx[S_1]\big|_{\tilde{\mu}}}{dS_1} = \frac{z'}{z'[S_1]}x[S_1]\big|_{\tilde{\mu}} + z[S_2](z[S_2] - z[S_1]) \tag{75}$$

and

$$\frac{d y[S_1]|_{\bar{\mu}}}{d S_1} = \frac{z'}{z'[S_1]} y[S_1]|_{\bar{\mu}} + z[S_2](z[S_2] - z[S_1]). \tag{76}$$

Denoting by $S_1[\bar{\mu}]$ the value of S_1 at the intersection of the stable locus and the level curve of (70), $\bar{\mu} = \bar{\mu}[S_1, S_2]$, we obtain, from (75) and (76):

$$x[S_1]|_{\bar{\mu}} = \exp[A[S_1]]\{x[S_1[\bar{\mu}]]$$
$$+ \int_{S_1[\bar{\mu}]}^{S_1} \exp[-A[S_1]] z[S_2^{\bar{\mu}}[\tau]](z[S_2^{\bar{\mu}}[\tau]] - z[\tau]) \, d\tau\}, \tag{77}$$

$$y[S_1]|_{\bar{\mu}} = \exp A[S_1]]\{y[S_1[\bar{\mu}]]$$
$$+ \int_{S_1[\bar{\mu}]}^{S_1} \exp[-A[S_1]] z[S_2^{\bar{\mu}}[\tau]](z[S_2^{\bar{\mu}}[\tau]] - z[\tau]) \, d\tau\}, \tag{78}$$

where $S_2^{\bar{\mu}}[\tau]$ is the solution S_2 to $\bar{\mu} = \bar{\mu}[\tau, S_2]$ and

$$A[S_1] \equiv \int_{S_1[\bar{\mu}]}^{S_1} (z'/z'[x]) \, dx.$$

This enables us to state the following lemma.

Lemma 9. Divide the regions *OEK* and *CEJ* into the six subregions of fig. 5.13: I, II_1, II_2, III, IV_1, and IV_2. Then,
  (i) $x[S_1]|_{\bar{\mu}} > (<) 0$ in III, IV_1, and IV_2 (I, II_1, and II_2).
  (ii) $y[S_1]|_{\bar{\mu}} > (<) 0$ in I, II_1, and IV_2 (III, IV_1, and II_2).

Proof. Notice that, from (59):

$$\mu_1(t) - \mu_2(t) = \begin{cases} -\dfrac{t^2 z'(\bar{\mu} - v_2)}{2 z[S_1[\bar{\mu}]]} x[S_1[\bar{\mu}]], & \text{when } \mu_1(t) < \mu_2(t), \\[2mm] -\dfrac{t^2 z'(\bar{\mu} - v_2)}{2 z[S_1[\bar{\mu}]]} y[S_1[\bar{\mu}]], & \text{when } \mu_1(t) > \mu_2(t), \end{cases} \tag{79}$$

where t is negative and sufficiently near zero, at which $\bar{\mu} = \mu_1(0) = \mu_2(0)$. Therefore, if $\bar{\mu} > \mu_e$, i.e. $S_1[\bar{\mu}] < S_e$, then $x[S_1[\bar{\mu}]] < 0$ and $y[S_1[\bar{\mu}]] > 0$. Similarly, if $\bar{\mu} < \mu_e$, i.e. $S_1[\bar{\mu}] > S_e$, then $x[S_1[\bar{\mu}]] > 0$ and $y[S_1[\bar{\mu}]] < 0$. Considering (77) and (78), and taking $x[S_e]|_{\bar{\mu}} = y[S_e]|_{\bar{\mu}} \doteq 0$ into account, we can easily verify (i) and (ii). For example, take a value of μ which is greater than μ_e. A level curve $\bar{\mu} = \bar{\mu}[S_1, S_2]$ can be depicted as the straight line *PEP'* in fig. 5.14. Since $\exp[A]$ and $z[S_2](z[S_1])$ are positive, $y[S_e]|_{\bar{\mu}}$ is positive everywhere on *PEP'* except at $S_1 = S_e$ where, from (78), $y[S_e]|_{\bar{\mu}} = 0$. (It may be wondered whether (74) and (78) are

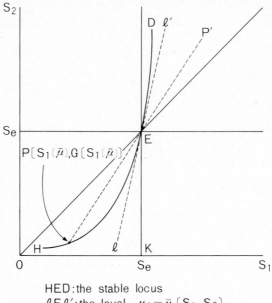

HED: the stable locus
$\ell E\ell'$: the level $\mu_e = \bar{\mu}\,[S_1, S_2]$
PEP': the level $\bar{\mu} = \bar{\mu}\,[S_1, S_2]$

Figure 5.14

consistent with each other. However, considering the definition of $A[S_1]$:

$$\lim_{S_1 \to S_e} A[S_1] = \lim_{S \to S_e} \int_{S_1[\bar{\mu}]}^{S_1} \frac{z'}{z[\tau]} \, d\tau$$

$$= \lim_{S_1 \to S_e} \int_{S_1[\bar{\mu}]}^{S_1} \frac{d(-z[\tau])/d\tau}{(-z[\tau]} \, d\tau$$

$$= \lim_{S_1 \to S_e} \int_{-z[S_1[\bar{\mu}]]}^{-z[S_1]} \frac{d(-z[\tau])}{(-z[\tau])}$$

$$= [\log z]_{z=-z[S_1[\bar{\mu}]]}^{z=0} = -\infty.$$

therefore $\lim_{S_1 \to S_e} \exp[S_1] = 0$.)   Q.E.D.

Denote by $t[S_1[\bar{\mu}],\, G[S_1[\bar{\mu}]]]$ the time at which the optimal trajectory, which reaches the stable locus at $(S_1[\bar{\mu}],\, G[S_1[\bar{\mu}]],\, \bar{\mu})$ at time zero, enters one of the regions OEJ and KEC of fig. 5.13. Evidently $t[S_1[\bar{\mu}],\, G[S_1[\bar{\mu}]]] < 0$ and for any $t \in (t[S_1[\bar{\mu}],\, G[S_1[\bar{\mu}]]], 0)$, the optimal trajectory $(S_1(t), S_2(t))$ is in one of subregions I, II, III $\equiv$ III$_1 \cup$ III$_2$ or IV $\equiv$ IV$_1 \cup$ IV$_2$.

Lemma 10. Along the optimal trajectory, for any $t \in (t[S_1[\bar{\mu}]],$ $G[S_1[\bar{\mu}]]], 0)$:
  (i) $\mu_1(t) > \mu_2(t)$ if the optimal trajectory is in I or II,
  (ii) $\mu_1(t) < \mu_2(t)$ if the optimal trajectory is in II or IV.

Proof. We prove this lemma for the case in which the optimal trajectory is in region I. The other three cases can be handled by a similar argument. Suppose that there exists $t^* \in (t[S_1[\bar{\mu}], G[S_1[\bar{\mu}]]], 0)$ such that $\mu_1(t^*) = \mu_2(t^*)$. Without loss, $\mu_1(t)$ can be taken to be greater than $\mu_2(t)$ for any $t \in (t^*, 0)$. Now compare $\mu_2(t)$ with $\bar{\mu}[S_1(t), S_2(t)]$ when $t \in (t^*, 0)$. Obviously:

$$\mu_1(0) = \mu_2(0) = \bar{\mu}[S_1(0), S_2(0)](= \bar{\mu}(S_1[\bar{\mu}], G[S_1[\bar{\mu}]]] = \bar{\mu}). \tag{80}$$

Differentiating $\mu_2 - \bar{\mu}$ with respect to time, and recalling lemma 9, we obtain:

$$\lim_{t \to 0} (\dot{\mu}_2 - \dot{\bar{\mu}}) = \left(\frac{\bar{\mu} - v_2}{z[S_1(0)]}\right)^2 \times \frac{z' y[S_1(0)]|_{\bar{\mu}}}{(v_2 - v_1)} > 0. \tag{81}$$

Therefore, for any t which is negative and sufficiently near zero:

$$\mu_2(t) < \bar{\mu}(t). \tag{82}$$

On the other hand, since $\dot{\mu}_1(t^*) \geq \dot{\mu}_2(t^*)$ and $\mu_1(t^*) = \mu_2(t^*)$, considering $\dot{\mu}_i = (\mu_i - v_i)z[S_i]$, $i = 1, 2$, and $S_1 > S_2$ in the region I, we have:

$$\mu_1(t^*) = \mu_2(t^*) \geq \bar{\mu}[S_1(t^*), S_2(t^*)]. \tag{83}$$

Therefore, from (82) and (83) there must be $t^{**} \in [t^*, 0)$ such that $\mu_2(t^{**}) = \bar{\mu}[S_1(t^{**}), S_2(t^{**})]$ and such that $\dot{\mu}_2(t^{**}) \leq \dot{\bar{\mu}}(t^{**})$. But this is impossible. For at t^{**} (81) must hold; hence $\dot{\mu}_2(t^{**}) > \dot{\mu}_1(t^{**})$ because $y[S_1(t^{**})]|_{\bar{\mu}} > 0$ from lemma 9. Q.E.D.

Building on the results obtained in this and earlier sections we now can state the following basic propositon:

Proposition 4. Along the optimal trajectory:
  (i) if $S_2(t) > G[S_1(t)]$, then $\mu_2(t) < \mu_1(t)$,
  (ii) if $S_2(t) < G[S_1(t)]$, then $\mu_2(t) > \mu_1(t)$.

Proof. There remain for consideration the regions S_2BOEC and S_1KEJ of fig. 5.13. Suppose that the optimal trajectory lies in the region OEB in fig. 5.13 and that there is $t^0 < 0$ such that $\mu_1(t^0) > \mu_2(t^0)$. Then:

$$\dot{\mu}(t^0) - \dot{\mu}_2(t^0) = (\mu_1(t^0) - v_1)z[S_1(t^0)] - (\mu_2(t^0) - v_2)z[S_2(t^0)]$$
$$< (\mu_2(t^0) - v_1)z[S_1(t^0)] - (\mu_2(t^0) - v_2)z[S_2(t^0)]$$
$$= (v_2 - v_1)z[S_1(t^0)] + (\mu_2(t^0) - v_2)(z[S_1(t^0)] - z[S_2(t^0)])$$
$$< 0. \tag{84}$$

Therefore, for any $t < t^0$, $\mu_1(t) > \mu_2(t)$ as long as the optimal trajectory is in the region OEB. Next, suppose that the optimal trajectory is in the region S_2BEC in fig. 5.13 and that there is $t^0 < 0$ such that $\mu_1(t^0) > \mu_2(t^0)$. Then, for any $t < t^0$, $\mu_1(t) > \mu_2(t)$, as long as the optimal trajectory is in S_2BEC. For in this region $\dot{\mu}_1(t) < \dot{\mu}_2(t)$.

Furthermore, it is impossible that the optimal trajectory, after leaving region I or III, returns to I or III when $t \to -\infty$. For suppose that it crosses OE in fig. 5.13; then, since $\mu_1 > \mu_2$ at the crossing point on OE, the optimal trajectory must be depicted as bb' in fig. 5.13. But this is impossible, for at the crossing point b:

$$\frac{dS_2}{dS_1} = \frac{g[S] - \phi[\mu]}{g[S]} < 1. \tag{85}$$

Since $\mu_1 > \mu_2$, $\dot{S}_1 = g[S_e] > 0$ on CE. Therefore, it is also impossible that the optimal trajectory, after leaving region III, returns to III when $t \to -\infty$.

Therefore, in view of (i) of lemma 10, in the region to the left of the stable locus HED in fig. 5.13, $\mu_1(t) > \mu_2(t)$. That is, if the point $(S_1(t), S_2(t))$ is in this region, then only the second deposit is extracted.

By similar logic we can prove that, in the region to the right of the stable locus HED in fig. 5.13, $\mu_1(t) < \mu_2(t)$.   Q.E.D.

Finally, let us examine the properties of the optimal trajectory inside the two regions depicted by $G[S_1] = S_2$. Here we consider in detail only the region $\{(S_1, S_2) \mid S_2 < G[S_1]\}$. The other region $\{(S_1, S_2) \mid S_2 > G[S_1]\}$ may be considered similarly. In the region $\{(S_1, S_2) \mid S_2 < G[S_1]\}$ μ_1 is always smaller than μ_2 along the optimal trajectory. Therefore, S_i and μ_i, $i = 1, 2$, follow the system of differential equations:

$$\dot{S}_1 = g[S_1] - \phi[\mu_1], \tag{86}$$

$$\dot{\mu}_1 = (\mu_1 - v_1)z[S_1], \tag{87}$$

$$\dot{S}_2 = g[S_2], \tag{88}$$

$$\dot{\mu}_2 = (\mu_2 - v_2)z[S_2]. \tag{89}$$

We now concentrate on the subsystem (86) and (87). Fig. 5.15 is the diagram of the subsystem. Suppose, for example, that the initial value of S_1 is $S_1(0)$. If the initial value of S_2, $S_2(0)$, is equal to FJ in fig. 5.16, then $\mu_1(0)$ takes the value $FS_1(0)$ in fig. 5.15. If $S_2(0)$ is less than FJ in fig. 5.16, say GJ, then $\mu_1(0)$ takes the value $GS_1(0)$ in fig. 5.15. The arrows, GD and AE, etc. in fig. 5.15 correspond to those in fig. 5.16. One of the interesting cases is that in which $S_2(0)$ is less than $AS_1(0)$ in fig. 5.16. For example, let $S_2(0)$ be $HS_1(0)$. Then the optimal trajectory is HLE in both figures, with the first deposit alone extracted until S_1 is less than S_e ($H \rightarrow L$), thereafter both deposits extracted ($L \rightarrow E$). S_1 decreases below S_e at first and then increases to S_e. That is, "overshooting" occurs along the optimal trajectory.

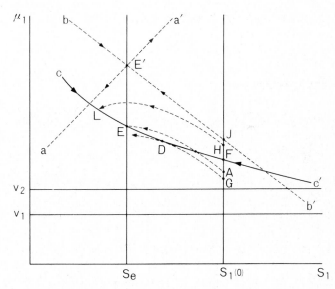

aE′ a′: the unstable locus of (86) and (87)
bE′ b′: the stable locus of (86) and (87)
cEc′: the stable locus of (36)

Figure 5.15

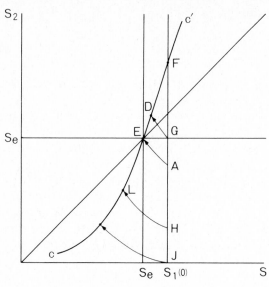

cEc′: the stable locus $\mu = \tilde{\mu} [S_1, \mu e, S_e]$

Figure 5.16

6. Concluding remarks

Figure 5.17 is the phase diagram which we obtain as the end-product of our argument. Inspection of fig. 5.17 yields the following conclusions, of which (i), (ii), and (iii) are noteworthy.

(i) In contrast to Herfindahl's finding, the deposit which is extracted first depends on the extent of the initial deposits as well as the relative costs of extraction.

(ii) If the initial extent lies in the second or fourth "quadrant" (regarding (S_e, S_e) as "origin") of fig. 5.17 but not in trajectory x or y, then there is "overshooting" of the steady state by either $S_1(t)$ or $S_2(t)$, but not both.

(iii) If extraction costs are the same for both deposits, i.e. $v_1 = v_2$, then the stable locus coincides with the 45° straight line from the origin O.

(iv) We have discussed case (21). If (21) is not satisfied, in other words if the extraction cost is high, then, depending on the initial extent of the deposits, it is possible that along the optimal trajectory only one of the deposits is extracted and that the other deposit is never extracted. Let us

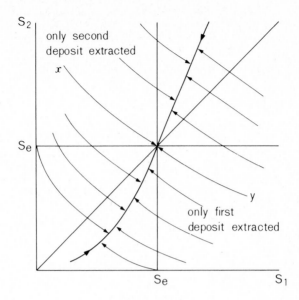

Figure 5.17

take one example. For simplicity we assume that $v_1 = v_2 = v$. If $g[S_A]$ is greater then $\phi[v]$, there is an interval $[S_{**}, S_*]$ in which $g[S] > \phi[v]$. If one of $S_1(0)$ and $S_2(0)$ is in the interval, then the optimal trajectory is as follows. Only the deposit whose initial stock is in the interval is extracted. The outstanding stock is described by the equation $\dot{S} = g[S] - \phi[v]$. Consumption is $c = \phi[v]$. Obviously S converges to S_* and the other deposit is never extracted.

References

Herfindahl, O. C. (1967), Depletion and economic theory, in M. M. Gaffney, ed., Resources and Taxation (University of Wisconsin Press, Madison) pp. 63–90.

Kemp, M. C. and N. V. Long (1980a), On the optimal order of exploitation of deposits, in: M. C. Kemp and N. V. Long, eds., Exhaustible Resources, Optimality, and Trade (North-Holland Publishing Company, Amsterdam) essay 3.

Kemp, M. C. and N. V. Long (1980b), On two folk theorems concerning the extraction of exhaustible resources, Econometrica 48, 663–674.

Kemp, M. C. and N. V. Long (1980c), On the optimal order of exploitation of deposits of an exhaustible resource: The case of certainty, in: H. Siebert, ed., Erschöpfbare Ressourcen, Schriften des Vereins für Socialpolitik, New Series, 108 (Duncker and Humblot, Berlin).

Pontryagin, L. S. (1962), Ordinary Differential Equations (Addison-Wesley, Reading, Mass.).

Shimomura, K. (1982), On the optimal order of exploitation of deposits of a renewable resource, Doctoral thesis, University of New South Wales.

Solow, R. M. and F. Y. Wan (1976), Extraction costs in the theory of exhaustible resources, Bell Journal of Economics 7, 359–370.

On the transition from an exhaustible resource-stock to an inexhaustible substitute

NGUYEN MANH HUNG, MURRAY C. KEMP and NGO VAN LONG*

1. Introduction

A country posseses an exhaustible and non-renewable resource-stock, say oil. It also knows how to produce a perfect flow-substitute, say solar energy. Sooner or later the country must look to the sun rather than its oil wells as its primary or only source of energy. Both the extraction of oil and the harnessing of the sun may be costly. In particular, the production of solar energy may entail set-up costs as well as conventional scale-dependent costs.[1]

Several questions present themselves.

(i) When should the transition from oil to solar energy begin?

(ii) Should the transition be abrupt or gradual; and, if gradual, should it terminate in finite time?

(iii) How should the price of energy behave before, after, and at the point of introduction of solar energy?

(iv) Should the stock of oil be exhausted?

(v) Are there circumstances in which it is optimal to extract oil indefinitely?

We shall interpret these questions from the social or "planning" point of view. However, other points of view are possible; for example, that of

*We thank Hans-Werner Sinn for comments which prompted us to add the remark of section 5; and we thank an anonymous referee for useful comments concerning the scope of the paper. This essay first appeared in A. Ulph and A. Ingham, eds., *Demand, Equilibria and Trade. Essays in Honour of Professor Ivor Pearce* (Macmillan, London, 1984).

[1]For an earlier analysis of set-up costs in a context of exhaustible resources, see Hartwick, Kemp and Long (1980).

Essays in the Economics of Exhaustible Resources, edited by M. C. Kemp and N. V. Long
© *Elsevier Science Publishers B.V., 1984*

the monopolist with exclusive access both to the available oil and to the known means of harnessing the sun.[2]

We do not attempt at this stage to provide a detailed statement of conclusions. The latter have been collected in a series of formal propositions. Here we simply note that, depending on the assumptions made about cost and demand, the transition may begin immediately, never, or after the lapse of finite time; the transition may be abrupt or phased over finite or infinite time; the stock of oil may be exhausted, only partly used, or left untouched; and the price of energy may jump in either direction at the beginning of the transition. That a jump in price may be required is perhaps a little surprising, but can be appreciated in terms of the optimality condition that the sum of consumers' and producers' surpluses be a continuous function of time.

We find it useful to conduct our exposition in the concrete terms of oil and solar power. However, the analysis applies wherever production can be based either on a finite resource-stock or on a never-ending resource-flow. Moreover, the resource-stock may be interpreted quite broadly: by holding to a particular method of production a country might run down its stock of unpolluted air or water if there are no means of disposing of noxious by-products; or by sticking to intensive methods of agriculture it might deplete its stock of arable land. Finally, the analysis applies when production entails the accumulation (rather than depletion) of a resource-stock, as when a commodity can be produced by either of two processes, one of which involves learning-by-doing and the accumulation of a stock of "knowledge".

2. The model and some preliminary calculations

The rate of energy consumption at time t is $q(t)$ and the inverse demand function is

$$p = D(q), \tag{1a}$$

where

$$D(q) > 0, \quad \text{for all } q > 0; \quad D'(q) \equiv dD/dq < 0, \tag{1b}$$

and p is the price of energy in terms of utility or, equivalently, in terms of

---

[2]We do not attempt a descriptive analysis of the paths of oil extraction and of solar-energy production in mixed competitive–imperfectly-competitive economies. For such analyses the reader is referred to Hoel (1978) and Gilbert and Goldman (1978).

some other good with constant marginal utility. The rate of oil extraction and the rate of production of solar energy at time t are, respectively, $y(t)$ and $z(t)$. After careful choice of quantity units, and on the assumption that neither extracted oil nor captured solar energy can be stored,

$$q(t) = y(t) + z(t). \tag{2}$$

The total cost of oil extraction is $C(y, Y)$, where $Y(t)$ is the stock of oil surviving to time t. It is assumed throughout that:

$$C(0, Y) = 0, \qquad C_y \equiv \partial C/\partial y \geqq 0, \qquad C_Y \equiv \partial C/\partial Y \leqq 0. \tag{3a}$$

The production of solar energy entails variable costs $S(z)$, with

$$S(0) = 0, \qquad S'(z) \equiv dS/dz \geqq 0, \tag{3b}$$

as well as a set-up cost K which, for simplicity, is taken to be completely independent of z. We do not at this stage rule out the possibility that $K = 0$.[3] Nor do we rule out the possibility that there is an upper bound on the rate of production of solar energy; that possibility can be accommodated by letting $S(z)$ go to infinity as z approaches the least upper bound from below.

We seek the socially optimal trajectories of y and z. Now if during some interval of time it is optimal to produce solar energy only, then it is optimal to never again extract oil, for at the end of the interval the future will look just as at the beginning. In particular, this is true of any interval beginning at time zero. Thus, we seek the optimal trajectories of y and z, the trajectory of y beginning at time zero and the trajectory of z beginning at some time $T \geqq 0$ when the solar plant is installed. The value of the *transition time T* is to be determined.[4]

The social benefit derived from consumption $q(t)$ is:

$$B(q(t)) \equiv \int_0^{q(t)} D(\tilde{q}) \, d\tilde{q}, \tag{4a}$$

where, from (1):

$$B'(q) \equiv dB/dq \geqq 0, \qquad B''(q) \equiv d^2B/dq^2 = D'(q) < 0 \tag{4b}$$

---

[3] The analysis could be reworked to accommodate the possibility that K is negative, as when some aesthetic or social value attaches to the production of solar energy and attracts a once-over government subsidy.

[4] If $K = 0$, so that within limits it may be a matter of indifference when the solar plant in installed, T will be taken to be the latest point in time at which installation can take place without social loss.

and, to avoid trivality, it is assumed that:

$$B'(0) > S'(0), \qquad C_y(0, Y(0)). \tag{4c}$$

Thus, if r is the constant rate of time preference, the social problem is to find

(P1) $\max\limits_{T, \{y, z\}} \int_0^\infty \exp(-rt)[B(y(t) + z(t) - C(y(t), Y(t))$

$\qquad - S(z(t))] \mathrm{d}t - \exp(-rT)K$

s.t. $y(t) \geqq 0, \qquad z(t) \geqq 0, \qquad z(t) = 0, \quad \text{if } t < T,$

$\qquad \dot{Y}(t) \equiv \mathrm{d} Y/\mathrm{d}t = -y(t),$

$\qquad Y(0) = Y_0, \qquad \lim\limits_{t \to \infty} Y(t) \geqq 0.$

(Notice that $y(t)$ is not required to be zero for $t \geqq T$. The simultaneous extraction of oil and production of solar energy is not ruled out.)

It is convenient to approach (P1) in stages. Let us begin by considering the subproblem, defined for given T and $Y(T)$, of finding

(P2) $\max\limits_{\{y\}} \int_0^T \exp(-rt)[B(y) - C(y, Y)] \mathrm{d}t$

s.t. $y(t) \geqq 0,$

$\qquad \dot{Y}(t) = -y(t),$

$\qquad Y(0) = Y_0, \text{ given}; \qquad Y(T) = Y_T, \text{ given}.$

Introducing the Hamiltonian:

$$H_1 = \exp(-rt)[B(y) - C(y, Y)] - p_1 y, \tag{5}$$

we have, as necessary conditions for a maximum:

$$\partial H_1/\partial y = \exp(-rt)[B'(y) - C_y(y, Y)] - p_1 \leqq 0 \quad (=0, \text{ if } y > 0), \tag{6}$$

$$\dot{p}_1 = -\partial H_1/\partial Y = \exp(-rt)C_Y(y, Y). \tag{7}$$

Let $W_1(Y_T, T)$ be the required maximum value. It is well known that:

$$\partial W_1/\partial Y_T = -p_1(T^-) \equiv - \lim\limits_{t \to T^-} p_1(t), \tag{8a}$$

$$\partial W_1/\partial T = H_1(T^-) \equiv \lim\limits_{t \to T^-} H_1(t). \tag{8b}$$

(See, for example, Hadley and Kemp (1971, pp. 117–120)).)

Let us consider next the subproblem, again defined for given T and Y_T, of finding

(P3) $\max\limits_{\{y,z\}} \int\limits_{T}^{\infty} \exp(-rt)[B(y+z) - C(y, Y) - S(z)]\,\mathrm{d}t$

   s.t. $y(t) \geqq 0, \qquad z(t) \geqq 0,$

   $\dot{Y}(t) = -y(t),$

   $Y(T) = Y_T, \qquad \lim\limits_{t\to\infty} Y(t) \geqq 0.$

Introducing the Hamiltonian:

$$H_2 = \exp(-rt)[B(y+z) - C(y, Y) - S(z)] - p_2 y, \tag{9}$$

we have, as necessary conditions:

$$\partial H_2/\partial y = \exp(-rt)[B'(y+z) - C_y(y, Y)] - p_2 \leqq 0 \quad (\doteq 0, \quad \text{if } y > 0), \tag{10}$$

$$\partial H_2/\partial z = \exp(-rt)[B'(y+z) - S'(z)] \leqq 0 \quad (=0, \quad \text{if } z > 0), \tag{11}$$

$$\dot{p}_2 = -\partial H_2/\partial Y = \exp(-rt)C_Y(y, Y) \tag{12}$$

$$\lim\limits_{t\to\infty} p_2(t)\,Y(t) = 0, \qquad \lim\limits_{t\to\infty} p_2(t) \geqq 0. \tag{13}$$

Let $W_2(Y_T, T)$ be the required maximum value. It has been shown elsewhere that:

$$\partial W_2/\partial Y_T = p_2(T^+) \equiv \lim\limits_{t\to T^+} p_2(t), \tag{14a}$$

$$\partial W_2/\partial T = -H_2(T^+) \equiv -\lim\limits_{t\to T^+} H_2(t). \tag{14b}$$

(See Hadley and Kemp (1971, pp. 117–120).)

Returning to (P1) we find that it can be recast in the simple Kuhn–Tucker form:

(P4) $\max\limits_{T, Y_T} W_1(Y_T, T) + W_2(Y_T, T) - \exp(-rt)K$

   s.t. $Y_T \geqq 0, \qquad T \geqq 0.$

Any solution to (P4) must satisfy:

$$\sum \partial W_i / \partial Y_T \leqq 0 \quad (=0, \quad \text{if } Y_T > 0), \tag{15}$$

$$(\sum \partial W_i / \partial T) + r \exp(-rT)K \leqq 0 \quad (=0, \quad \text{if } T > 0). \tag{16}$$

Defining the current-value Hamiltonians:

$$\bar{H}_i(t) \equiv \exp(rt)H_i(t), \qquad i = 1, 2, \tag{17}$$

and the current-value shadow prices:

$$\psi_i(t) \equiv \exp(rt)p_i(t), \qquad i = 1, 2, \tag{18}$$

we can re-write (15) and (16) as:

$$\psi_1(T^-) \geqq \psi_2(T^+) \quad (=\text{if } Y_T > 0) \tag{19}$$

and

$$\bar{H}_1(T^-) \leqq \bar{H}_2(T^+) - rK \quad (=\text{if } T > 0). \tag{20}$$

Condition (19) tells us that if Y_T is positive, then the shadow price of unextracted oil is continuous at the transition time T and that otherwise it might jump down. Condition (20) tells us that if T is positive, then net national income is continuous at T.[5] (Notice that, for $t > T$, net national income consists of $\bar{H}_2(t)$ less the interest cost of the solar plant.) Clearly T is finite if and only if:

$$B(z^*) - S(z^*) > rK, \tag{21}$$

where z^* maximizes $B(z) - S(z)$. We shall assume in what follows that (21) is satisfied and that z^* is positive and unique.

Two general propositions follow easily from (19) and (20).

Proposition 1. For an upward jump in price at T it is necessary that $C(y, Y)$ be strictly concave in y over some interval.

Proof. From (6) and (10), respectively:

$$p_1(T^-) = \exp(-rt)[B'(q^-) - C_y(q^-, Y_T)] \tag{22}$$

and

$$p_2(T^+) \geqq \exp(-rt)[B'(q^+) - C_y(y^+, Y_T)], \tag{23}$$

---

[5]For the interpretation of the current-value Hamiltonian as a measure of national income, see Kemp and Long (1981).

where $q^- \equiv q(T^-) \equiv \lim_{t \to T^-} q(t)$, etc. From (18) and (19), however:

$$p_2(T^+) \leqq p_1(T^-). \tag{24}$$

Hence:

$$B'(q^+) - C_y(y^+, Y_T) \leqq B'(q^-) - C_y(q^-, Y_T). \tag{25}$$

Now, if $q^- > q^+$, then $B'(q^-) < B'(q^+)$ which, with (25), implies that:

$$C_y(q^-, Y_T) < C_y(y^+, Y_T). \tag{26}$$

But if $q^- > q^+$, then $q^- > y^+$ which, in view of (26), implies that C_y is a decreasing function of y over some interval. Q.E.D.

Proposition 2. If $C(y, Y)$ and $S(z)$ are convex in y and z, respectively, and if $rK = 0$, then the price is continuous at T.

Proof. In view of Proposition 1, it suffices to rule out downward jumps in price.

Suppose that T is positive. Evidently $z(t) = 0$ if $t < T$, and $z(T^+) > 0$. Since $rK = 0$:

$$B'(q(t)) < S'(z), \quad \text{for all } z < q(t) \text{ and } t < T, \tag{27}$$

and

$$B'(q(T^+)) = S'(z(T^+)). \tag{28}$$

From (27), (28), and the fact that $B'' < 0$:

$$q(t) > q(T^+), \quad \text{for } t < T,$$

whence

$$q(T^-) \geqq q(T^+), \tag{29}$$

and any price jump must be upward. Q.E.D.

3. The case in which no oil is extracted after T

In this section we concentrate on a particular type of optimal program, namely that in which no oil is extracted after the transition time T (so that any oil remaining at T is abandoned). For such an outcome we provide three distinct sufficient conditions. The following definitions are a useful preliminary.

Definition 1. z^* is that value of z which maximizes $B(z) - S(z)$; $p^* \equiv B'(z^*)$. It will be assumed that z^* is positive and unique.

Definition 2.

(a) $N(q) \equiv B(q) - qB'(q)$.
(b) $M(y, Y) \equiv yC_y(y, Y) - C(y, Y)$.
(c) $I(z) \equiv zS'(z) - S(z)$.

One may interpret $N(q)$ as the consumers' surplus, $M(y, Y)$ as the producers' surplus from oil extraction (to be distinguished from the scarcity rent $y[B'(q) - C_y(y, Y)]$), and $I(z)$ as the producers' surplus from the production of solar energy. In view of (3), $I(0) = M(0, Y) = 0$.

Definition 3. $\bar{q}$ is that value of q which satisfies

$$N(\bar{q}) = N(z^*) + I(z^*) - rK \tag{30}$$

and $\bar{p} \equiv D(\bar{q})$.

Condition A.[6]   For all $y \in [0, z^*]$, all $z \in [0, z^*]$ and all $Y \leq Y(0)$:

$$C_y(y, Y) > S'(z). \tag{31}$$

Condition B.[7] $C(y, Y)$ and $S(z)$ are weakly concave in y and z, respectively.

Condition C. $C_y(y, Y) = a(Y)$, $a'(Y) \leq 0$; $S''(z) > 0$; $p > p^*$.

Thus, condition A restricts the relative positions of the two cost curves, condition B restricts their shapes, and condition C does both.

It is obvious that if condition A is satisfied it is optimal to abandon any oil surviving at T. That the same is true of conditions B and C requires a brief demonstration. Consider condition B. If $C(y, Y)$ and $S(z)$ are concave functions in y and z, respectively, then, for any shadow price $\psi \geq 0$ and any given $q \geq 0$, the cost-minimization problem,

---

[6]If, for all $y \in [0, z^*]$ and all $Y \leq Y(0)$, $C_{yY}(y, Y) \leq 0$, then (31) can be replaced by the less stringent condition:

$$C_y(y, 0) > S'(z).$$

[7]Condition B does not exclude the possibility that the Hamiltonian $\bar{H}_i = B(y + z) - C(y, Y) - S(z) - \psi_i y$ is concave in y and z.

$$\min_{y,z} C(y, Y) + S(z) - \psi y$$

$$\text{s.t.} \quad z + y \geqq q,$$

has one or both of the corner solutions $(y = 0, \ z = q)$ and $(y = q, \ z = 0)$. But if it is optimal to install the solar plant at $t = T$, then clearly $(y = 0, \ z = q)$ is optimal at T (and also after T for if, in any interval $[T, T + \varepsilon]$, $y = 0$, then the future will look the same at $t = T + \varepsilon$ as at $t = T$). Thus, condition B suffices for an optimal program with all surviving oil abandoned at T.

Consider condition C. The condition is illustrated by fig. 6.1. Thus, the consumers' surplus $N(\bar{q})$ may be identified with the area CDE, the consumers' surplus $N(z^*)$ with the area BDF, and the producers' surplus $I(z^*)$ with the area ABF. It follows that (30) is satisfied if and only if rK

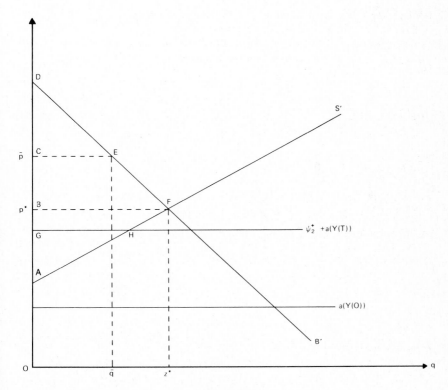

Figure 6.1

can be identified with the area *ACEF*. Evidently z^* is positive; for, if not, it cannot have been optimal to build the solar plant at T. Suppose that y^+ also is positive. Then ψ_2^+ is positive and, from (10) and (11):

$$B'(y^+ + z^+) = S'(z^+) = \psi_2^+ + a(Y(T)). \tag{32}$$

Evidently (32) is satisfied only if $\psi_2^+ + a(Y(T))$ is less than p^*, as shown in fig. 6.1. But then the variable costs saved by solar energy (which may be identified with the area *AGH* of fig. 6.1) are less than rK, implying that $H(T^-)$ is greater than $H(T^+) - rK$, violating (20). Hence $y^+ = 0$.

    None of the conditions A, B, and C is inconsistent with $T = 0$, i.e. with the abandonment of the oil deposit at the outset. To rule out that uninteresting outcome we introduce an additional condition.

Condition D. $C(z^*, Y(0)) < S(z^*) + rK$.

With the condition A, B, or C, condition D ensures that $T > 0$. Notice, however, that if $rK = 0$, then conditions A and D (but not B and D) are incompatible; and, of course, condition C implies that $rK > 0$.

    For the remainder of this section it will be assumed that one of the above sufficient conditions (A and D, B and D, C and D) is satisfied, so that $T > 0$ and any oil surviving to T is abandoned. The transversality condition (20) then reduces to:

$$[B(q^-) - q^- B'(q^-)] + [q^- C_y(q^-, Y_T) - C(q^-, Y_T)]$$
$$= B(q^+) - S(q^+) - rK, \tag{33}$$

or, since $q^+ = z^*$ and $B'(z^*) = S'(z^*)$, to:

$$N(q^-) + M(q^-, Y_T) = N(q^+) + I(q^+) - rK. \tag{34a}$$

    Equation (34a) contains the three unknowns q^-, q^+, and Y_T. With the aid of the additional equations,

$$q^+ = z^* \tag{34b}$$

and

$$[B'(q^-) - C_y(q^-, Y_T)]Y_T = 0, \tag{34c}$$

a solution may be found, in principle. The first of the additional equations is a direct consequence of the conditions, already discussed, which guarantee that there is no oil extraction after T. The second equation is a "complementary slackness" condition. Thus, if Y_T is positive but it is suboptimal to extract after T, then $\psi_2(T^+) = 0$, implying that $\psi_1(T^-) = 0$;

and, from (19), if $\psi_2(T^+) = 0$, then $\psi_1(T^-) = 0$, implying that $B'(q^-) - C_y(q^-, Y_T) = 0$.

We can now introduce and prove the most important result of this section.

Proposition 3. If $T > 0$ and $y(t) = 0$ for $t > T$ and if $B(q) - C(q, Y)$ is strictly concave in q, then:

(a) $q^- > q^+$ (so that the price of energy jumps up at T) if and only if

$$I(q^+) - rK > M(q^+, Y_T); \tag{35a}$$

(b) $q^- = q^+$ (so that the price of energy is continuous at T) if and only if

$$I(q^+) - rK = M(q^+, Y_T); \tag{35b}$$

(c) $q^- < q^+$ (so that the price of energy jumps down at T) if and only if

$$I(q^+) - rK < M(q^+, Y_T). \tag{35c}$$

Proof. It suffices to prove (a). From the assumed concavity of $B(q) - C(q, Y)$, $N(q) + M(q, Y)$ is increasing in q. From this fact and from (34a) it follows that if (35a) holds, then:

$$N(q^-) + M(q^-, Y_T) = N(q^+) + I(q^+) - rK$$
$$> N(q^+) + M(q^+, Y_T),$$

whence $q^- > q^+$.

Conversely, if $q^- > q^+$, then:

$$N(q^-) + M(q^-, Y_T) > N(q^+) + M(q^+, Y_T).$$

With (34a), this inequality implies (35a). Q.E.D.

Corollary.

(a) If conditions A and D are satisfied, then the price of energy jumps downward at the transition time T.

(b) If $C(y, Y)$ is strictly concave in y and $S(z)$ linear (so that condition B is satisfied), if condition D is satisfied, and if rK is sufficiently small, then the price of energy jumps upward at T.

(c) If $C(y, Y)$ is linear in y and $S(z)$ concave, and if $rK > 0$, then the price of energy jumps downward. (If $C(y, Y)$ is linear in y and $S(z)$ strictly concave, then the price of energy jumps down if $rK \geq 0$.)

(d) If conditions C and D are satisfied, then the price of energy jumps downward.

Proof.

(a) From conditions A and D:

$$C(q^+, Y_T) \leqq S(q^+) + rK$$

(for otherwise it would be optimal to produce solar energy earlier) and, from condition A:

$$C_y(q^+, Y_T) > S'(q^+).$$

Hence:

$$q^+ C_y(q^+, Y_T) - C(q^+, Y_T) > q^+ S'(q^+) - S(q^+) - rK,$$

which is (35c).

(b) Since $C(y, Y)$ is strictly concave in y, $M(q^+, Y)$ is negative; and since $S(z)$ is linear, $I(q^+) = 0$. Hence (35a) is satisfied if rK is sufficiently small.

(c) Since $C(y, Y)$ is linear in y, $M(q, Y) = 0$; and since $S(z)$ is concave, $I(q) \leqq 0$. Hence (35c) is satisfied if $rK > 0$. (If $S(z)$ is strictly concave, then $I(q) < 0$ and (35c) is satisfied if $rK \geqq 0$.)

(d) Since $C(y, Y)$ is linear in y, $M(q, Y) = 0$; and in verifying the sufficiency of condition C it was shown that $I(z^*) - rK < 0$. Hence (35c) is satisfied.   Q.E.D.

Parts (b) and (c) of the corollary are of special interest in showing that a jump in price is possible even if the set-up cost is zero, and that the jump may be in either direction.

4. The case in which oil is extracted after T

One might be tempted to conjecture that if $T > 0$ and if $y(T^+) > 0$, then the price of energy must be continuous at T. We begin this final section with an example for which the price is indeed continuous. Nevertheless the conjecture is false, as will be shown by means of two additional examples.

Condition E. $C_y(y, Y) = a(Y)$, $a'(Y) \leqq 0$; $S''(z) > 0$; $a(Y(0)) < S'(0)$; $\bar{p} \leqq p^*$.

Proposition 4. If condition E is satisfied and if the initial stock of oil is sufficiently large, then $T > 0$, $Y(T) > 0$, $y(T^+) > 0$, and $q^- = q^+$.

Proof.   If condition E is satisfied, then so is condition D. From condition D and (30), $a(Y(0)) < \bar{p}$, as in fig. 6.2. From the definitions of $\bar{p}$ and $\bar{q}$, rK can be identified with the area of ACK less the area of KFE, with this difference in turn equal to the area of, say, AGH. Thus, if $\psi_1(0) + a(Y(0))$ is less than the distance OG, then initially oil is the sole source of energy. However,

$$\frac{d}{dt}[\psi_1 + a(Y)] = \dot{\psi}_1 + a'(Y)\dot{Y}$$

$$= \dot{\psi}_1 - y\,a'(Y),$$

and, from (7) and (18):

$$\dot{\psi}_1 = r\psi_1 + y\,a'(Y),$$

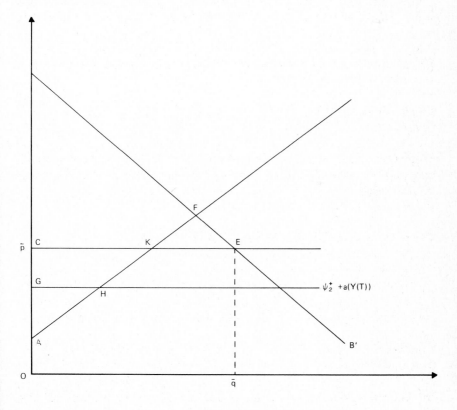

Figure 6.2

so that

$$\frac{d}{dt}[\psi_1 + a(Y)] = r\psi_1 \geqq 0.$$

Thus, eventually $\psi_1(t) + a(Y(t))$ rises and the rate of extraction declines until $\psi_1(t) + a(Y(t))$ equals the distance OG at $t = T$. Then the saving in variable cost achieved by switching to solar energy is just equal to rK and the solar plant is installed. The total output of energy is continuous at T but the rate of extraction of oil drops by GH to make way for solar power. Thereafter, $\psi_2(t) + a(Y(t))$ steadily rises to p^*, $z(t)$ steadily increases to z^*, and $y(t)$ steadily declines to zero, with all the journeys completed in finite time. If $a(0) > p^*$, then some oil will be left underground permanently; otherwise, the oil deposit will be exhausted.

It remains to note that if the initial stock of oil is sufficiently large, then $\psi_1(0) + a(Y(0))$ must be less than the distance OG, implying that $T > 0$.

Q.E.D.

Definition 4. $\hat{q}$ is that value of q such that $C'(\hat{q}) = B'(\hat{q})$; $\hat{q}^0$ is that value of q such that $C_y(\hat{q}^0, 0) = B'(\hat{q}^0)$.

Condition F. $C = C(y)$, $C'(y) > 0$, $C''(y) > 0$, $C'(\infty) = \infty$; $S(z) = b$, $b > 0$; $C'(0) < b < B'(0)$; $\hat{q} > z^*$.

Proposition 5. If condition F is satisfied and if rK is sufficiently small, then $y(t) > 0$ during some finite and non-degenerate interval beginning at T. If, in addition, the initial stock of oil is sufficiently great, then $T > 0$. If $T > 0$, then the price of energy jumps down at T.

Proof. From condition F, for any $\psi_1 \in (0, b - C'(0))$ the equation

$$C'(y) + \psi_1 = b$$

has a unique solution $\bar{y}(\psi_1)$, and the equation

$$C'(y) + \psi_1 = B'(y)$$

has a unique solution $\tilde{y}(\psi_1)$. If the initial stock of oil is sufficiently large, then $\psi_1(0)$ will be close to zero and $y(0) = \bar{y}(\psi_1(0)) = q(0)$ will be greater than z^* (see fig. 6.3). As the stock is depleted, $\psi_1(t)$ rises until both $\tilde{y}(\psi_1)$ and $\bar{y}(\psi_1)$ lie to the left of z^*. If rK is sufficiently small, there is a unique $\psi_1^* \in (0, b - C'(0))$ such that:

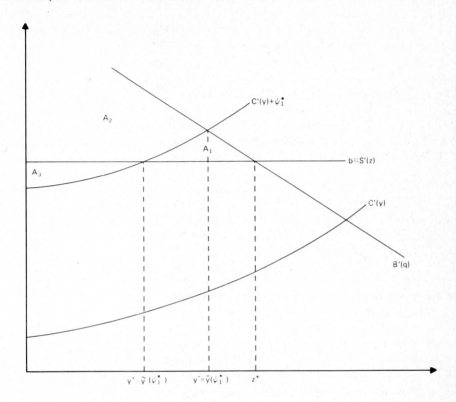

Figure 6.3

$$B(\bar{y}(\psi_1^*)) - C(\bar{y}(\psi_1^*)) - \psi_1^* \bar{y}(\psi_1^*)$$

$$= B(z^*) - C(\tilde{y}(\psi_1^*)) - b[z^* - \tilde{y}(\psi_1^*)] - \psi_1^* \tilde{y}(\psi_1^*) - rK,$$

that is, the transversality condition,

$$H_1(T^-) = H_2(T^+) - rK,$$

is satisfied.

(In terms of fig. 6.3, area A_2 plus area A_3 = the sum of the areas A_1, A_2, and A_3 less rK; that is, area A_1 is equal to rK.) When $\psi_1(t)$ reaches ψ_1^* the solar plant is installed. Clearly:

$$q^- = y^- = \bar{y}(\psi_1^*); \qquad q^+ = y^+ + z^+ = \tilde{y}(\psi_1^*) + z^+ = z^*,$$

so that $q^- < q^+$ and the price of energy jumps down. After T, $y(t)$ is positive but declining until the stock of oil is exhausted at finite time

$T' \equiv T + \theta$, when ψ_1 reaches $b - C'(0)$. Evidently T' is uniquely determined by the equation

$$b - C'(0) = \psi_1^* \exp(r\theta).$$

Over the time interval θ accumulated extraction is:

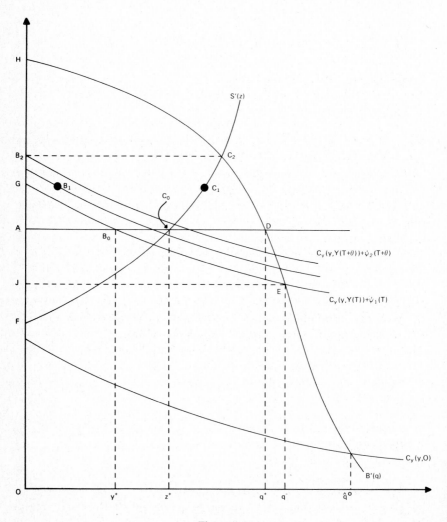

Figure 6.4

$$A \equiv \int_0^\theta y(s)\,ds,$$

where

$$C'(y(s)) + \psi_1^* \exp(rs) = b - C'(0).$$

If and only if $Y(0) > A$, $\psi_1(0) < \psi_1^*$ and the solar plant is installed at $T > 0$.

Q.E.D.

Condition G. $S'(0) \geqq C_y(0, 0)$; $S''(z) > 0$, $C_{yy}(y, Y) < 0$, $S''(z) + C_{yy} \geqq 0$.

Proposition 6. If condition G is satisfied, if rK is sufficiently small, and if the initial stock of oil is sufficiently large, then $T > 0$, $y^+ > 0$, and the price of energy jumps up at $t = T$.

Proof. If the initial stock of oil is sufficiently large, then $\psi_1(0)$ is small and $y(0) = q(0)$ close to $\hat{q}^0$ (see fig. 6.4). As the stock is depleted, $\psi_1(t)$ rises and possibly $C_y(y, Y)$ rises for given y. If rK is sufficiently small, then eventually, at finite time T, (20) is satisfied: $H(T^-)$, represented by the area GHE, is equal to the difference between $H(T^+)$, represented by the sum of the areas FAC_0 and B_0GHD, and rK; that is, the area FAC_0 less rK is equal to the area B_0DE.

At $t = T$ the solar plant is installed and output jumps down from q^- to $q^+ = y^+ + z^+$ (see fig. 6.4 again). For, from the assumption that $S''(z) + C_{yy} \geqq 0$, if $q = q^+$, then any increase in y beyond y^+ (implying an equal reduction in z below z^+) is wasteful; and the same is true of any reduction of y below y^+ (and an equal increase of z above z^+). Associated with the downward jump of output, the price of energy jumps up from OJ to OA. Thereafter the price of energy steadily rises with the depletion of the stock of oil until, at finite time $T + \theta$, it reaches $p^* \equiv B'(z^*)$. During the interval θ, $y(t)$ declines to zero along the path $B_0B_1B_2$ and $z(t)$ rises to z^* along the path $C_0C_1C_2$.

Q.E.D.

5. Final remark

It has been assumed that neither extracted oil nor captured solar energy can be stored. That is an extreme assumption. To relax it might be thought to be fatal to the possibility of upward jumps in price. However, reflection shows that this is not so. Thus, consider the possibility of holding extracted oil across the transition point T. Since the period of storage is degenerate, only set-up costs, possibly dependent on the amount stored, are relevant. Evidently the social cost-of-storage function and the optimal $p(T^-)$ and $p(T^+)$ of sections 2–4 might allow some profitable storage across T. However, provided only that the function is positive for all positive quantities stored, some residual post-storage upward price jump must remain.[8]

[8]Suppose that the total storage cost incurred by an *individual arbitrageur* is $a(x)$, where x is the quantity stored. Then an arbitrage profit can be made, however small the price jump, if and only if:

$$\lim_{x \to 0^+} a(x) = 0 = \lim_{x \to 0^+} a'(x),$$

that is, if and only if the *social* cost of storage is zero for all positive quantities stored.

References

Gilbert, R. J. and S. M. Goldman (1978), Potential competition and monopoly price of an exhaustible resource, Journal of Economic Theory 17, 319–331.

Hadley, G. and M. C. Kemp (1971), Variational Methods in Economics (North-Holland Publishing Company, Amsterdam).

Hoel, M. (1978), Resource extraction, substitute production, and monopoly, Journal of Economic Theory 19, 28–37.

Hartwick, J. M., M. C. Kemp and N. V. Long (1980), Set-up costs and the theory of exhaustible resources, University of New South Wales.

Kemp, M. C. and N. V. Long (1981), On the evaluation of social income in a dynamic economy, in: G. R. Feiwel, ed., Samuelson and Neoclassical Economics (Kleewer–Nijhoff Publishing, Boston) pp. 185–189.

On the development of a substitute for an exhaustible natural resource

MURRAY C. KEMP and NGO VAN LONG*

1. Introduction

The exhaustibility of stocks of natural resources causes societies to search for flow substitutes for those resources, and it causes them to invest in physical capital and to undertake research-and-development expenditures designed to improve the quality or reduce the production cost of the substitutes. What then are the socially optimal trajectories of resource-extraction, of output of the substitutes, and of investment in equipment and in research and development? And how do the socially optimal trajectories compare with those generated by various alternative market structures? In this essay we examine these questions.

Assumptions must be made. In particular, it is assumed that there is just one natural resource and just one perfect flow substitute for it. The average cost of producing the substitute depends on the amount produced and also on the state of the arts. At any moment, the state of the arts is given, but it can be changed gradually by expenditure on research and development. On the other hand, the average cost of extracting the resource is constant, independent both of the rate of extraction and of the outstanding stock of the resource.

After calculating the socially optimal trajectory (in section 2), we describe the trajectory associated with each of several alternative market situations. Thus (in section 3) we treat the case of universal monopoly, in which the resource is owned by a single firm and the same firm has the

*First published in W. Eichhorn et al., eds., *Economic Theory of Natural Resources* (Physica-Verlag, Würzburg, 1982) pp. 47–63.

Essays in the Economics of Exhaustible Resources, edited by M. C. Kemp and N. V. Long
© *Elsevier Science Publishers B.V., 1984*

exclusive legal right to develop and produce the substitute. Then (in section 5) we visit the opposite pole and examine the case of universal competition, in which ownership of the resource is dispersed over many small firms and in which there is complete freedom of entry to the activity of developing and producing the substitute. As a preliminary to the analysis of section 5, we examine (in section 4) the mixed case in which ownership of the resource is dispersed but the right to develop and produce the substitute is legally restricted to a single firm.

Our work builds on that of Vousden (1977). Vousden developed a model of social optimization slightly more general than ours, but he stopped short of comparing the socially optimal trajectory with the outcomes of alternative market structures. Our work also bears an affinity to that of Stiglitz and Dasgupta (1982) and Dasgupta, Gilbert and Stiglitz (1982). They do compare the socially optimal trajectory with the outcomes when decisions and asset-holdings are decentralized in various market situations. However, whereas we suppose that expenditure on research and development generates reductions of cost continuously and without delay, they see the objective of such expenditure as the reduction of the period of waiting for an invention of given characteristics.

Unlike Vousden, but like Dasgupta and Stiglitz, we ignore the possibility that there is uncertainty about the size of the resource-stock, about the returns to expenditure on research and development, and about future demand.

2. The social optimum

A single natural resource is available in known amount Q_0. It can be extracted at the constant average cost k, where k may be zero. The total cost of extraction at time t is therefore $kq(t)$, where q is the rate of extraction.

A perfect substitute for the resource can be produced at a total cost of $c(R,y)$, where y is the rate of output and R represents the state of the arts. Expenditure on research and development is $g(r)$, where $r \equiv \dot{R} \equiv dr/dt$.

Total revenue from the sale of the resource and its substitute is $\pi(q + y) \equiv \pi(x)$, so that average revenue is $p(x) \equiv \pi(x)/x$. Subject to the usual qualifications, the social surplus is:

$$u(x) - c(R,y) - kq - g(r),$$

where

$$u(x) \equiv \int_0^x p(z)\,\mathrm{d}z.$$

Evidently, $u'(x) \equiv \mathrm{d}u(x)/\mathrm{d}x = p(x)$.

It is supposed that all functions are continuous and that all second derivatives exist. Moreover, it is assumed that:

$c(R, y)$ is convex in (R, y),

$c_R \leqq 0$, $\quad c_{RR} \geqq 0$, $\quad c_y > 0$, $\quad c_{yy} \geqq 0$, $\quad c_{yR} < 0$,

$c(R, y)$ is bounded by $\underline{c}(y) > 0$ and $\bar{c}(y)$

$c_y(R, 0) < p(0)$,

$g' > 0$, $\quad g'' \geqq 0$,

$\pi(x)$ is strictly concave.

The social problem is to find:

$(P^s) \quad \max_{q,y,r} \int_0^\infty \exp(-\rho t)[u(q+y) - c(R, y) - kq - g(r)]\,\mathrm{d}t$

s.t. $\dot{Q} = -q$, $\quad Q(0) = Q_0 > 0$, $\quad \lim_{t \to \infty} Q(t) \geqq 0$,

$\dot{R} = r$, $\quad R(0) = R_0$,

$q, y, r \geqq 0$.

The Lagrangian is:

$$L = u(q+y) - c(R, y) - kq - g(r) - \psi_1 q + \psi_2 r,$$

where ψ_1 and ψ_2 are the co-states associated with Q and R, respectively. Among the first-order conditions we have:

$\partial L/\partial q = u' - k - \psi_1 \leqq 0 \quad (=0, \text{ if } q > 0),$ \hfill (1)

$\partial L/\partial y = u' - c_y \leqq 0 \quad\quad (=0, \text{ if } y > 0),$ \hfill (2)

$\partial L/\partial r = -g' + \psi_2 \leqq 0 \quad\quad (=0, \text{ if } r > 0),$ \hfill (3)

$\dot{\psi}_1 = \rho\psi_1$ \hfill (4)

$\dot{\psi}_2 = \rho\psi_2 + c_R.$ \hfill (5)

Both ψ_1 and ψ_2 are non-negative. For let us define $V(Q(t), R(t))$ as:

$$\max_{q,y,r} \int_0^\infty \exp(-\rho(z-t))[u(q+y) - c(R, y) - kq - g(r)]\,dz$$

s.t. $\dot{Q} = -q, \qquad Q(t) \geqq 0, \qquad \lim_{z \to \infty} Q(z) \geqq 0,$

$\dot{R} = r,$

$q, y, r \geqq 0.$

Then it is well known that $\partial V/\partial Q = \psi_1 \geqq 0$ and that $\partial V/\partial R = \psi_2 \geqq 0$. Let x^s be defined by:

$$u'(x^s) = p(x^s) = k,$$

and R^s by:

$$c_y(R^s, x^s) = k;$$

let $y^s(R)$ be defined by:

$$c_y(R, y^s) = p(y^s),$$

and $p^s(R)$ by:

$$p^s \equiv p(y^s);$$

and let R^{s*} be defined by:

$$-c_R(R^{s*}, y^s(R^{s*}))/\rho = g'(0).$$

It will be shown that, if R^{s*} exists, it is unique (see the proof of proposition 3(c)).

Proposition 1 (Social optimum).

(a) If $R_0 \geqq R^s$, then the resource is of no value and it is optimal to set $q(t) = 0$ always.

(b) If $R_0 < R^s$, then either (i) $x(t) \geqq x^s$ always and $p(x)$ is non-increasing always, or (ii) $x(0) < x^s$ and $p(x)$ rises until the resource-stock is exhausted and thereafter is non-increasing.

(c) After exhaustion of the resource-stock, the optimal output of the substitute is $y^s(R)$, if it exists. If $y^s(R)$ does not exist, the optimal output is zero. If the optimal output is positive, it is an increasing function or R.

(d)(i) It is optimal to invest in research (that is, $r(t) > 0$ for some t) if $|c_R(R_0, y^s(R_0))/\rho| > g'(0)$. (ii) No investment in research will take place after time t if and only if $R(t) \geqq R^{s*}$. (iii) Investment in research and development can occur before production of the substitute begins, that is, it may be optimal to allow the product of research and development to lie dormant for a season.

Proof.

(a) This part of the proposition is obvious. It is illustrated by Figs. 7. 1(a) and 7. 1(b).

(b) Either $\psi_1(0) = 0$ so that, from (4), $\psi_1(t) = 0$ always; or $\psi_1(0) > 0$ so that $\psi_1(t) > 0$ always. Suppose that $\psi_1(0) = 0$. Then, from (1), $x(t) = x^s$ and $p(t) = k$ until $R(t)$ reaches R^s; at that time, any remaining resource-stock can be abandoned.

If $\psi_1(0) = 0$, it is suboptimal to exhaust the resource-stock before $R(t)$ reaches R^s; for, if that did occur, price would jump up from k, implying that the path to exhaustion is suboptimal. Moreover, if $\psi_1(0) = 0$, $R(t)$

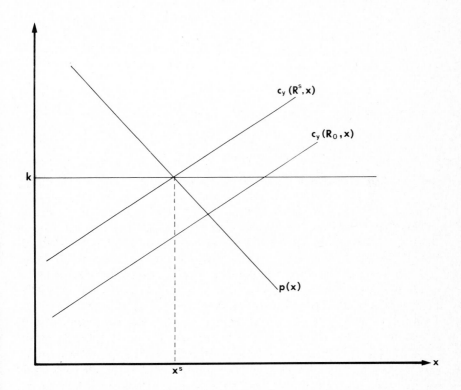

Figure 7.1(a): $c_{yy} > 0$

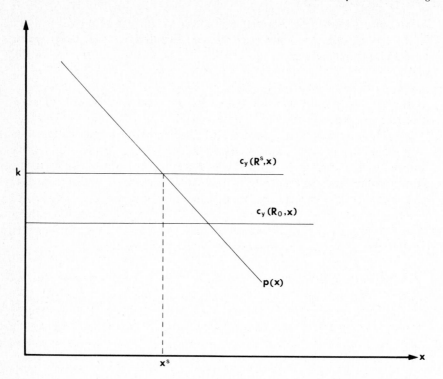

Figure 7.1(b): $c_{yy} = 0$

must reach R^s, at least asymptotically; for, otherwise, $q(t) \geqq \varepsilon > 0$, implying exhaustion in finite time and, in particular, exhaustion before $R(t)$
reaches R^s. If $R(t)$ is asymptotic to R^s but never reaches R^s, then the
resource-stock is never exhausted and there must exist an unbounded
interval of time during which extraction of the resource and production
of the substitute proceed simultaneously. If $R(t)$ rises beyond R^s, then
$p(t)$ steadily falls and $x(t)$ steadily rises as $R(t)$ increases.

   Suppose, alternatively, that $\psi_1(0) > 0$. Since $\partial V/\partial Q = \psi_1(t) > 0$, the
resource-stock will never be abandoned before it is exhausted. If $q(t) > 0$,
then, from (1), price must be rising: $p(t) = k + \psi_1(0)\exp(\rho t)$. After
exhaustion (which may or may not occur) price is non-increasing, falling
if and only if R is increasing. If exhaustion does not occur, there must be
an interval during which extraction and production of the substitute
occur simultaneously; if exhaustion does occur, there may be such an
interval.

(c) This proposition is obvious.

(d) (i) Suppose that the inequality is satisfied but $r(t) = 0$ always. Eventually either the resource-stock will be exhausted or the rate of extraction will be arbitrarily small. Then the marginal gain from an increase of knowledge is $c_R(R_0, y^s(R_0))/\rho$, while the cost of such an increment is $g'(0)$. Hence, the trajectory $r(t) \equiv 0$ is suboptimal. (ii) This proposition follows from (d)(i) by treating time t as the origin. (iii) From the strict concavity of π, p is a declining function of x. Hence, the average utility cost of investment in research and development is an increasing function of the rate of investment. Any investment therefore should take place over an interval of time; in particular, this is true of investment before production of the substitute begins. Q.E.D.

3. A single monopoly of the resource and of its substitute

We have described those trajectories which are optimal from the vantage point of society (viewed, for example, as a collection of individuals with identical preferences and endowments). We now swing to the opposite extreme and examine the policies which are optimal from the point of view of a single individual or subgroup of individuals with exclusive control both of the resource itself and of the development and production of its substitute.

The problem of the monopolist is to find:

$$(\mathrm{P}^m) \quad \max_{q,y,r} \int_0^\infty \exp(-\rho t)[\pi(q+y) - c(R, y) - kq - g(r)]\,\mathrm{d}t$$

s.t. the constraints of (P^s).

Let x^m be defined by:

$$\pi'(x^m) = k,$$

and R^m by:

$$c_y(R^m, x^m) = k;$$

let $y^m(R)$ be defined by:

$$c_y(R, y^m) = \pi'(y^m),$$

and $p^m(R)$ by:

$$p^m \equiv p(y^m);$$

and let R^{m*} be defined by:

$$-c_R(R^{m*}, y^m(R^{m*}))/\rho = g'(0).$$

It will be shown that, if R^{m*} exists, it is unique (see the proof of proposition 3(c)).

Proposition 2 (Monopolist's optimum).

(a) If $R_0 \geqq R^m$, then the resource is of no value and it is optimal to set $q(t) = 0$ always.

(b) If $R_0 < R^m$, then either (i) $x(t) \geqq x^m$ always and $\pi'(x)$ is non-increasing always, or (ii) $x(0) < x^m$ and $\pi'(x)$ rises until the resource-stock is exhausted and thereafter is non-increasing.

(c) After exhaustion of the resource-stock, the optimal output of the substitute is $y^m(R)$, if it exists. If $y^m(R)$ does not exist, the optimal output is zero. If the optimal output is positive, it is an increasing function of R.

(d) (i) It is optimal to invest in research (that is, $r(t) > 0$ for some t) if $-c_R(R_0, y^m(R_0))/\rho > g'(0)$. (ii) No investment in research will take place after time t if and only if $R(t) \geqq R^{m*}$. (iii) Investment in research and development can occur before production of the substitute begins; that is, it may be optimal to allow the product of research and development to lie dormant for a time.

Proof. The proof is similar to that of proposition 1.

Proposition 3 (Comparison of social optimum and monopolist optimum).

(a) $x^s > x^m$.

(b) $R^s > R^m$ if $c_{yy} > 0$, $R^s = R^m$ if $c_{yy} = 0$.

(c) $R^{s*} > R^{m*}$.

Proof. (a) and (b) are obvious.

(c) Let us define:

$$F^s(R) = -c_R(R, y^s(R))/\rho - g'(0),$$

$$F^m(R) = -c_R(R, y^m(R))/\rho - g'(0),$$

so that R^{s*} is the solution of $F^s = 0$ and R^{m*} is the solution of $F^m = 0$. Now

$$dF^m/dR = -(c_{RR} + c_{Ry}(dy^m/dR))/\rho.$$

But

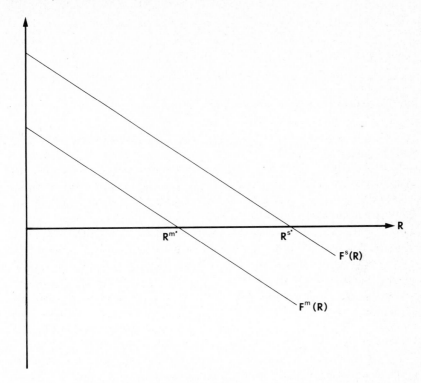

Figure 7.2

$$d y^m/dR = c_{Ry}(\pi'' - c_{yy}).$$

Hence:

$$dF^m/dR = -(c_{RR} + (c_{Ry})^2/(\pi'' - c_{yy}))/\rho$$

$$\leqq (\pi'' c_{RR} - (c_{Ry})^2))/(\rho(c_{yy} - \pi''))$$

$$< 0 \quad \text{[from the convexity of } c(R, y)\text{]}$$

Similarly, $dF^s/dR < 0$. Moreover, $y^m(R) > y^s(R)$ and $c_{Ry} < 0$, implying that the curve $F^m(R)$ lies everywhere below the curve $F^s(R)$, as in fig. 7.2. Q.E.D.

Corollary. A resource-stock is socially valuable but worthless to a monopolist if $R^s > R_0 > R^m$. In that case, the monopolist over-conserves to the point of never using the resource. On the other hand, if $R^{s*} > R_0 > R^{m*}$, it is socially optimal to eventually invest in research and development but suboptimal for a monopolist to do so.

4. Dispersed ownership of the resource, monopoly of the substitute

In section 3 we characterized the trajectories which emerge when both ownership of the resource and the right to develop and produce a substitute lie with a single firm or individual. We now review the analysis of that section on the revised assumption that ownership of the resource is dispersed (competitive) while the development and production of the substitute remain subject to monopoly.

The monopolist faces a large number of small price-taking resource-owners and therefore is in a position to play the role of Stackelberg leader. We suppose that at the outset the leader announces a path $\{p(t)\}$ of selling prices, i.e. prices for the extracted resource or its substitute, and then, given the assumption of perfect foresight, sticks to it. We also suppose that the leader buys the entire stock of the (unextracted) resource at the outset, paying whatever in-the-ground price $P_0 - k$ is optimal for him. Of course the announced price path is then constrained by the requirement that over any interval of time beginning at the initial moment the in-the-ground price rises at an average rate not greater than ρ. It might seem that it would suit the leader to announce a zero in-the-ground price. However, such an announcement, in a context of perfect foresight, would bind the leader to charge a selling price of k for ever. Evidently the leader must strive for the best compromise between the desire to keep the buying price low and the desire to minimize the transition to the monopoly-selling price of section 3.

Formally, the task of the leader is to find:

$$(\text{P}^{m*}) \quad \max_{q,y,r,p_0} \int_0^\infty \exp(-\rho t)[\pi(q+y) - kq - c(R, y) - g(r)]\, dt - p_0 Q_0$$

$$\text{s.t.} \quad \dot{Q} = -q, \qquad Q(0) = Q_0, \qquad \lim_{t\to\infty} Q(t) \geqq 0,$$

$$\dot{R} = r, \qquad R(0) = R_0,$$

$$\dot{p}/(p - k) \leqq \rho,$$

$$q, y, r, p_0 \geqq 0.$$

Until the matter is mentioned again, it will be supposed that, everywhere on the optimal path, $r = 0$. We also rule out the trivial case in which $p^m(R_0) \leqq k$, so that the resource-stock has no value. There remain for consideration three cases, defined by the relative values of R_0, R^s, and R^m.

Case 1 ($R_0 \geqq R^s$). In this case $c_y(R_0, y^m(R_0)) \leqq k$, as in fig. 7.3. The resource-stock would be of no value to the monopolist of section 3, for it is cheaper to produce the substitute than to extract the resource. However, in the hands of competitive owners the resource is a threat to the leader. Hence, it is optimal for the leader to buy the entire un-extracted resource-stock at the present-value price $p_0 - k$, $p_0 \leqq p^m(R_0)$, then permanently withdraw the stock from the market, producing only the less costly substitute commodity. Until $p^m(R^0)$ is reached, the leader's optimal selling price rises from p_0 according to the formula

$$\dot{p}/(p-k) = \rho. \tag{6}$$

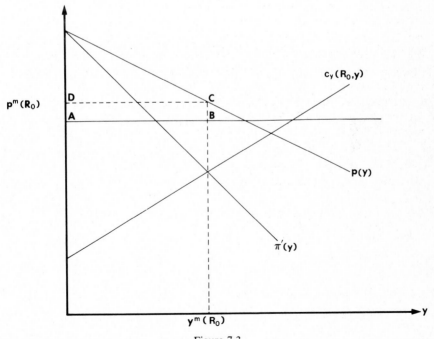

Figure 7.3

Thereafter, price is constant at the level p^m. Of course, if $p_0 = p^m$, then the leader's selling price is equal to p^m from the outset.

It remains to determine the optimal p_0. If p_0 were set equal to p^m, the leader would receive the same amount, represented by the area *ABCD* of fig. 7.3, during each period. If P_0 were set below p^m, then, by virtue of the constraint (6), profits would be lower during some initial interval; but the amount paid for the resource stock also would be less. The optimal p_0 equates marginal gain and loss. Setting $p_0 = p^m - \delta$, $\delta > 0$, the gain from setting p_0 below p^m is:

$$G(\delta) \equiv \delta Q_0,$$

so that

$$G'(\delta) = Q_0. \tag{7}$$

On the other hand, the loss of revenue while the leader's selling price rises to p^m is:

$$L(\delta) \equiv \int_0^{T(\delta)} \exp(-\rho)[p^m y^m - py) - (c(R_0, y^m) - c(R_0, y))]\, dt, \tag{8}$$

where

$$p(t) = (p_0 - k)\exp(\rho t) + k$$
$$= (p^m - \delta - k)\exp(\rho t) + k, \tag{9}$$
$$y = y(p) = y((p_0 - k)\exp(\rho t) + k),$$

and T is the solution of $p^m = p(T)$, that is, of

$$p^m = (p_0 - k)\exp(\rho T) + k$$
$$= (p^m - \delta - k)\exp(\rho T) + k. \tag{10}$$

Solving (10):

$$T(\delta) = (1/\rho)[\log(p^m - k) - \log(p^m - \delta - k)]. \tag{11}$$

Substituting from (11) into (8), and differentiating:

$$L'(\delta) = T'(\delta)\exp(-\rho T)(p^m y^m - p(T)y(T))$$
$$- (c(R_0, h^m) - c(R_0, y(T)))]$$
$$- \int_0^{T(\delta)} \exp(-\rho T)[d(py - c(R_0, y))/d\delta]\, dt.$$

However, $p^m y^m = p(T)y(T)$ and $c(R_0, y^m) = c(R_0, y(T))$; hence:

$$L'(\delta) = - \int_0^{T(\delta)} \exp(-\rho t)[d(py - c(R_0, y))/d\delta]\,dt$$

$$= - \int_0^{T(\delta)} \exp(-\rho t)[d(py - c(R_0, y))/dp][dp/d\delta]\,dt.$$

Moreover, $dp/d\delta = -\exp(\rho t)$; hence:

$$L'(\delta) = - \int_0^{T(\delta)} [\pi'(y) - c_y(R_0, y)][dy/dp]\,dt.$$

For $p < p^m$, $\pi' > c_y$; and, of course, $dy/dp < 0$. Hence:

$$L'(\delta) \geqq 0 \quad (=0, \quad \text{if } T = 0, \text{ that is, if } \delta = 0).$$

The choice of optimal δ, say δ^*, is illustrated by fig. 7.4. Clearly, δ^* is positive, implying that the optimal p_0, say p_0^*, is less than p^m. Moreover,

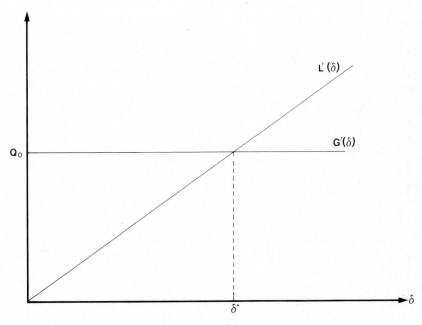

Figure 7.4

from (9), $(p_0 - k) \exp(\rho T) = p^m - k$, implying that $p_0^* > k$. Thus:

$$k < p_0^* < p^m.$$

Case 2 $(R_0 < R^m)$. In this case, evidently, it is never optimal to retire the resource-stock, either in whole or in part. It is convenient to distinguish two subcases, according as (a) $c_y(R_0, 0) > k$, as in fig. 7.5(a), or (b) $c_y(R_0, 0) \leqq k$, as in fig. 7.5(b).

(a) Suppose that $c_y(R_0, 0) > k$ so that, whatever the level of sales, it is less costly to extract the resource than to produce the substitute. As in case 1, the leader may be supposed to purchase the entire resource-stock at the outset, at price $p_0 - k$. The stock is then extracted and sold at a net price $p - k$ which grows exponentially, beginning at $p_0 - k$, until $p = p^m(R_0)$. Before $p = p^m$, the resource-stock will be exhausted and production of the substitute begun. For, suppose that, at the point of exhaustion,

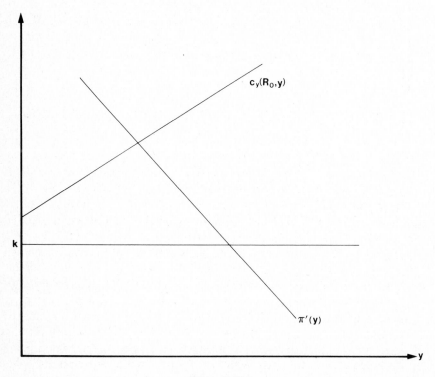

Figure 7.5(a)

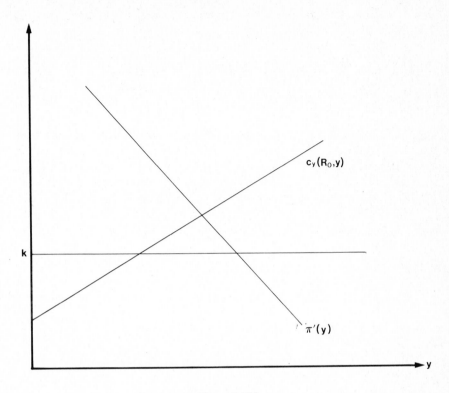

Figure 7.5(b)

$p > p^m$. Then the cost of purchase is unnecessarily high and the period during which no profit is earned unnecessarily long. Suppose that, at the point of exhaustion, $p = p^m(R_0)$, as in section 3. Again the cost of purchasing the resource stock and the period of no profit could be reduced; but these considerations are now more or less offset by the need (imposed by (6)) to sell for a time at a price less than p^m. It can be shown, by an argument similar to that developed for case 1, that if at the point of exhaustion p is sufficiently close to p^m, then the offset is incomplete, and that if at the point of exhaustion p is sufficiently far below p^m, the offset is more than complete, implying that, along the optimal trajectory, exhaustion occurs at a price below p^m. Thus, the optimal policy consists of three phases. During the first phase the entire market is supplied by the resource-stock at a price which obeys (6); that phase ends with the exhaustion of the stock. During the second phase, price continues to obey (6) but the entire market is supplied by the substitute. In the third phase the price is constant at p^m.[1]

(b) Suppose alternatively that $c_y(R_0, 0) \leqq k$. Then it is optimal always to produce the substitute commodity. The first phase of the optimal policy (a) is replaced by a phase during which the market is supplied partly from the resource-stock and partly by the substitute. Otherwise, the new policy has the same characteristics as the old.

Case 3 ($R^m \leqq R_0 < R^s$). This case is illustrated by fig. 7.6. It might seem that the optimal policy must have the same characteristics as in case 1: buy the resource-stock at the outset, at price $p_0 - k$, retire the entire stock, and let $p - k$ climb exponentially until $p = p^m(R_0)$. However, reflection reveals that such a policy is not always optimal. Let us define $\bar{y}$ by:

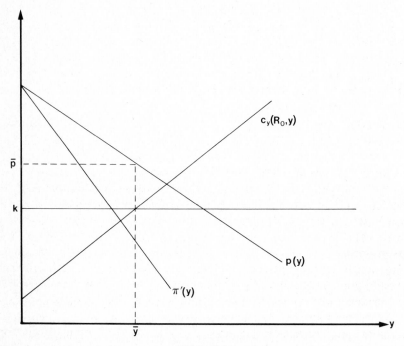

Figure 7.6

$$c_y(R_0, \bar{y}) = k,$$

and $\bar{p}$ by:

$$\bar{p} = p(\bar{y}).$$

Clearly, $\bar{p} > k$ because $R_0 < R^s$. Let us suppose that $\bar{p} > p_0$. Then, during an initial interval of time, the leader will wish to sell more than $\bar{y}$ and it is optimal to extract some of the resource. That first phase ends when $p = \bar{p}$. Thereafter the optimal policy is as in case 1.

We have proceeded to this point on the strong assumption that $R_0 \geq R^{m*}$ so that, everywhere along the optimal trajectory, $r = 0$. Let us now drop that assumption. Again we consider three cases, the first of which is a generalization of case 1, the second of case 2 and the third of case 3.

Case 1' ($R_0 \geq R^s$). In its general outline, the optimal policy of the leader is the same as in case 1. The resource-stock is purchased by the leader at a present-value price $p_0 - k$, with $p_0 < p^m(R_0)$, but is then withheld. Until $p^m(R)$ is reached, the leader's optimal selling price rises from p_0 according to formula (6) and thereafter falls with increases in R.

Case 2' ($R_0 < R^m$).
 (a) Suppose that $c_y(R_0, 0) > k$. It is possible that the optimal policy will consist of three phases similar to those of case 2(a). However, things might be otherwise. It is possible that, along the optimal trajectory, $c_y(R, 0)$ will dip below k before the resource is exhausted, implying the existence of an interval during which extraction and production take place simultaneously. It is even possible that, before exhaustion, $c_y(R, y^m(R)) \leq k$, implying that any remaining resource-stock will be abandoned.
 (b) Suppose that $c_y(R_0, 0) < k$. As in case 2(b), the substitute is produced from the outset. As in case 2'(a), but in contrast to the outcome in case 2(b), it may be optimal to abandon part of the resource-stock.

Case 3' ($R^m \leq R_0 < R^s$). The outcome is as in case 1' except that there may exist an initial interval of time during which the resource is extracted.

The conclusions of this section are summarized in

Proposition 4 (Dispersion of resource-holding, monopoly of the development and production of the substitute). During an initial phase, the selling price is bound by (6) and rises; thereafter, it is non-increasing, falling with increases in R. If $R_0 \geqq R^s$, the resource-stock will be abandoned in its entirety; if $R_0 > R^m$, the resource-stock has value to the leader and will be exploited, in whole or in part, during the initial price phase; if $R^m \leqq R_0 < R^s$, the resource-stock may or may not have value to the leader and therefore may or may not be extracted. While the resource-stock is being exploited, production of the substitute may take place simultaneously, and must do so if $c_y(R_0, 0) < k$.

5. Dispersed ownership of the resource, freedom of entry to the development and production of the substitute

In section 4 it was supposed that the development and production of a substitute for the resource is in the hands of a single, legally protected firm. We now vary that assumption by supposing that the development and production of the substitute is open to any and every firm. We suppose, further, that inventions are protected by unlimited patent.

One can imagine that there takes place an initial meeting of all firms and individuals. At that meeting a complete set of contracts for present and future delivery are formed. The characteristics of an equilibrium price path will depend on the nature of the game played at the meeting. Since there is complete freedom of entry one feels justified in insisting that the price path is such that any firm which develops and produces the substitute will just break even. Beyond that, various possibilities present themselves. Here we follow as closely as possible the analysis of section 4 and suppose that, although bound by the no-profit restriction, each firm seeks to play the role of Stackelberg leader. Detailed analysis is organized under the three subheadings of section 4.

Case 1″ ($R_0 \geqq R^s$). We can imagine that each firm, seeking to secure the role of leader, bids for the resource-stock. Bidding stops when the price reaches that level, say $p_0^{**} - k$, at which the present value of the net cash flow is exactly offset by the cost of buying the resource-stock. Since all firms have the same information, all firms will have the same maximum bid. Which firm makes the purchase is of no importance; we can imagine that it is determined by a random device.

The price paid may be greater or less than $p^m(R_0) - k$, depending on the cost function $c(R, y)$, on the size of the stock Q_0, and on the rate of interest. If $p_0^{**} > p^m(R_0)$, then the price path contains a jump at the initial moment. If $p_0^{**} < p^m(R_0)$, then the price path is as in case 1′: there is an interval during which p is bounded by (6) and which terminates when $p(T)$ equals $p^m(R(T))$; thereafter, $p(t) = p^m(R(t))$. The two possibilities are illustrated by figs. 7.7(a) and 7.7(b), respectively.

Case 2″ ($R_0 < R^m$). Again we can imagine that at the initial point of time some particular firm purchases the entire resource-stock at the break-even price $p_0^{**} - k$.

(a) Suppose that $c_y(R_0, 0) > k$. If $p_0^{**} > p^m(R_0)$, then, as in case 1″, there is an initial jump in price; thereafter $p(t) = p^m(R(t))$. If $p_0^{**} < p^m(R_0)$, then, as in case 2′(a), the equilibrium path has two phases: an initial phase with price bound by (6) and a later phase with price $p^m(R(t))$ not increasing. The initial phase may consist of two specialized sub-phases, as in case 2(a), with only the extracted resource being sold in the first subphase and only the substitute in the second subphase. However, that is not inevitable: as in case 2′(a), there may be an interval of

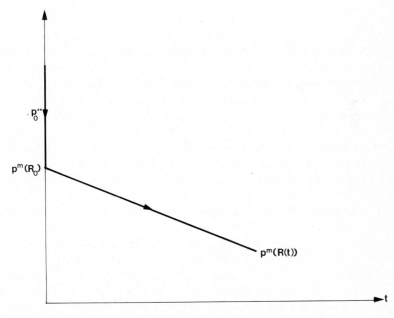

Figure 7.7(a): $p_0^{**} > p^m(R_0)$

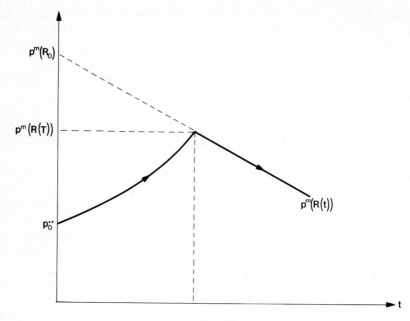

Figure 7.7(b): $p_0^{**} < p^m(R_0)$

simultaneous extraction and production, and it may be optimal to with-draw part of the resource-stock. Moreover, as in case $1''$, there may be no interval during which the substitute is produced under conditions of rising price; in fact, at the point of exhaustion there may be a dis-continuous drop in the price.

(b) Suppose that $c_y(R_0, 0) \leqq k$. Again there will be an initial dis-continuous drop in price if $p_0^{**} > p^m(R_0)$. As in case $2'(b)$, the substitute will be produced from the outset, and the resource-stock may be aban-doned before its exhaustion. In contrast to our conclusion concerning case $2''(a)$, there can be no discontinuous drop in price at any time after the initial moment, for the substitute is produced always.

Case $3''$ $(R^m \leqq R_0 < R^s)$. The outcome is the same as in case $3'$ except that there will be an initial discontinuous drop in price if $p_0^{**} > p^m(R_0)$.

Proposition 5. If the purchase price of the resource-stock $p_0^{**} - k$ is less than $p^m(R_0) - k$, that is, if p_0^{**} is less than $p^m(R_0)$, then the equili-brium price, production, and extraction paths have the qualitative properties described in section 4. If $p_0^{**} \geqq p^m(R_0)$, there is no initial phase with increasing price; indeed, if $p_0^{**} > p^m(R_0)$, then the price path begins with an abrupt jump from p_0^{**} down to $p^m(R_0)$.

References

Dasgupta, P., R. J. Gilbert and J. E. Stiglitz (1982), Invention and innovation under alternative market structures: The case of natural resources, Review of Economic Studies 44, 567–582.

Stiglitz, J. E. and P. Dasgupta (1982), Market structure and resource depletion: A contribution to the theory of intertemporal monopolistic competition, Journal of Economic Theory 28, 128–164.

Vousden, N. J. (1977), Resource scarcity and the availability of substitutes: A theoretical model, in: M. D. Intriligator, ed., Frontiers of Quantitative Economics, vol IIIB (North-Holland Publishing Company, Amsterdam) pp. 507–532.

The optimal restriction of resource imports and the optimal investment in capacity for substitute production

MURRAY C. KEMP and NGO VAN LONG

1. Introduction

Both resource deposits and manufacturing capacity are unevenly distributed across the globe. With theoretical license one can pretend that there are just two types of country, the resource-poor and the resource-rich, the former importing raw materials to feed their manufacturing industries and the latter offering raw materials in exchange for manufactured goods.

Some years ago we examined the interaction of a competitive resource-poor and a competitive resource-rich country, under alternative assumptions about the policies of governments: universal non-intervention or free trade, monopolistic behaviour by the government of the resource-rich country combined with non-intervention by the resource-poor country, and monopsonistic behaviour by the resource-poor country combined with non-intervention by the resource-rich country (see Kemp and Long (1979)). The models developed at that time were quite primitive. It was supposed that two countries traded in a single raw material, extracted from an exhaustible stock, and in a single consumption good, produced by means of the raw material and of other factors. The first of the two countries owned the entire world stock of the resource but had neither the facilities nor the aptitudes and skills needed to produce the consumption good. The second country had both facilities and aptitudes but lacked the resource. International borrowing and lending were ruled out; so was domestic investment, both in physical capital and in research and development.

Essays in the Economics of Exhaustible Resources, edited by M. C. Kemp and N. V. Long
© *Elsevier Science Publishers B.V., 1984*

We now extend our earlier paper, in two directions. First, we allow for the possibility that, by investment in plant and equipment or by investment in research and development, the resource-poor country can develop the capacity to produce a substitute for the imported raw material. And, second, we introduce a passive third country, to provide an additional circuit through which the countries of primary interest can interact and thus to moderate some of the more extreme conclusions flowing from the two-country models.

The extended formulation allows us to ask a broader range of questions than in our earlier paper. In particular, questions relating to the timing of investment can be posed.

2. La mise en scène

We distinguish three countries. The home or *resource-poor country* imports a raw material, say oil; it produces and exports a commodity which can be consumed or accumulated as physical capital or invested in research and development; and, potentially, it can produce a non-tradeable perfect substitute for the imported raw material. The *resource-rich country* simply extracts oil (without cost) and exchanges it on the world market for the manufactured consumption good. The *rest of the world*, like the home country, is resource-poor. It imports oil and exports the manufactured good; but it cannot produce the resource-substitute.

The production function for manufacturing in the home country is:

$$Q = F(R + S) \qquad F'(0) > 0, \; F'' < 0,$$

where R is the amount of oil imported and used in production and S is the amount of resource-substitute produced and used in the manufacturing sector. By assumption, neither the resource-substitute nor the raw material can be stored. There may be other inputs (labour and land, for example) but they are used in fixed amounts and so are subsumed in the form of F. Output of the resource-substitute is:

$$S = K,$$

where K may be interpreted as the stock of physical capital or as accumulated investment in research and development. In either case, interpretation allows other factors to be hidden behind the scenes. Ignoring depreciation, the rate of investment is:

$$I = \dot{K} \geq 0.$$

It will be assumed that there is an upper bound $\bar{I}$ on I, unrelated to the properties of F or to the level of the terms of trade. International borrowing and lending are ruled out, so the balance of trade is zero at each moment of time. Denoting by $p(t)$ the international terms of trade (the price of the raw material in terms of the manufactured consumption good) at time t, and by r_H the positive and constant home rate of time preference, the task of the home country is to find:

$$\max \int_0^\infty [F(R(t) + S(t)) - p(t)R(t) - I(t)] \exp(-r_H t) \, \mathrm{d}t.$$

Of course this is not yet a well-defined maximum problem, for the controls have not been specified. The missing information will be provided when we choose from alternative policy mixtures in sections 3–5.

We turn our attention to the resource-rich country. If $X(t)$ is the stock of oil outstanding at time t, so that

$$E(t) = -\dot{X}(t)$$

is the rate of extraction, and if r_O is the positive and constant rate of time preference in the resource-rich country, then the task of that country is to find:

$$\max \int_0^\infty p(t)E(t) \exp(-r_O t) \, \mathrm{d}t$$

subject to given $X(0)$ and to the requirement that $X(t)$ be always non-negative. Again, the control variables will be specified in sections 3–5.

Finally, we consider the rest of the world. Let the production function for manufacturing in the rest of the world be:

$$Q_W = F_W(R_W) \qquad F_W'(0) > 0,$$

where R_W is the rate at which oil is imported and used. Then the task of the rest of the world is to find:

$$\max \int_0^\infty [F_W(R_W(t)) - p(t)R_W(t)] \exp(-r_W t) \, \mathrm{d}t,$$

where r_W is, of course, the positive and constant rate of time preference.

For simplicity, and without appreciable loss, it will be assumed henceforth that $r_H = r_O = r_W = r$.

Three distinct situations will be considered, one in each of the next three sections; but our primary interest lies in the first two.

(1) All countries take $p(t)$ as given: the "free trade" case.

(2) The resource-poor home country behaves aggressively, restricting its demand for oil in the knowledge that this will turn the terms of trade in its favour; the other countries continue to trade freely.

(3) The oil-producer exercises its monopoly power, restricting sales and raising price; the remaining countries trade freely.

In all cases we shall be interested in the equilibrium time paths of oil imports, investment, production of the resource-substitite, and the home and foreign price of energy. We shall be especially interested in the timing of investment expenditures – when they begin, how they progress, when they end – and in the timing of complete self-sufficiency in energy. And, of course, we shall want to compare cases, especially cases 1 and 2, thus determining the impact of government intervention on the several quantities of interest. Our principal conclusions in sections 3 and 4 will be summarized in three formal propositions.

3. Case 1: Universal free trade

Since the rest of the world is competitive and free-trading, the marginal product of oil is equal to the price of oil at each moment of time, yielding the demand function:

$$R_{\mathrm{W}}(t) = F_{\mathrm{W}}'^{-1}(p(t)) \equiv D_{\mathrm{W}}(p(t)).$$

And competitive oil producers are content to meet any demand, for as long as the stock lasts, if only

$$\dot{p}(t)/p(t) = r.$$

The task of the home country, then, is to find:

(P1) $\displaystyle \max_{\{I(t),R(t)\}} \int_0^\infty F(R + K) - Rp_0 \exp(rt) - I] \exp(-rt)\, \mathrm{d}t$

$$\text{s.t. } \bar{I} \geqq I = \dot{K} > 0,$$

$$K(0) \quad \text{and} \quad p_0 \text{ given.}$$

Without loss of generality we can set $\dot{K}(0) = 0$.

The Hamiltonian for (P1) is :

$$H = F(R + K) - Rp_0\exp(rt) - I + \psi I + \lambda(\bar{I} - I),$$

and as necessary conditions we have:

$$F' - p_0 \exp(rt) \leqq 0 \quad (=0, \quad \text{if } R(t) > 0), \tag{1}$$

$$-1 + \psi - \lambda \leqq 0 \quad (=0, \quad \text{if } I(t) > 0), \tag{2}$$

$$\lambda \geqq 0 \quad (=0, \quad \text{if } I(t) < \bar{I}), \tag{3}$$

$$\dot{\psi} = r\psi - F', \tag{4}$$

where ψ is the positive shadow price of oil. From (1)–(4):

$$\text{if } \psi(t) \gtreqless 1, \quad \text{then } I(t) \begin{cases} = \bar{I}, \\ \in [0, \bar{I}], \\ = 0, \end{cases} \tag{5}$$

and

$$\text{if } \dot{\psi} \gtreqless 0, \quad \text{then } F'/r \lesseqgtr \psi. \tag{6}$$

From (1)–(6) we may deduce the typical path of ψ. This is displayed in fig. 8.1 for the case in which oil is initially so plentiful that both ψ and p_0 are less than 1; other cases can be illustrated by moving the curves to the left and ignoring those parts of the curves which project into the second quadrant. In fig. 8.1, ψ first rises, reaches its maximum at time t_2, then declines. During the interval $(0, t_3)$ oil is imported; hence, the home price

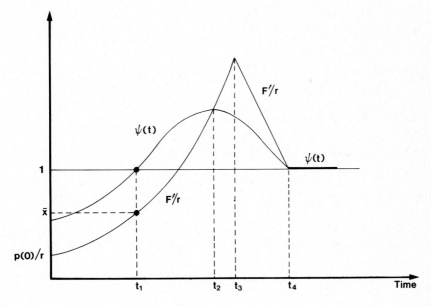

Figure 8.1

of oil, and therefore F'/r, rises exponentially at the constant rate r. On the other hand, during that interval:

$$\dot{\psi}/\psi = r - p/\psi < r.$$

During the interval $(0, t_3)$, therefore, F'/r rises faster than ψ and cuts ψ from below. After the attainment of self-sufficiency in energy at t_3, both F'/r and the home price of energy fall as the stock of capital continues to grow, until at t_4 a steady state is reached with $K = \bar{K}$, where $\bar{K}$ is defined by:

$$F'(\bar{K}) = r.$$

Thereafter investment is zero and the home price of energy is constant. Of course, the home country ceases to trade at t_3. To complete our qualitative history of a free-trading world economy it remains only to note that investment begins at t_1, when $\psi = 1$ (or, if $\psi(0) > 1$, at $t = 0$), and thereafter continues at the maximum rate $\bar{I}$ until $K = \bar{K}$ at t_4. (This follows from the linearity of the utility function.) The interval (t_1, t_4) therefore has a duration of $\bar{K}/\bar{I}$ time periods.

Proposition 1. A free-trading world economy passes through two phases, each divided into two subphases. In the first phase, phase A, the home country relies upon imports of oil. In an initial subphase A1, perhaps degenerate, there is no investment for substitute production ($\psi < 1$). In a subsequent subphase A2, lasting less than $\bar{K}/\bar{I}$ time periods, $\psi > 1$ and investment takes place at the maximum rate I. In the second phase, phase B, the home country is self-sufficient in energy. In an initial subphase B1, investment continues at rate $\bar{I}$, output of the oil substitute increases at a constant rate, and the home price of energy falls. In a subsequent subphase B2, a steady state prevails, with investment zero, outputs constant and relative prices constant.

Additional precision is provided by a second proposition. Let K_3 be the value of K at t_3, when the home country achieves self-sufficiency.

Proposition 2. The value of K_3 and hence the length of the time interval (t_1, t_3) are independent of p_0, provided p_0 is less than a calculable $\bar{x} > 0$.

Proof. Defining:

$$q(t) \equiv \psi(t) \exp(-rt), \tag{7}$$

we have:

$$\dot{q} = (\dot{\psi} - r\psi)\exp(-rt) = -F'(R + K)\exp(-rt),$$

and, for any t_1 and t_3:

$$q(t_3) - q(t_1) = \int_{t_1}^{t_3} -F(R(t) + K(t))\exp(-rt)\,dt. \tag{8}$$

If $\psi(t_1) = 1$, then, from (7) and (8):

$$1 = \psi(t_3)\exp(-r(t_3 - t_1)) + \int_{t_1}^{t_2} F'(R(t) + K(t))\exp(-r(t - t_1))\,dt. \tag{9}$$

For $t \leq t_3$, $F' = p(t)$; hence:

$$F'(R(t) + K(t)) = F'(K_3)\exp(-r(t_3 - t)). \tag{10}$$

Let

$$\theta \equiv t_3 - t_1. \tag{11}$$

Substituting from (10) and (11) into (9):

$$1 = [\psi(t_3) + \theta F'(K_3)]\exp(-r\theta). \tag{12}$$

On the other hand:

$$\theta\bar{I} = K(t_3) - K(t_1) = K(t_3) \equiv K_3. \tag{13}$$

Equations (12) and (13) can be solved for θ and K_3 provided that $\psi(t_3)$ can be expressed as a function of K_3. Now at any time t during phase B the home country solves the autarkic and therefore time-independent problem:

(P2)   max $V = \int_{t}^{\infty} [F(K(s)) - I(s)\exp(-r(s - t))]\,ds$

s.t. $\dot{K}(s) = I(s)$,

$K(t) = K_t$,   given,

and the solution to this problem implies the existence of a shadow price μ_t such that:

$$\mu_t = V'(K_t).$$

Since $V(K_t)$ is strictly concave in K_t, we can write:

$$\mu_t = \mu_t(K_t),$$

with

$$d\mu_t/dK_t = V''(K_t) < 0.$$

From the Principle of Optimality applied to (P1) it is clear that, for $t \geq t_3$:

$$\psi(t) = \mu_t = \mu_t(K_t) = V'(K_t), \tag{14}$$

as required.

Substituting from (14) into (12):

$$1 = [V'(K_3) + \theta F'(K_3)] \exp(-r\theta). \tag{15}$$

Eqs. (13) and (15) determine the optimal values of θ and K_3, say θ^* and K_3^*.

The price at time t_1 is

$$p(t_1) = p(t_3) \exp(-r\theta^*) = F'(K_3^*) \exp(-rK_3^*/\bar{I}). \tag{16}$$

Hence, if

$$p_0 < F'(K_3^*) \exp(-rK_3^*/\bar{I}) \equiv \bar{x}, \tag{17}$$

then there exists a non-degenerate time interval $(0, t_1)$ over which $I(t) = 0$.   Q.E.D.

To this point we have concentrated on the home country's problem, taking the time path $p(t)$ as exogenous. We complete our discussion of the case of universal free trade by pinning down the world equilibrium price path.

If (17) is satisfied, then, from (16) and the Hotelling condition that $\dot{p}/p = r$, we obtain t_1 as a function of $p(0)$:

$$p_0 \equiv p(0) = p(t_1) \exp(-rt_1) = [F'(K_3^*) \exp(-rK_3^*/\bar{I})] \exp(-rt_1).$$

Thus:

$$t_1 = t_1(p_0), \qquad t_1'(p_0) < 0.$$

Now the total demand for oil from the rest of the world is a function of p_0:

$$Y_W(p_0) = \int_0^\infty D_W(p(t)) \, dt = \int_0^\infty D_W(p_0 \exp(rt)) \, dt,$$

where

$$d Y_W(p_0)/dp_0 = \int_0^\infty (\partial D_W/\partial p_0) \, dt < 0.$$

In equilibrium, world demand equals world supply:

$$X_0 - Y_W(p_0) = \int_0^\infty R(t)\,dt, \qquad (18)$$

where

$$R(t) = F'^{-1}(p(t)), \qquad t \leq t_1,$$

and

$$R(t) + (t - t_1)\bar{I} = F'^{-1}(p(t)), \qquad t \in [t_1, t_3].$$

Hence:

$$\int_0^{t_3} R(t)\,dt = \int_0^{t_1(p_0)} F'^{-1}(p_0 \exp(rt))\,dt$$

$$+ \int_{t_1(p_0)}^{t_1(p_0)+\theta^*} [F'^{-1}(p(t_1)\exp(r(t - t_1))) - (t - t_1)\bar{I}]\,dt. \qquad (19)$$

Let $\gamma = t - t_1$. Then, making use of (16), the second integral on the right-hand side of (19) is:

$$\int_0^{\theta^*} [F'^{-1}(F'(K_3^*)\exp(r\gamma - rK_3^*/\bar{I})) - \gamma\bar{I}]\,d\gamma \equiv \text{constant} \equiv \Omega,$$

where Ω is accumulated demand during the period of transition (t_1, t_3). Thus, condition (18) becomes:

$$X_0 - Y_W(p_0) - \Omega = \int_0^{t_1(p_0)} F'^{-1}(p_0 \exp(rt))\,dt,$$

which determines the free-trade equilibrium price p_0^F. That p_0^F is unique is easily checked. Let:

$$Y(p_0) \equiv \int_0^{t_1(p_0)} F'^{-1}(p_0 \exp(rt))\,dt \equiv \int_0^{t_1(p_0)} D(p_0 \exp(rt))\,dt. \qquad (20)$$

Then

$$dY/dp_0 = \int_0^{t_1} D'(p_0 \exp(rt))\exp(rt)\,dt + D(p(t_1))(dt_1/dp_0).$$

The first term on the right-hand side is negative, and the second term is the product of positive and negative components. Hence, $dY/dp_0 < 0$. Fig. 8.2 provides an illustration.

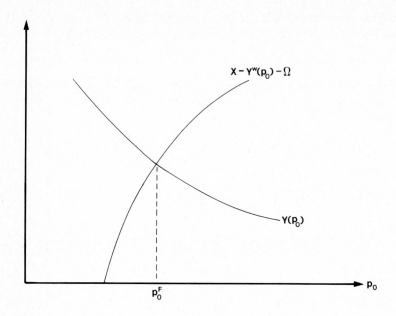

Figure 8.2

4. Case 2: Intervention by the government of the resource-poor home country

We now approach the heart of our analysis.

Suppose that the home government intervenes to influence world prices, simply announcing at $t = 0$ the path of prices at which it will trade. Suppose, further, that it binds itself to adhere to the announced path. (The significance of this undertaking will be discussed below.) Then the home government seeks:

(P3) $\max_{p_0,\{R(t),I(t)\}} \int_0^\infty [F(R(t) + K(t)) - R(t)p_0 \exp(rt) - I(t)] \exp(-rt)\, dt$

$$\text{s.t. } C(p_0) \equiv -[X_0 - Y_w(p_0)] + \int_0^\infty R(t)\, dt = 0,$$

$$\bar{I} \geq I = \dot{K} \geq 0,$$

$$K(0) = 0,$$

with the initial price treated as a control parameter (see Long and Vousden (1977, p. 15)). The Hamiltonian associated with (P3) is:

$$H = [F(R + K) - Rp_0^* \exp(rt) - I] \exp(-rt) + qI + \lambda(\bar{I} - I) + \mu R,$$

where μ is the constant multiplier associated with the integral constraint and an asterisk indicates an optimal value. The necessary conditions associated with R and I are:

$$[F' - p_0^* \exp(rt)] \exp(-rt) - \mu \leqq 0 \quad (=0, \quad \text{if } R(t) > 0), \tag{21}$$

$$-\exp(-rt) + q - \lambda \leqq 0 \quad\quad\quad (=0, \quad \text{if } I > 0), \tag{22}$$

$$\lambda \geqq 0, \quad\quad \bar{I} - I \geqq 0, \quad\quad \lambda(\bar{I} - I) = 0, \tag{23}$$

$$\dot{q} = -F' \exp(-rt). \tag{24}$$

The necessary condition associated with the control parameter p_0 is:

$$-\mu(\mathrm{d}\, Y_W/dp_0) = \int_0^\infty (\partial H/\partial p_0)\, \mathrm{d}t \equiv \int_0^\infty - R \exp(-rt)\, \mathrm{d}t. \tag{25}$$

Now

$$\int_0^\infty R(t)\, \mathrm{d}t = X_0 - Y_W(p_0^*) \geqq 0.$$

In the uninteresting case in which $X_0 - Y_W(p_0^*) = 0$, we deduce from (25) that $\mu = 0$ which, in view of (21), implies that :

$$F' - p_0 \exp(-rt) \leqq 0 \quad (=0, \quad \text{if } R(t) > 0).$$

Hence, $R(0) = 0$ only if $F'(0) \leqq p_0^*$; and this in turn is the case only if the free-trade price p_0^F exceeds $F'(0)$. It follows that:

$$\text{if } F'(0) > p_0^F, \quad \text{then } X_0 - Y_W(p_0^*) > 0. \tag{26}$$

It is reasonable to assume that the condition of (26) is satisfied. If it is satisfied, then $\mu = 0$, implying that if the home country's optimal path is to be decentralized, then the government must impose a tariff at a rate of $\mu \exp(rt)$ per unit of imported raw material. Since $p(t) = p_0 \exp(rt)$, this implies that the ad valorem rate of tariff is constant.

Replacing p_0 with

$$\pi_0 \equiv p_0^* + \mu, \tag{27}$$

we now see that conditions (21)–(24) are formally identical to conditions (1)–(4). In particular, the optimal investment, import, and production policies are of the same form as in case 1.

The optimal p_0^* and μ are determined by the equations:

$$X_0 - Y_W(p_0^*) - \Omega = \int_0^{t_1(\pi_0)} F'^{-1}(\pi_0 \exp(rt)) \, dt,$$

$$-\mu(d\,Y_W/dp_0) = X_0 - Y_W(p_0^*),$$

and (27). Let

$$Y(\pi_0) = \int_0^{t_1(\pi_0)} F'^{-1}(\pi_0 \exp(rt)) \, dt. \tag{28}$$

Since $Y(p_0)$ defined by (20) and $Y(\pi_0)$ defined by (28) are the same function, for any $\mu > 0$ the tariff-ridden cumulative domestic demand curve lies to the left of its free-trade counterpart (see fig. 8.3). Thus, not unexpectedly, the initial world price p_0^* which prevails when the home country imposes an optimal tariff is lower than the initial world price p_0^F under free trade. The initial domestic price $p_0^* + \mu$, on the other hand, is greater than p_0^F. Hence, the home country begins to invest at an earlier date t_1, ceases to invest at an earlier date t_4, and becomes independent of imports at an earlier date t_3.

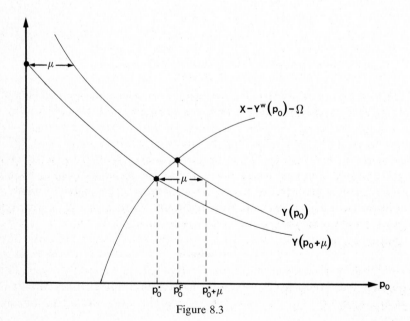

Figure 8.3

Proposition 3. If $F'(0) > p_0^F$, then the home country can with advantage exploit its position as a large buyer and restrict its trade with the resource-rich supplier of oil. The optimal tariff is at a constant ad valorem rate. Along its optimal path, the home country advances the date at which substitute production begins and, therefore, the date at which it becomes self-sufficient.

We have specified that at $t = 0$ the home country announces p_0^* and binds itself to adhere to the price path $p(t) = p_0^* \exp(rt)$. We now briefly explain why it was found necessary to stipulate that the announcement is binding. Suppose that μ and p_0^* are announced at $t = 0$, so that at time t_3^* the home country stops importing. At t_3^* the domestic price satisfies the condition:

$$\pi(t_3^*) = F'(K_3^*),$$

and the world price is:

$$p(t_3^*) < F'(K_3^*).$$

It is clear that if at t_3^* the home country replans, then it is optimal to take advantage of the low world price and continue trading. The world price will be bid up and the rate of duty reduced. More generally, the home country may wish to replan before t_3^*.

5. Case 3: Intervention by the resource-rich country

We now pass to the other extreme and briefly consider the possibility that the resource-rich country exercises its monopoly power by restricting its oil sales, knowing that the home country will begin investing in the resource-substitute as soon as the price of oil reaches the critical level defined by (16). Evidently the problem facing the aggressive resource-rich country is asymmetrical to that facing the aggressive home country. In particular, the optimal ad valorem rate of export duty is not generally a constant. We therefore simplify slightly by assuming that the resource-rich country cannot impose export duties or their equivalent, export quotas, but can determine at $t = 0$, once and for all, the proportion of the resource-stock to be made available for commercial exploitation. (Alternately, we might have assumed that the oil-exporting country also uses oil and then restricts its policy options to a constant ad valorem rate of export duty.)

Given that assumption, the same price ratio prevails everywhere. The problem facing the government of the supplying country is, therefore:

(P4) $\max \int\limits_{0}^{\infty} [-\dot{X}p_0 \exp(rt)] \exp(-rt)\, dt$

   s.t. $X^* = Y_W(p_0) + \Omega + Y(p_0),$

   $\int\limits_{0}^{\infty} (-\dot{X})\, dt \equiv X^* \leq X_0,$

where X^* is the amount of the resource to be made available for commercial exploitation, or, simplifying:

(P4') $\max\limits_{p_0} [Y_W(p_0) + \Omega + Y(p_0)]p_0$

   s.t. $Y_W(p_0) + \Omega + Y(p_0) \leq X_0,$

or, letting Z denote total world demand,

   $Z = Z(p_0) \equiv Y_W(p_0) + \Omega + Y(p_0),$

and inverting $Z(p_0)$ to obtain:

   $p_0 = G(Z), \qquad G'(X) < 0,$

(P4'') $\max\limits_{Z} ZG(Z)$

   s.t. $Z \leq X_0.$

Let Z^{**} be the solution to

   $ZG'(Z) + G(Z) = 0.$

Then Z^*, the solution to (P4''), is given as:

   $Z^* = \min\{X_0, Z^{**}\}$

The solution is illustrated by fig. 8.4.

Suppose that $Z^{**} < X_0$. Then the supplying country receives a greater total of discounted revenue than under free trade. Moreover, the world price is higher than P_0^F; hence, the home country begins to invest in substitute capacity at an earlier date. Of course, none of these conclusions is surprising.

The problem of dynamic inconsistency arises again. Suppose that at time $t' > 0$ an accumulated amount $X_0 - Z^{**}$ has been sold and that

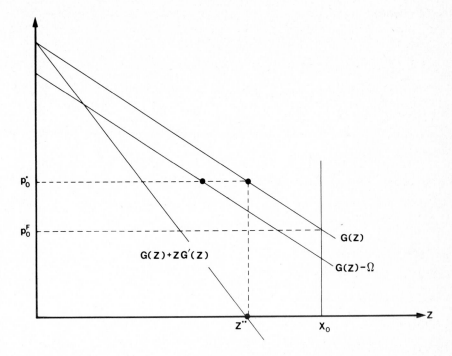

Figure 8.4

substitute investment is about to begin. If then the supplying country reviews its plan, the price will fall from $p_0^* \exp(rt')$ to p_0^*, and the investment plan will be deferred. More interesting is the case in which at t' (with accumulated extraction of $X_0 - Z^{**}$) substitute production has begun. If then the supplying country revises its plan it will find that the world demand function has moved to the left by a constant $k\Omega$, $0 < k < 1$; that is, the new world demand function will be:

$$\bar{G}(Z) = G(Z) - k\Omega.$$

The new optimal price will be p_0^{***} which may be *less* than p_0^*. (This is indeed the case if $G(Z)$ is linear.) The producers of the substitute will then, for the time being, stop all investment. Indeed, if there were a sufficiently large constant marginal cost of producing the substitute, then producers would even shut down existing plants.

References

Kemp, M. C. and N. V. Long (1979), The interaction of resource-rich and resource-poor economies, Australian Economic Papers 18, 258–257; reprinted in: M. C. Kemp and N. V. Long, eds., Exhaustible Resources, Optimality, and Trade (North-Holland Publishing Company, Amsterdam, 1980) essay 17.
Long, N. V. and N. Vousden (1977), Optimal control theorems, in: J. D. Pitchford and S. J. Turnovsky, eds., Applications of Control Theory to Economic Analysis (North-Holland Publishing Company, Amsterdam) pp. 11–34.

PART IV

THE ECONOMICS OF FORESTS AND FISHERIES

On the economics of forests

MURRAY C. KEMP and NGO VAN LONG*

1. Introduction

In this essay we describe a productive process involving the point input of labour, the repeated input of land, and the point output of forest products, and then imbed the process in a model of the economy as a whole. The optimal duration or "maturity" of the process is to be determined in terms of the parameters of the model.

The well-known formulae of Jevons (1957)–Wicksell (1938) and Faustmann (1968) are introduced and assigned their appropriate spheres of application, thus making clear that the two formulae are not competitive but complementary. In this respect we add only marginally to the earlier papers of Samuelson (1976) and Wan (1966). It is shown also that, even if the utility function is linear, it may be optimal to diversify maturities and suboptimal to fail to do so. This finding appears to be new.

Our model is very simple. In particular, both labour and land are specialized to forestry. However, additional products would merely complicate the analysis without destroying our conclusion about optimal maturities.

2. The model

A central planner (or a set of competitive markets) has the disposal of a homogeneous tract of land, of given size and good only for growing trees of a particular kind, and of a homogeneous work force, of given size and

*This essay first appeared in the *International Economic Review* 24 (1983) 113–131.

Essays in the Economics of Exhaustible Resources, edited by M. C. Kemp and N. V. Long

good only for planting trees. Trees need no tending and can be harvested without labour. Harvested timber is a homogeneous but perishable consumption good. It may not be the only consumption good. However, it is the only produced consumption good; any other consumption goods are available at constant rates of flow, given by Nature. The land is initially empty. Let $c(t)$ be the rate of flow of harvested timber and the rate of consumption at time t, $u(c)$ the instantaneous social utility function, and ρ the constant and positive rate of time preference. Then the task of the planner is to find the feasible paths of planting and harvesting which yield:

(P) $\max \int\limits_{0}^{\infty} \exp(-\rho t) \cdot u(c(t)) \, dt.$

The solution to the above problem depends qualitatively on the relative supplies of labour and land, on the manner in which individual trees grow, on the efficiency of labour in planting, and on the curvature of the utility function. Until section 5 it is assumed that to plant a tree takes b units of labour one period of time (or $b/2$ units of labour two periods of time) and that each tree occupies a plot the size of which is taken as a datum. Thus, the technology is one of fixed coefficients. It is assumed that the growth of an individual tree is described by a function $f(\theta)$, where θ is the age of the tree and where (i) $f(\theta)$ is differentiable for all $t \in (0, \infty)$, (ii) there exists $s \geqq 0$ such that

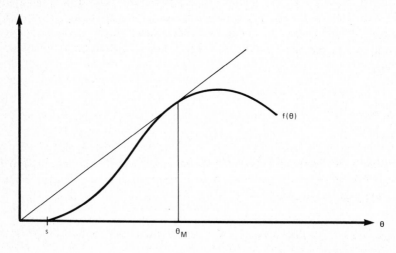

Figure 9.1

$$f(\theta)\begin{cases} = 0, & \text{if } \theta \in [0, s], \\ > 0, & \text{if } \theta \in (s, \infty), \end{cases}$$

and (iii) $\lim_{\theta\to\infty} \exp(-\rho\theta) \cdot f(\theta) = 0$. The function $f(\theta)$ may, but need not, have the conventional convex–concave structure displayed in fig. 9.1; nor is it assumed that eventually $f(\theta)$ is a declining function. It is assumed also that the labour force L and the available land area (number of one-tree plots) N are given constants, independent both of time and of the use to which they are put. Finally, it is assumed, until the brief final section, that the utility function $u(c)$ is linear, so that to solve (P) is to maximize the present value of the flow of harvests.

Initially the land is bare. If the entire labour force is devoted to planting, it takes $\bar{\theta} \equiv bN/L$ periods of time to completely cover the land. The number $\bar{\theta}$ will play a key role in the analysis of section 3.

3. Linear utility

If no labour is needed for planting, if $u(c)$ is linear, and if all trees are cut at the same maturity, (P) reduces to:

$$\text{(P1)} \quad \max_{\theta} \sum_{t=1}^{\infty} \exp(-\rho\theta t) \cdot f(\theta) = \max_{\theta} f(\theta)/[\exp(\rho\theta) - 1] \equiv \max_{\theta} F(\theta),$$

where $F(\theta)$ is the present value of a harvesting–replanting sequence in which a tree is planted today and then replanted at intervals of θ periods. (Here, and below, F is for Faustmann.) The solution to (P1) is found by solving the following first-order condition, which in section 1 we have referred to as Faustmann's formula:[1]

$$f'(\theta)/f(\theta) = \rho/[1 - \exp(-\rho\theta)]. \tag{1}$$

Suppose for the time being that $F(\theta)$ attains its global maximum only once, at $\theta_F(\rho)$.

If, on the other hand, no land is required (a rather far-fetched assumption in a forestry context), and if all trees are cut at the same maturity, then (P) reduces to the problem of maximizing the average rate of return on each unit of labour invested in planting; that is, (P) reduces to:

---

[1]Faustmann did not himself derive eq. (1). The first-order conditions were later worked out by Ohlin, Preinreich, and others. For brief histories of the formula, see Samuelson (1976) and Wan (1966).

(P2) $\max_{\theta} \exp(-\rho\theta) \cdot f(\theta) \equiv \max_{\theta} J(\theta),$

where $J(\theta)$ is the present value of a tree planted today and harvested after θ periods and therefore bears a relationship of constant proportionality to the return on labour applied today. (Here, and later, J is for Jevons.) The solution to (P2) is found by solving the following first-order condition, which may be found in Jevons (1957), Wicksell (1938), and Fisher (1930):

$$f'(\theta)/f(\theta) = \rho. \tag{2}$$

Suppose, again for the time being, that $J(\theta)$ attains its global maximum only once, at $\theta_J(\rho)$.[2] It is easy to verify that $\theta_F(\rho) < \theta_J(\rho)$.

Given the analysis of Faustmann and of Jevons–Wicksell, it is tempting to conjecture that if both factors are required for planting but labour is "redundant", then the optimal maturity for (P) is θ_F, at least asymptotically; and that if both factors are required for planting but land is "redundant", then the optimal maturity for (P) is θ_J, at least asymptotically.

Now it is a feature of our analysis that the redundancy or otherwise of each factor is treated as a matter of *choice* by the planning authority, not as a datum of Nature. It will emerge that there are circumstances in which the optimal maturity is a *constant*, equal to θ_F or θ_J, and in which labour or land, respectively, is redundant. However, there are other circumstances in which it is optimal either to set θ equal to a constant intermediate in value to θ_F and θ_J, with both factors eventually fully employed, or to diversify maturities, possibly with labour periodically unemployed. In the balance of this section we shall be occupied in making good these assertions.

Suppose that there is no diversification, so that θ is unique, that $\theta \geqq \bar{\theta}$, and that the available land area is planted as quickly as possible and thereafter maintained in a fully planted state. (The assumption that $\theta \geqq \bar{\theta}$ ensures that it is feasible to fully plant the available land.) The present value of the flow of harvests is then:

$$\frac{L}{b} F(\theta) \int_0^{\bar{\theta}} \exp(-\rho t)\, dt = a_F F(\theta), \tag{3}$$

where L/b is the rate of planting per period and

---

[2]The question of uniqueness seems to have been neglected in the literature. Wicksell (1938, p. 178) gave a local second-order condition which, however, does not ensure uniqueness.

$$a_F \equiv \frac{N}{\rho\theta}[1 - \exp(-\rho\bar{\theta})] \qquad (4)$$

is a positive constant.

Suppose, alternatively, that θ is unique, but that $\theta \leqq \bar{\theta}$. Then, at most, a proportion $\theta/\bar{\theta}$ of the available land can be maintained in a forested state. The present value of the flow of harvests is:

$$\frac{L}{b}F(\theta) \int_0^\theta \exp(-\rho t)\, \mathrm{d}t = a_J J(\theta), \qquad (5)$$

where

$$a_J \equiv N/\rho\bar{\theta} \qquad (6)$$

is a positive constant. Of course, $a_F < a_J$.

Let us pause to consider some of the properties of the functions $a_F F(\theta)$ and $a_J J(\theta)$. In view of the restrictions placed on $f(\theta)$:

$$a_F F(\theta) = 0 = a_J J(\theta), \quad \text{if } \theta \leqq s, \qquad (7a)$$

$$a_F F'(\theta) = 0 = a_J J'(\theta), \quad \text{if } \theta = s, \qquad (7b)$$

$$\lim_{\theta \to \infty} a_F F(\theta) = 0 = \lim_{\theta \to \infty} a_J J(\theta). \qquad (7c)$$

Moreover, defining

$$k(\theta) \equiv \frac{a_J J(\theta)}{a_F F(\theta)} = \frac{1 - \exp(-\rho\theta)}{1 - \exp(-\rho\bar{\theta})} \qquad (\theta > s), \qquad (8)$$

we easily verify that, for $\theta > s$:

$$k(\bar{\theta}) = 1, \qquad (9)$$

$$k'(\theta) > 0, \qquad (10)$$

$$\lim_{\theta \to \infty} k(\theta) = 1/[1 - \exp(-\rho\bar{\theta})]. \qquad (11)$$

From (9) and (10):

$$a_F F(\theta) \gtreqless a_J J(\theta), \quad \text{as } \theta \lesseqgtr \bar{\theta}. \qquad (7d)$$

By definition:

$$a_F F(\theta) = \left[\frac{1 - \exp(-\rho\bar{\theta})}{1 - \exp(-\rho\theta)}\right] a_J J(\theta). \qquad (12)$$

Hence, differentiating:

$$a_F F'(\theta) = a_J[1 - \exp(-\rho\bar{\theta})]\left[\frac{J'(\theta)}{1 - \exp(-\rho\theta)} - \frac{\rho J(\theta)\exp(-\rho\theta)}{(1 - \exp(-\rho\theta))^2}\right]$$

$$= \frac{N}{\rho\bar{\theta}}\frac{J}{\theta}\frac{1 - \exp(-\rho\bar{\theta})}{1 - \exp(-\rho\theta)}\left[\frac{\theta J'(\theta)}{J(\theta)} - \frac{\rho\theta}{\exp(\rho\theta) - 1}\right]. \tag{13}$$

It follows that:

$$F'(\theta) \gtreqless 0, \quad \text{as} \quad \frac{\theta J'(\theta)}{J(\theta)} \gtreqless \frac{\rho\theta}{\exp(\rho\theta) - 1}, \tag{7e}$$

where $\rho\theta < \exp(\rho\theta) - 1$. The properties described by (7a)–(7e) are incorporated in figs. 9.2–9.4, 9.6, and 9.7. For example, figs. 9.2(a) and 9.2(b) are drawn with $F(\theta)$ attaining a second local maximum at $\theta = \hat{\theta}$, $\hat{\theta} > \theta_F$. To verify that a second maximum exists we observe that, from property (7e), $F'(\theta) > 0$ for θ between θ^{**} and θ^{***} and then, bearing in mind (7c), infer that $F(\theta)$ reaches a local maximum to the right of θ^{***}. (The asterisks indicate those values of θ at which $J'(\theta) = J(\theta)/\theta$, i.e. those values of θ at which $J(\theta)/\theta$ attains a local maximum or minimum or which are points of inflection for $J(\theta)/\theta$.) Of course that part of the curve $a_F F(\theta)$ which lies to the left of $\bar{\theta}$ is irrelevant if all trees are cut at the same age; similarly with that part of the curve $a_J J(\theta)$ which lies to the right of $\bar{\theta}$.

Let us now return to problem (P). We have noted that, under the assumption of linear utility, solving (P) is equivalent to maximizing the present value of the flow of harvests. This suggests that we should piece together the relevant parts of the functions $a_F F(\theta)$ and $a_J J(\theta)$ to form a consolidated function, say $H(\theta)$, and then seek that value of θ which maximizes $H(\theta)$. We shall see that whether this procedure does indeed yield an optimal choice of maturity depends on the value of $\bar{\theta}$. Figs. 9.2–9.4 illustrate three possibilities, of which the first is by far the most troublesome.

Case 1: $\theta_F \leq \bar{\theta} \leq \theta_J$. In figs. 9.2(a)–9.2(c) the curves $a_F F(\theta)$ and $a_J J(\theta)$ intersect between θ_F and θ_J. It is tempting to conjecture that, in this case, the present value of the flow of future harvests is maximized by cutting all trees at the same maturity $\bar{\theta}$, fully planting the land as soon as possible, and thereafter maintaining a balanced forest with constant maturity $\bar{\theta}$ and full employment of both land and labour. Under that policy the present value of harvests is simply:

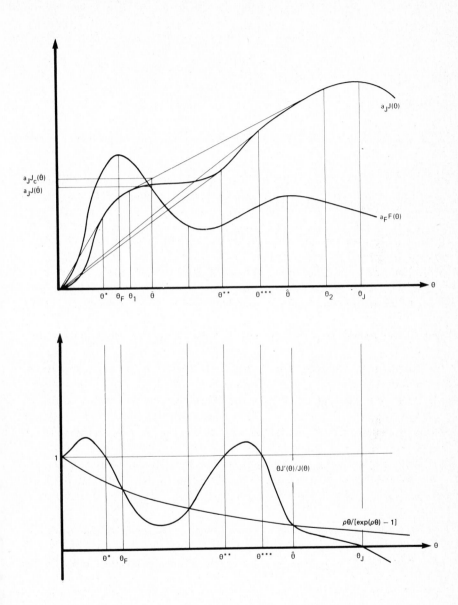

Figure 9.2(a)

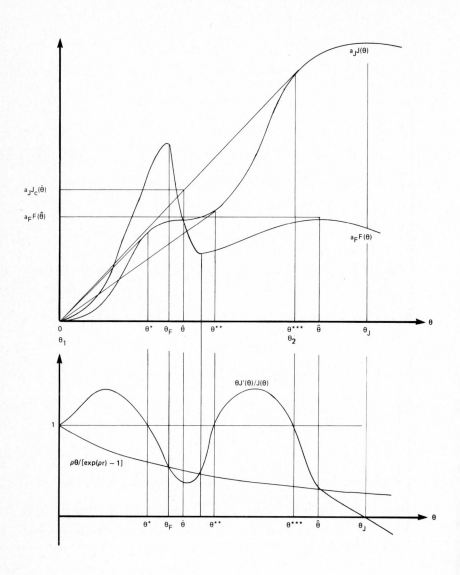

Figure 9.2(b)

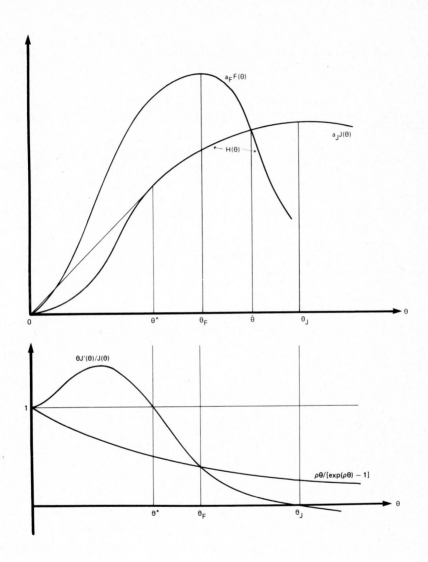

Figure 9.2(c)

$$a_J J(\bar{\theta}) = \frac{L}{\rho b} J\left(\frac{bN}{L}\right), \tag{14}$$

as indicated by the tip of the cusp at $\bar{\theta}$ on $H(\theta)$. However, it will be shown that only in the subcase depicted in fig. 9.2(c) is that policy sometimes (not always) optimal, and that in the remaining subcases, depicted in figs. 9.2(a) and 9.2(b), the policy is always suboptimal. Indeed, it will be shown that, in the subcase depicted in fig. 9.2(b), the policy is suboptimal even under the restriction that all trees be cut at the same maturity.

Consider fig. 9.2(a). A glance at the figure reveals that $a_J J(\theta)$ is not uniformly concave and suggests the conjecture that (14) will be surpassed if maturities are suitably diversified.[3] We now verify the conjecture.

Let us define $\mathscr{J}$ as the set of points bounded by the θ-axis and the curve $J(\theta)$, $\mathscr{H}(\mathscr{J})$ as the convex hull of $\mathscr{J}$, and $J_c(\theta)$ as the upper boundary of $\mathscr{H}(\mathscr{J})$. And let θ_1 and θ_2 be such that:

(i) $0 \leqq \theta_1 < \bar{\theta} < \theta_2$, i.e. $\alpha_1 \theta_1 + \alpha_2 \theta_2 = \bar{\theta}$ for some $\alpha_i \in (0, 1)$ and $\alpha_1 + \alpha_2 = 1$,

(ii) $J(\theta_i) = J_c(\theta_i)$ $(i = 1, 2)$,

(iii) $J_c(\theta)$ is linear over $[\theta_1, \theta_2]$.

Dividing the available labour and land into two bundles with

$$L_i = \alpha_i L, \qquad N_i = \theta_i L_i / b \qquad (i = 1, 2), \tag{15}$$

so that

$$L_1 + L_2 = L \quad \text{and} \quad N_1 + N_2 = N, \tag{16}$$

we then obtain the larger present value:

$$\frac{\alpha_1 L}{\rho b} J(\theta_1) + \frac{\alpha_2 L}{\rho b} J(\theta_2) = \frac{L}{\rho b}[\alpha_1 J_c(\theta_1) + \alpha_2 J_c(\theta_2)]$$

$$= \frac{L}{\rho b} J_c(\bar{\theta})$$

$$> \frac{L}{\rho b} J(\bar{\theta}). \tag{17}$$

While (17) is greater than (14), it is not necessarily the greatest

---

[3]It is easy to verify, from the definition of $J(\theta)$, that if $J'(\theta) > 0$, then $J''(\theta) > 0$ implies $f''(\theta) > 0$.

possible present value. Before beginning the demonstration of this fact, we observe that it is not possible by "concavifying" $F(\theta)$ to find a preferred policy with both factors fully employed. For, given any θ_1' and θ_2' such that $\alpha_1'\theta_1' + \alpha_2'\theta_2' = \bar{\theta}$ for some $\alpha_1' \in (0, 1)$ and $\alpha_1' + \alpha_2' = 1$, the present value of the post-diversification stream of harvests is:

$$\sum \frac{\alpha_i'L}{\rho b}[1 - \exp(-\rho\theta_i')]F(\theta_i') = \frac{L}{\rho b}\sum \alpha_i'J(\theta_i') \leqq \frac{L}{\rho b}J_c(\bar{\theta}), \qquad (18)$$

with strict equality if $\theta_i' = \theta_i$ $(i = 1, 2)$. We notice also that if some land is left empty, then the full employment of labour can be assured only by choosing a point on $J_c(\theta)$ to the left of $\bar{\theta}$, with a present value less than (14). There remains the possibility of improving on (14) by diversifying maturities with some labour eventually unemployed, that is, by diversifying à la Faustmann. Now $J_c(\bar{\theta})$ is the solution of

$$(P3) \quad \max_{L_i, N_i} \sum \frac{L_i}{b}J\left(\frac{bN_i}{L_i}\right)$$

$$\text{s.t.} \quad \sum N_i = N,$$

$$\sum L_i = L.$$

However $J(\theta) = [1 - \exp(-\rho\theta)]F(\theta)$; hence (P3) is a special case of:

$$(P4) \quad \max_{L_i, N_i, \theta_i'} \sum \frac{L_i}{b}\left[1 - \exp\left(-\rho\frac{N_ib}{L_i}\right)\right]F(\theta_i')$$

$$\text{s.t.} \quad \sum N_i \leqq N,$$

$$\sum L_i \leqq L,$$

$$\theta_i' \geqq bN_i/L_i.$$

If, for some i, $\theta_i' > bN_i/L_i$, then $J_c(\bar{\theta})$ is suboptimal and diversification à la Faustmann is optimal.[4] But, however that may be, optimality entails

---

[4]Even this conclusion needs mild qualification in so far as it relates to the initial period of maximal planting. Let (θ_1, θ_2) be the solution to (P3) and (θ_1', θ_2') the solution to (P4), with $\theta_1' > \theta_1$ and $\theta_1 < \theta_2$. Then notice that in (P4) there is no provision for the possibility, at time θ_1, of moving newly unemployed labour from the first parcel of land to the second (to assist with the planting there). If that possibility were allowed for, both $J_c(\bar{\theta})$ and the diversified Faustmann outcome could be surpassed.

diversification of maturities and the full employment of land.[5] Moreover, as fig. 9.2(a) makes clear, optimality never entails more than two maturities. (Of course, in singular cases it may be optional to employ more than two maturities).

Let us now turn our attention to fig. 9.2(b). In the subcase there depicted,

$$\bar{\theta} < \max\left\{ \tilde{\theta} : \frac{J(\tilde{\theta})}{\tilde{\theta}} > \frac{J(\theta)}{\theta}, \text{ all } \theta \right\}$$

and the diversification of maturities associated with $J_c(\bar{\theta})$ takes a degenerate form, with some labour effectively idle. (The idle labour fills the day planting seeds, on an infinitesimal scrap of land, immediately tearing them up and replacing them with new seeds.) But if labour is redundant, we are in Faustmann's world and it is optimal either to choose a single maturity, say $\hat{\theta}$, such that $\hat{\theta} > \bar{\theta}$ and $F(\hat{\theta}) \geq F(\theta)$ for all $\theta \geq \bar{\theta}$, or to diversify à la Faustmann with two maturities.[6] The maturity $\hat{\theta}$ may be greater or less than θ_2.

Finally, we consider fig. 9.2(c). In the subcase depicted there, and in that subcase only, it sometimes is optimal to set $\theta = \bar{\theta}$. Even in that subcase, however, it sometimes is optimal to diversify à la Faustmann with two maturities.

Case 2: $\bar{\theta} > \theta_J$. In fig. 9.3 the curves $a_F F(\theta)$ and $a_J J(\theta)$ intersect to the right of θ_J. Inspection of the figure suggests that the present value of future harvests is maximized by devoting the entire labour force to planting always but cutting each tree at the Jevons–Wicksell maturity θ_J, that is, by choosing θ_J on the Jevons branch of $H(\theta)$. If that policy is adopted, then, after an initial interval of forestation lasting θ_J periods, there is a balanced forest occupying $\theta_J/\bar{\theta}$, $\theta_J/\bar{\theta} < 1$, of the available land; that is, land is redundant always.

We proceed to show that the above policy is indeed optimal and, in particular, that it is superior to any alternative policy involving the diversification of maturities. From earlier arguments, no alternative policy

---

[5]From the first-order conditions for (P4):

$$(L_i/b)F'(\theta'_i)\exp(-\rho b N_i/L_i) - \lambda_N - \delta_i b/L_i = 0.$$

where λ_N and δ_i are the non-positive multipliers associated with the constraints $\sum N_i \leq N$ and $\theta'_i \geq bN_i/L_i$, respectively. It follows that $F'(\theta'_i) \leq 0$. Thus, if (θ_1, θ_2) is a solution to (P4), then F' must be non-positive at those values. In this respect, fig. 9.2(a) is consistent with the optimality of (θ_1, θ_2).

[6]In the later case, the qualification of footnote 4 applies.

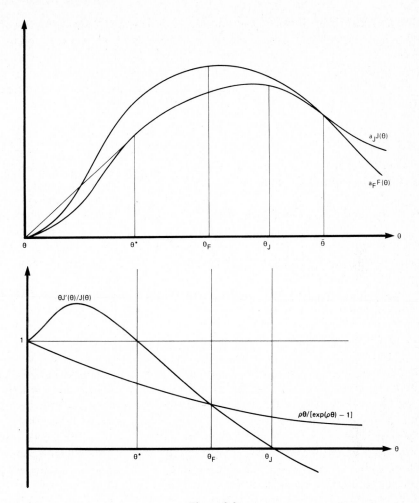

Figure 9.3

with both factors fully employed, with or without diversification, can yield a present value as large as that of the policy described. To establish the optimality of that policy it therefore suffices to show that under an optimal policy labour must be fully employed. Now without diversification of maturities we have, for $\theta > \bar{\theta}$:

$$a_F F(\theta) < \frac{L}{\rho b} J(\theta) \leqq \frac{L}{\rho b} J(\theta_J). \tag{19}$$

We therefore may confine our attention to policies of diversification with labour less than fully employed. Let θ_1 and θ_2, θ_1^* and θ_2^* be such that:

$$\alpha_1\theta_1 + \alpha_2\theta_2 = \bar{\theta}, \quad \text{for some } \alpha_i \in (0, 1) \text{ with } \alpha_1 + \alpha_2 = 1, \tag{20a}$$

$$\theta_i^* \gtreqqless \theta_i \quad (i = 1, 2), \quad \text{with a strong inequality for some } i, \tag{20b}$$

and let

$$L_i = \alpha_i\theta_i, \quad N_i = \theta_i L_i / b. \tag{21}$$

Choosing maturities θ_i^* so that labour is underemployed, the present value of future harvests is:

$$R \equiv \sum \frac{L_i}{\rho b}[1 - \exp(-\rho\theta_i)]F(\theta_i^*)$$

$$< \sum \frac{L_i}{\rho b} J(\theta_i^*) \quad [\text{from (20b)}]$$

$$\leqq \sum \frac{L_i}{\rho b} J(\theta_J). \tag{22}$$

Case 3: $\bar{\theta} < \theta_F$. In figs. 9.4(a) and 9.4(b), at the other extreme, the curves $a_F F(\theta)$ and $a_J J(\theta)$ intersect to the left of θ_F. Inspection of fig. 9.4(a) suggests the choice of θ_F as maturity, with a present value $a_F F(\theta_F)$ read from the Faustmann branch of the consolidated curve. In fact it has already been argued, in the course of our treatment of case 1, that such a policy is, in the subcase illustrated by fig. 9.4(a), optimal. Thus, in that subcase, the present value of the flow of harvests is maximized by devoting the entire labour force to planting until, at time $\bar{\theta}$, all available land is covered, and then refraining from planting until, at time θ_F, the oldest trees reach the limiting Faustmann maturity θ_F. Thereafter, intervals of harvesting–planting (of duration $\bar{\theta}$ periods) alternate with intervals of growth (of duration $\theta_F - \bar{\theta}$ periods) during which there is neither harvesting nor planting (see fig. 9.5). If this policy is adopted, then, after the initial interval of forestation lasting $\bar{\theta}$ periods, the available land is always fully planted and the age distribution of trees is periodical. Thus, eventually labour is redundant.

Inspection of fig. 9.4(b) suggests that, in the subcase there depicted, it might be possible by diversification to achieve a present value greater than $a_F F(\theta_F)$. We now show that this is not so, that the Faustmann policy is optimal in this subcase also. Let θ_i, α_i, L_i, and N_i be defined as in our

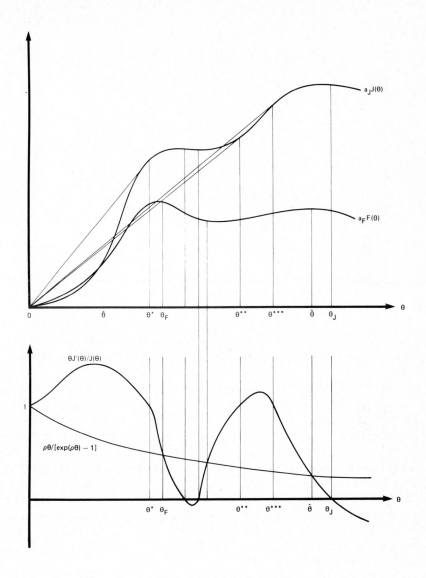

Figure 9.4(a)

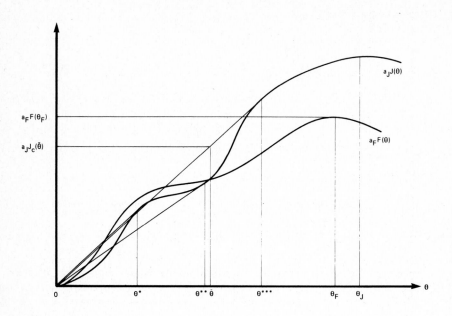

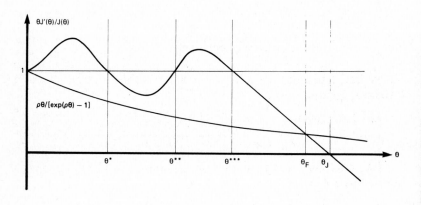

Figure 9.4(b)

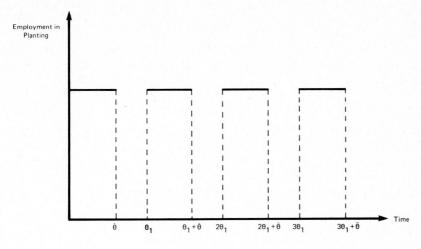

Figure 9.5

discussion of case 1. Then the present value of future harvests under a policy of diversified maturities, with both factors fully employed, is:

$$\sum \frac{\alpha_i L}{\rho b} J(\theta_i) = \frac{L}{\rho b} \sum \alpha_i [1 - \exp(-\rho\theta_i)] F(\theta_i)$$

$$< \frac{L}{\rho b} \{\sum \alpha_i [1 - \exp(-\rho\theta_i)]\} F(\theta_F)$$

$$< \frac{L}{\rho b} [1 - \exp(-\rho\bar{\theta})] F(\theta_F), \tag{23}$$

where in the last step use is made of the fact that $1 - \exp(-\rho\theta)$ is strictly concave, implying that:

$$1 - \exp(-\rho\bar{\theta}) \equiv 1 - \exp(-\rho\sum\alpha_i\theta_i)$$

$$> \sum \alpha_i [1 - \exp(-\rho\theta_i)]. \tag{24}$$

That completes our analysis of the three cases. Our findings are summarized in

Proposition 1. Suppose that $F(\theta)$ and $J(\theta)$ attain their global maxima once only.

(a) Let $\bar{\theta} > \theta_J$. Then it is optimal to cut all trees at the Jevons maturity θ_J, with some land permanently unemployed.

(b)) Let $\bar{\theta} < \theta_F$. Then it is optimal to cut all trees at the Faustmann maturity θ_F, with labour periodically unemployed.

(c) Let $\theta_F \leqq \bar{\theta} \leqq \theta_J$. Then (i) if $J(\bar{\theta}) = J_c(\bar{\theta})$, either it is optimal to cut all trees at the same maturity $\bar{\theta}$, with both factors fully employed after an initial interval of $\bar{\theta}$ periods, or it is optimal to diversify à la Faustmann, with some labour unemployed after an initial interval of intensive planting; (ii) if $J(\bar{\theta}) < J_c(\bar{\theta})$ and $\bar{\theta} > \max\{\tilde{\theta}: J(\tilde{\theta})/\tilde{\theta} > J(\theta)/\theta,$ all $\theta\}$, either it is optimal to diversify maturities, with both factors fully employed after an initial interval of $\bar{\theta}$ periods, or it is optimal to diversify à la Faustmann; if $J(\bar{\theta}) < J_c(\bar{\theta})$ and $\bar{\theta} \leqq \max\{\tilde{\theta}: J(\tilde{\theta})/\tilde{\theta} > J(\theta)/\theta,$ all $\theta\}$, either it is optimal to cut all trees at the Faustmann maturity θ_F, with labour periodically unemployed, or it is optimal to diversify à la Faustmann.

Remark. For the diversification of maturities to be optimal it is necessary that over some interval either $J(\theta)$ or $F(\theta)$ be strictly convex. However, for diversification to be optimal it is neither necessary nor sufficient that the underlying growth function $f(\theta)$ be somewhere strictly convex; in particular, it is neither necessary nor sufficient that $f(\theta)$ have the convex–concave structure displayed in fig. 9.1.

So far we have ruled out the possibility that $J(\theta)$ attains its global maximum at more than one value of θ. For completeness we now consider that singular possibility. It will be shown that the policies described in proposition 1 remain optimal but are not necessarily the only optimal solutions. The main changes are in the appropriately generalized versions of cases 2 and 3. In those cases it is now possible that diversification of maturities may be optimal. Thus let Θ_F be the set of θ-values which yield the global maximum of $F(\theta)$, and let Θ_J be the set of θ-values which yield the global maximum of $J(\theta)$. It can be shown each member of Θ_J exceeds all members of Θ_F.[7] Instead of cases 1–3, therefore, we can consider:
    Case 1′: $\max \Theta_F \leqq \bar{\theta} \leqq \min \Theta_J$.
    Case 2′: $\bar{\theta} > \min \Theta_J$.
    Case 3′: $\bar{\theta} < \max \Theta_F$.
Only cases 2′ and 3′ present new possibilities.

Case 2′: $\bar{\theta} > \Theta_J$. In fig. 9.6 there are two values of θ, θ_{J1} and θ_{J2}, at which $a_J J(\theta)$ reaches its global maximum. it is optimal to set $\theta = \theta_{J1} = \min \Theta_J$, leaving some land empty (as it was optimal to do in case 2). But it also is optimal to diversify maturities, allowing some trees to remain standing for θ_{J2} periods, and to maintain the full employment of both factors. (By an argument given in the course of our study of case 2, it is suboptimal to leave some labour idle.)

Case 3': $\bar{\theta} < \max \Theta_F$. In fig. 9.7 there are two values of θ, θ_{F1} and θ_{F2}, at which $a_F F(\theta)$ attains its global maximum. It is optimal to set $\theta = \theta_{F1}$; it is optimal to set $\theta = \theta_{F2}$; and it is optimal to diversify over the two maturities. However, whatever policy is adopted, labour is periodically unemployed.

4. The possibility of decentralization

Any competitive equilibrium is optimal if a suitable transversality condition is satisfied. But the possibility that $J(\theta)$ and $F(\theta)$ are not uniformly concave and that optimality implies diversification suggests that not all optimal programs can be decentralized. We now show that any optimum with diversification of maturities à la Jevons can be decentralized. Whether all optima with diversification can be decentralized is left as an open question.

Suppose that social optimality implies diversification of maturities, with both labour and land fully employed after an initial period of aforestation. The optimal program is obtained as the solution of (P3). For that

---

[7] Let θ_F be any member of Θ_F and θ_J any member of Θ_J. We wish to show that $\theta_F < \theta_J$. Suppose that $\theta_F > \theta_J$. Then:

$$1 - \exp(-\rho\theta_F) > 1 - \exp(-\rho\theta_J), \tag{i}$$

and, from the definition of θ_J:

$$\exp(-\rho\theta_F) \cdot f(\theta_F) < \exp(-\rho\theta_J) \cdot f(\theta_J). \tag{ii}$$

It follows from (i) and (ii) that:

$$\frac{\exp(-\rho\theta_F) \cdot f(\theta_F)}{1 - \exp(-\rho\theta_F)} < \frac{\exp(-\rho\theta_J) \cdot f(\theta_J)}{1 - \exp(-\rho\theta_J)}, \tag{iii}$$

which is impossible. Alternatively, suppose that $\theta_F = \theta_J$. Then, from (1):

$$\frac{f'(\theta_F)}{f(\theta_F)} = \frac{\rho}{1 - \exp(-\rho\theta_F)}, \tag{iv}$$

and, from (2):

$$\frac{f'(\theta_J)}{f(\theta_J)} = \rho. \tag{v}$$

Since θ_F is finite, (iv) and (v) are mutually inconsistent.

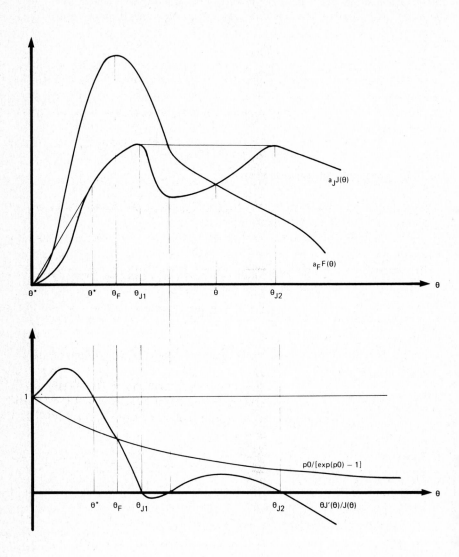

Figure 9.6

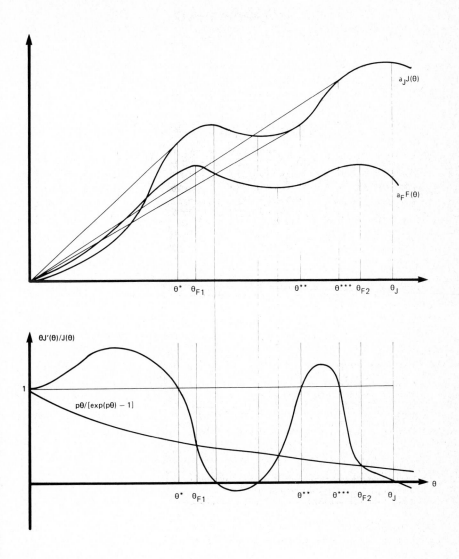

Figure 9.7

problem there are six first-order conditions, the two resource constraints, and:

$$\frac{\partial \mathcal{L}}{\partial N_i} = \frac{J'(bN_i/L_i)}{\rho} - \gamma = 0, \qquad\qquad i = 1,2, \qquad\qquad (25a)$$

$$\frac{\partial \mathcal{L}}{\partial L_i} = \frac{J(bN_i/L_i)}{\rho b} - \frac{N_i}{\rho L_i} J'\left(\frac{bN_i}{L_i}\right) - \lambda = 0, \qquad i = 1,2, \qquad (25b)$$

where $\mathcal{L}$ is the Lagrangian defined by (P3) and γ and λ are multipliers associated with the constraints of the problem. And to match those conditions are the six unknowns N_i, L_i, γ, and λ. Let asterisks indicate their values at a social optimum. Given γ^* and λ^* we can contemplate a competitive economy in which the fth firm chooses L_{if} and N_{if} to maximize

$$\sum_{i=1}^{2} [L_{if} J(bN_{if}/L_{if})/\rho b] - \lambda^* \sum_{i=1}^{2} L_{if} - \gamma^* \sum_{i=1}^{2} N_{if}, \qquad (26)$$

where γ^* and λ^* may be interpreted as the (asset) prices of labour and land. Since $L_{if} J(bN_{if}/L_{if})$ is homogeneous of degree one, only the ratios N_{if}/L_{if} are determinate, and they are precisely the ratios which emerge from (P3).

It remains to find the equilibrium rental and wage rates of the competitive economy. Since production takes time, land must be rented on a long-term basis, either for θ_1 periods or for θ_2 periods. The rental payable at $t = 0$ for a lease to run for θ_i periods, beginning at $t = 0$ or $t = k\theta_i$ (k a positive integer), is $r_i(0)$, where $r_i(0)$ is determined by:

$$\gamma^* = r_i(0) + r_i(0) \exp(-\rho\theta_i) + r_i(0) \exp(-2\rho\theta_i) + \cdots$$

$$= r_i(0)\left[\frac{\exp(\rho\theta_i)}{\exp(\rho\theta_i) - 1}\right]. \qquad (27)$$

If a unit of land is left vacant until time ε, $0 < \varepsilon < \theta_i$, then the rental payable at time ε for a lease to run for θ_i periods is $r_i(\varepsilon)$, where $r_i(\varepsilon)$ is given by:

$$\gamma^* = r_i(\varepsilon) \exp(-\rho\varepsilon) + r_i(\varepsilon) \exp(-\rho\varepsilon - \rho\theta_i) + r_i(\varepsilon) \exp(-\rho\varepsilon - 2\rho\theta_i) + \cdots$$

$$= r_i(\varepsilon) \exp(\rho\varepsilon)[\exp(\rho\theta_i)/(\exp(\rho\theta_i) - 1)]. \qquad (28)$$

It follows from (27) and (28) that $r_i(\varepsilon) = r_i(0) \exp(\rho\varepsilon)$. Thus, landowners are indifferent between leases beginning to run at $t = 0$ and at $t = \varepsilon$,

$0 < \varepsilon < \theta_i$. The wage rate is easier to determine. It is simply w, where $w/\rho = \lambda^*$.

5. Relaxing the assumption of fixed coefficients

Throughout sections 3 and 4 we have maintained the assumption of fixed coefficients of production. In the present section we briefly indicate that even without that assumption it may be suboptimal not to diversify.

Suppose then that b is no longer a given constant but a control which must be optimally set and which, with θ, enters the growth function f. (It is plausible that $\partial f/\partial b > 0$ and $\partial^2 f/\partial b^2 < 0$ if $f > 0$.) For each θ there exists a unique b, say $\hat{b}(\theta)$, which yields the largest present value of the stream of harvests, say $V(\theta)$. Thus, for given θ, we can define $\tilde{b}(\theta) \equiv \theta L/N$, the value of b such that it is just possible to cover the available land with the available labour in θ periods. Given $b = \tilde{b}(\theta)$, the present value of the stream of outputs is:

$$\frac{L}{\tilde{b}(\theta)} F(\theta, \tilde{b}(\theta)) \int_0^\theta \exp(-\rho t)\, dt,$$

where $F(\theta, b) \equiv f(\theta, b)/(\exp(\rho\theta) - 1)$. But, given θ, it might be optimal to choose a value of b greater than $\tilde{b}(\theta)$, in which case it will be impossible to cover all of the available land. (It is never optimal to choose a value of b less than $\tilde{b}(\theta)$, with less than full employment.) Thus, given θ, we have the problem:

(P5) $\quad \max_{b \geq \tilde{b}(\theta)} G(\theta, b),$

where

$$G(\theta, b) \equiv \frac{L}{b} F(\theta, b) \int_0^\theta \exp(-\rho t)\, dt. \tag{29}$$

The solution to (P5) is $\hat{b}(\theta)$. Substituting $\hat{b}(\theta)$ for b in G, we obtain the function:

$$V(\theta) \equiv G(\theta, \hat{b}(\theta)), \tag{30}$$

which, like $J(\theta)$ and $F(\theta)$, may be strictly convex over some θ-intervals. Thus, even when b is a control it may be optimal to diversify maturities and suboptimal not to do so.

6. Concave utility

If the utility function is concave, (P) immediately becomes much more complicated. Suppose, for example, that:

$$\lim_{c \to 0} u(c) > -\infty, \tag{31a}$$

$$\lim_{c \to 0} u'(c) = \infty. \tag{31b}$$

Then clearly it will be suboptimal to delay cutting on any particular plot of land until the oldest trees on that plot reach some time-independent maturity. It will be optimal to begin cutting as soon as growth occurs; and, at least in the early stages, the optimal cutting age will not be constant. In fact it has not been possible to prove any propositions concerning even the asymptotic pattern of harvesting and planting when the utility function is increasing and strictly concave but otherwise unrestricted and when production functions are only weakly restricted, as in section 2. However, on the basis of the numerical analysis of special cases carried out by Kemp and Moore (1980) it is reasonable to conjecture that on each plot the optimal rates of harvesting and planting approach the same constant.[8]

7. Variations and generalizations

It has been assumed that each tree or productive process yields its harvest at a single point in time, determined by the chosen maturity for that tree or duration of the process. However, the analysis of section 3 is more general than is apparent. In particular, it can be made to apply to trees or processes which yield a succession of harvests; one need only bring into play the constant discount or growth factor ρ and work with the *cumulative* current amount of the harvests. On the other hand, the analysis can be reworked to allow for the possibility that labour is needed not at the time of planting but at the time of felling or, indeed, at any other point in the life cycle of a tree.

---

[8]Samuelson (1976, p. 484) advances a similar conjecture for his slightly more general model.

References

Faustmann, M. (1968), Calculation of the value which forestry land and immature stands possess for forestry. English translation from the original German of 1849 in M. Gane, ed., Martin Faustmann and the Evolution of Discounted Cash Flow, Institute Paper no. 42 (Commonwealth Forestry Institute, University of Oxford) pp. 27–55.
Fisher, I. (1930), The Theory of Interest (Macmillan and Company, New York).
Jevons, W. S. (1957), The Theory of Political Economy, 5th edn. (Kelley and Millman, New York) (1st edn. 1871).
Kemp, M. C. and E. J. Moore (1980), Biological capital theory: A question and a conjecture, Economics Letters 4, 141–144.
Samuelson, P. A. (1976), Economics of forestry in an evolving society, Economic Inquiry 14, 466–492.
Wan, H. Y., Jr. (1966), A generalized Wicksellian capital model: An application to forestry, in: Institute of Economics, Academia Sinica, Teipei, Economic Papers, Selected English Series, vol. 1, pp. 1–13.
Wicksell, K. (1938), Lectures on Political Economy, vol. 1, 2nd edn. (George Routledge and Sons, London). (English translation from the original German of 1911.)

On the economics of international fisheries

CARL CHIARELLA, MURRAY C. KEMP, NGO VAN LONG
and KOJI OKUGUCHI*

1. Introduction

It has long been believed that, when several countries share access to a fishery, the total catch is suboptimal; that, in particular, for each fish population the catch is too high and the steady-state population and catch too low. Careful analyses by Khalatbari (1977) and Levhari and Mirman (1980) show that the traditional view is valid under a variety of institutional arrangements and solution concepts. Thus, Levhari and Mirman focused their attention on the case of *direct commonality*, in which each country enjoys immediate access to the entire fish population, and adopted a feedback or perfect closed-loop solution-concept. Khalatbari, on the other hand, examined the polar case of *indirect commonality*, in which each country has immediate access only to that part of the fish population in its coastal waters but in which fish move across international boundaries from regions of high population density to regions of low density, and adopted an open-loop solution-concept.[1] However, both Khalatbari and Levhari–Mirman relied on very special assumptions. Thus, to ensure the existence of closed-loop solutions, Levhari and Mirman resorted to a discrete-time formulation;[2] and to

---

*We gratefully acknowledge the helpful comments of Richard Hartl, John McMillan, and Hans-Werner Sinn. This essay first appeared in the *International Economic Review* 25 (1984).

[1]Khalatbari focused his attention on oil, a non-renewable resource. However, his analysis can be extended to accommodate renewability. See Kemp and Long (1980, Essay 10, section 3).

[2]In continuous time without delays the Levhari–Mirman problem has no solution. For proofs, see Reinganum and Stokey (1981) and McMillan and Sinn, Essay 11 of the present volume. The Reinganum–Stokey proof is set in the limiting context of non-renewable resources; the McMillan–Sinn proof relates to the special case of linear strategies.

Essays in the Economics of Exhaustigle Resources, edited by M. C. Kemp and N. V. Long
© *Elsevier Science Publishers B.V., 1984*

allow the calculation of explicit solutions they were driven to adopt log-linear growth and utility functions. Khalatbari, on the other hand, endowed countries with an implausible degree of myopia (the reader is referred to Kemp and Long (1980, Essay 10, section 4) for a full discussion). Thus, the domain of the traditional view remains an open question.

In the present essay we construct a very general model of fishing and then state four sets of conditions under each of which there is a socially optimal Nash equilibrium path, i.e. a path along which commonality of access does not matter. By perturbing the conditions one can generate conclusions of a traditional or non-traditional kind. Thus, the conditions go some way to marking out the domain of the traditional view. The solution-concept is open-loop; that is, strategies are taken to be functions of time only.[3]

2. Sufficient conditions for Nash optimality

Let n countries share access to each of m fish populations, with populations distinguished by species or by location. The net utility (or net revenue) of the kth country is:

$$u_k = u^{(k)}(c_{11}, \ldots, c_{1m}, \ldots, c_{k1}, \ldots, c_{km}, \ldots, c_{n1}, \ldots, c_{nm}; s_1, \ldots, s_m)$$
$$\equiv u^{(k)}(c_1, \ldots, c_k, \ldots, c_n; s_1, \ldots, s_m), \tag{1}$$

where c_{kj} is the rate of extraction by the kth country from the jth fish population, $c_k \equiv (c_{k1}, \ldots, c_{km})$ is the consumption or extraction vector of the kth country, and s_j is the jth fish population. The function $u^{(k)}$ is taken to be concave in the c_{kj}. Since u_k is interpreted as net utility or revenue, allowance is made for increasing or constant average costs of extraction. The population dynamics are described by the differential equations:

$$\dot{s}_j = \phi^{(j)}(c_1, \ldots, c_n; s_1, \ldots, s_m), \tag{2}$$

which accommodate predator–prey and other types of biological interaction. In the special case in which extraction is completely efficient (everything taken from the fishery reaches market) and does not impede reproduction, (2) reduces to:

---

[3]As we have noted in footnote 2, in continuous time there is no feedback or perfect closed-loop equilibrium.

$$\dot{s}_j = \tilde{\phi}^{(j)}(s_1, \ldots, s_m) - \sum_k c_{kj}. \tag{2a}$$

In an even more special case there is no interaction of populations and

$$\dot{s}_j = \hat{\phi}^{(j)}(s_j) - \sum_k c_{kj}. \tag{2b}$$

Consider first the joint or collective problem of finding:

(J) $\max\limits_{\{c_1,\ldots,c_n\}} \int_0^\infty \exp(-\rho t) \sum_k u^{(k)}(c_1, \ldots, c_n; s_1, \ldots, s_m)\, \mathrm{d}t$

s.t. $\dot{s}_j = \phi^{(j)}(c_1, \ldots, c_n; s_1, \ldots, s_m), \qquad j = 1, \ldots, m,$

$s_j(0)$ given, $c_k \geqq 0.$

The following conditions must be satisfied:

$$\sum_k (\partial u^{(k)}/\partial c_{ij}) + \sum_l \lambda_l(\partial \phi^{(l)}/\partial c_{ij}) = 0, \qquad i = 1, \ldots, n; j = 1, \ldots, m, \tag{3}$$

$$\dot{\lambda}_j = \rho\lambda_j - \sum_k (\partial u^{(k)}/\partial s_j) - \sum_l \lambda_l(\partial \phi^{(l)}/\partial s_j), \qquad j = 1, \ldots, m, \tag{4}$$

$$\lim_{t \to \infty} \exp(-\rho t)\lambda_j(t)s_j(t) = 0, \qquad\qquad j = 1, \ldots, m, \tag{5a}$$

$$\lim_{t \to \infty} \exp(-\rho t)\lambda_j(t) \geqq 0, \qquad\qquad j = 1, \ldots, m. \tag{5b}$$

Eqs. (2)–(5), with the initial values of the m fish populations, determine the trajectories of all fish populations and rates of catch. If, as we assume, the Lagrangian associated with (J) is strictly concave in the c_{ij} and s_j, then the solution is unique.

We seek now to characterize the Nash open-loop solution to the non-cooperative game. If ρ is the common rate of time preference, the task of the kth country is to find:

(N-C) $\max\limits_{\{c_k\}} \int_0^\infty \exp(-\rho t)u^{(k)}(c_1, \ldots, c_n; s_1, \ldots, s_m)\, \mathrm{d}t$

s.t. $\dot{s}_j = \phi^{(j)}(c_1, \ldots, c_n; s_1, \ldots, s_m), \qquad j = 1, \ldots, m,$

$s_j(0)$ given, $c_k \geqq 0.$

The following conditions must be satisfied:

$$\partial u^{(k)}/\partial c_{kj} + \sum_l \lambda_l^{(k)}(\partial \phi^{(l)}/\partial c_{kj}) = 0, \qquad\qquad j = 1, \dots, m, \qquad\qquad (6)$$

$$\dot{\lambda}_j^{(k)} = \rho \lambda_j^{(k)} - \partial u^{(k)}/\partial s_j - \sum_l \lambda_l^{(k)}(\partial \phi^{(l)}/\partial s_j), \qquad j = 1, \dots, m, \qquad (7)$$

$$\lim_{t \to \infty} \exp(-\rho t)\lambda_j^{(k)}(t)s_j(t) = 0, \qquad\qquad j = 1, \dots, m, \qquad\qquad (8a)$$

$$\lim_{t \to \infty} \exp(-\rho t)\lambda_j^{(k)}(t) \geqq 0, \qquad\qquad j = 1, \dots, m. \qquad\qquad (8b)$$

Given our earlier concavity assumptions, eqs. (2) and (6)–(8), together with the initial values of the m fish populations and of the mn rates of catch, uniquely determine the trajectories of all fish populations and rates of catch. However, the initial rates of catch are not supplied by history but must be chosen by the n players; and it is shown in the appendix that the choice of initial rates of catch is not uniquely determined. Thus, the equilibrium Nash trajectories are not unique.

Evidently the solution to (J) is Pareto optimal. What are the welfare properties of the Nash trajectories? In the appendix it is shown by example that not all Nash trajectories are Pareto optimal. It is now shown that there are circumstances in which some Nash trajectories are optimal.

Theorem 1. If $u^{(k)}$ is a function of c_k only and has infinite slope at the origin, then there exists an equilibrium Nash trajectory which coincides with the solution to (J) and hence is Pareto optimal.

Proof. By hypothesis, $\partial u^{(k)}/\partial s_j = 0$. Hence, (6)–(8) reduce to:

$$\partial u^{(k)}/\partial c_{kj} + \sum_l \lambda_l^{(k)}(\partial \phi^{(l)}/\partial c_{kj}) = 0, \quad k = 1, \dots, n; j = 1, \dots, m, \qquad (6')$$

$$\dot{\lambda}_j^{(k)} = \rho \lambda_j^{(k)} - \sum_l \lambda_l^{(k)}(\partial \phi^{(l)}/\partial s_j), \qquad k = 1, \dots, n; j = 1, \dots, m, \qquad (7')$$

$$\lim_{t \to \infty} \exp(-\rho t)\lambda_j^{(k)}(t)s_j(t) = 0, \qquad k = 1, \dots, n; j = 1, \dots, m, \qquad (8a')$$

$$\lim_{t \to \infty} \exp(-\rho t)\lambda_j^{(k)}(t) \geqq 0, \qquad k = 1, \dots, n; j = 1, \dots, m. \qquad (8b')$$

On the other hand, by hypothesis, (3)–(5) reduce to:

$$\partial u^{(k)}/\partial c_{kj} + \sum_l \lambda_l(\partial \phi^{(l)}/\partial c_{kj}) = 0, \qquad k = 1, \dots, n; j = 1, \dots, m, \qquad (3')$$

$$\dot{\lambda}_j = \rho\lambda_j - \sum_l \lambda_l(\partial\phi^{(l)}/\partial s_j), \qquad j = 1, \ldots, m, \qquad (4')$$

$$\lim_{t\to\infty} \exp(-\rho t)\lambda_j(t)s_j(t) = 0, \qquad j = 1, \ldots, m, \qquad (5a')$$

$$\lim_{t\to\infty} \exp(-\rho t)\lambda_j(t) \geqq 0, \qquad j = 1, \ldots, m. \qquad (5b')$$

Evidently any solution to (2), (3')–(5') is a solution to (2), (6')–(8'), with $\lambda_j^{(k)} = \lambda_j$ for all k and all j.   Q.E.D.

Remark 1 concerning theorem 1. If $u^{(k)}$ is a function of c_k only and if, in addition, all utility functions are the same, then the solution to (J) is symmetrical in the sense that the n paths of extraction coincide. From the proof of theorem 1 it then follows that the symmetrical Nash equilibrium path is Pareto optimal.

Remark 2 concerning theorem 1. The assumption that $u^{(k)}$ has infinite slope at the origin rules out the corner solution in which the entire fish population is taken on the first day. Evidently the assumption is unnecessarily strong for that purpose.

Theorem 2. If (a) $u^{(k)}$ takes the form $\sum_j c_{kj} v^{(j)}(\sum_i c_{ij})$, with $v^{(j)}$ of constant elasticity $1/\eta_j$, if (b) $\partial\phi^{(l)}/\partial s_j = 0$ for $j \neq l$, if (c) $\partial\phi^{(l)}/\partial c_{kj}$ is independent of k, and if (d) either (i) $\eta_j = \eta$ for all j or (ii) $\partial\phi^{(l)}/\partial(\sum_k c_{kj}) = 0$ when $j \neq l$, then the symmetrical Nash trajectory is optimal.

Proof. In view of (a) and (c), (3) reduces to:

$$v^{(j)} + \left[dv^{(j)}/d\left(\sum_s c_{sj}\right) \right] \sum_k c_{kj} + \sum_l \lambda_l \left[\partial\phi^{(l)}/\partial\left(\sum_s c_{sj}\right) \right] = 0, \quad j = 1, \ldots, m,$$

or

$$v^{(j)}[1 + 1/\eta_j] + \sum_l \lambda_l \left[\partial\phi^{(l)}/\partial\left(\sum_s c_{sj}\right) \right] = 0, \qquad j = 1, \ldots, m. \quad (3'')$$

On the other hand, applying (a) and (b) to (6) and confining attention to the symmetric solution, we have:

$$v^{(j)}[1 + 1/(n\eta_j)] + \sum_l \tilde{\lambda}_l \left[\partial\phi^{(l)}/\partial\left(\sum_i c_{ij}\right) \right] = 0, \qquad j = 1, \ldots, m. \quad (6'')$$

If (c)(i) is satisfied, we can set

$$\tilde{\lambda}_j = \frac{1 + 1/(n\eta)}{1 + 1/\eta} \lambda_j. \tag{9a}$$

If (c)(ii) is satisfied, we can set

$$\tilde{\lambda}_j = \frac{1 + 1/(n\eta_j)}{1 + 1/\eta_j} \lambda_j. \tag{9b}$$

In each case, (3″) and (6″) coincide. Moreover, from assumption (a) and (9), (4) and (7) coincide.   Q.E.D.

Theorem 2 accommodates the case in which there are m distinct species, with one "pool" for each species, and in which all countries enjoy direct access to each pool. Our next theorem covers the case in which there is a single species in m pools, with all countries enjoying direct access to each pool.

Theorem 2′. If (a) $u^{(k)}$ takes the form $(\sum_j c_{kj}) v (\sum_j \sum_i c_{ij})$, with v of constant elasticity $1/\eta$, and if (b) $\partial \phi^{(l)}/\partial c_{kj}$ is independent of k, then the symmetrical Nash trajectory is optimal.

Proof. Instead of (3″) we now have:

$$v[1 + 1/\eta] + \sum_l \lambda_l \left[\partial \phi^{(l)}/\partial \left(\sum_i c_{ij} \right) \right] = 0, \qquad j = 1, \ldots, m, \tag{3‴}$$

and instead of (6″) we have:

$$v[1 + 1/(n\eta)] + \sum_l \tilde{\lambda}_l \left[\partial \phi^{(l)}/\partial \left(\sum_i c_{ij} \right) \right] = 0, \qquad j = 1, \ldots, m. \tag{6‴}$$

Setting $\tilde{\lambda}_l = \lambda_l [1 + 1/(n\eta)]/[1 + 1/\eta]$, (3‴) and (6‴) are seen to be the same equation. Similarly, applying assumption (a) and confining attention to the symmetrical Nash solution, we see that (4) and (7) are the same equation.   Q.E.D.

Theorems 2 and 2′ provide sufficient conditions for the optimality of Nash trajectories when commonality of access is direct. We now seek sufficient conditions for optimality when commonality of access is indirect. To that end we set $m = n$ and assign the kth pool to the kth country.

Theorem 3. If (a) $u^{(k)} = c_{kk}v(\sum_j c_{jj})$ with v of constant elasticity $1/\eta$, if (b) $\dot{s}_j = \phi^{(j)}(c_{jj}; s_1, \ldots, s_n)$ with the $\phi^{(j)}$ symmetrical in the sense that (i) $\partial\phi^{(j)}/\partial c_{jj} = \partial\phi^{(k)}/\partial c_{kk}$ if $c_{jj} = c_{kk}$ and $s_1 = \cdots = s_n$ and that (ii) $\sum_i \partial\phi^{(j)}/\partial s_i = \sum_i \partial\phi^{(k)}/\partial s_i$ if all derivatives are evaluated at a symmetrical common point with $s_1 = \cdots = s_n$, and if (c) the n fish populations are initially of equal size, then the symmetrical Nash equilibrium is optimal.

Proof. Applying (a) and (b), (3) reduces to:

$$v[1 + 1/\eta] + \lambda_j[\partial\phi^{(j)}/\partial c_{jj}] = 0, \qquad j = 1, \ldots, n,$$

and (4) to:

$$\begin{bmatrix} \dot{\lambda}_1 \\ \vdots \\ \dot{\lambda}_n \end{bmatrix} = A \begin{bmatrix} \lambda_1 \\ \vdots \\ \lambda_n \end{bmatrix},$$

where

$$A(t) \equiv \begin{bmatrix} \rho & 0 & \cdots & 0 \\ 0 & \rho & \cdots & 0 \\ \vdots & \vdots & & \vdots \\ 0 & 0 & \cdots & \rho \end{bmatrix} - \begin{bmatrix} \partial\phi^{(1)}/\partial s_1 & \cdots & \partial\phi^{(n)}/\partial s_1 \\ \vdots & & \vdots \\ \partial\phi^{(1)}/\partial s_n & \cdots & \partial\phi^{(n)}/\partial s_n \end{bmatrix}.$$

And, again applying (a) and (b), (6) reduces to:

$$v[1 + 1/(n\eta)] + \lambda_j^{(j)}[\partial\phi^{(j)}/\partial c_{jj}] = 0, \qquad j = 1, \ldots, n,$$

and (7) to:

$$\begin{bmatrix} \dot{\lambda}_1^{(j)} \\ \vdots \\ \dot{\lambda}_n^{(j)} \end{bmatrix} = A \begin{bmatrix} \lambda_1^{(j)} \\ \vdots \\ \lambda_n^{(j)} \end{bmatrix}.$$

From (b)(ii) we may set $\lambda_j^{(j)} = \lambda_j^{(k)} = \lambda_j[1 + 1/n\eta)]/[1 + 1/\eta]$ for all j and all k; but then the two sets of necessary conditions coincide. Finally, from (c), $\lambda_j(0) = \lambda_k(0)$; hence, bearing in mind (b)(ii), $\lambda_j(t) = \lambda_k(t)$ for all t.
Q.E.D.

Remark 1 concerning theorem 3. Specification (b) of the growth-cum-migration functions $\phi^{(j)}$ is much more general than that proposed by

Khalatbari (1977) and Kemp and Long (1980, Essay 10). In particular, migration may be non-linearly related to stocks, and migration from the kth pool is not required to be evenly spread over the remaining pools.

Remark 2 *concerning theorem* 3.   If (a) and (b) are satisfied but (c′) the n initial fish populations stand in the ratios $(\tau_1, \tau_2, \ldots, \tau_n)$ with $\sum \tau_i = 1$, and if (d) there is a solution to the joint maximization problem (J) with rates of extraction in the same ratios, then the solution to (J) is a solution to (N-C). It can be shown that (d) is satisfied if $\phi^{(j)}(c_{jj}; s_1, \ldots, s_n)$ is linear, as in the formulations of Khalatbari (1977) and Kemp and Long (1980). However, in the case of renewable resources, like fish, the assumption of linearity is too strict.

Remark 1 *concerning theorems* 1–3.   Throughout the present section the planning horizon has been set at infinity. However, it is easy to verify that if time is continuous, then theorems 1–3 remain valid when the horizon is finite; the same for all countries and for the joint planner.

Remark 2 *concerning theorems* 1–3.   In each of the four theorems the assumptions suffice to rule out or neutralize technical and market externalities known to imply suboptimal extraction. Thus, theorem 1 applies when (i) each country either consumes its own catch or sells its catch on a world market in which, individually and collectively, the n countries under study are insignificant and when (ii) for each country the cost of extraction is independent of stocks and of the rates of extraction of other countries. By virtue of (ii) there are no stock or overcrowding externalities; and from (i) there are no "market share" problems. Theorems 2, 2′, and 3, on the other hand, apply to a world in which all countries have access to the same market and, individually and collectively, are able to influence prices. However, potential market externalities are suppressed, in familiar fashion (see Weinstein and Zeckhauser (1975) and Kemp and Long (1980, Essay 6)), by the assumption of constant elasticity of demand; and other externalities are either neutralized by assumptions of symmetry or are simply assumed away.

Appendix: The possible multiplicity and suboptimality of Nash equilibria

In this brief appendix we show by means of a simple example with

$m = n = 2$ that there may be more than one Nash equilibrium and that of the equilibria some may be Pareto suboptimal.

Let

$$u^{(k)}(c_{k1}, c_{k2}) = \gamma c \zeta_1 + \gamma c \zeta_2 \qquad (0 < \gamma < 1) \qquad k = 1, 2$$

$$\rho > 0,$$

$$\dot{s}_j = -c_{1j} - c_{2j}, \qquad\qquad\qquad\qquad j = 1, 2,$$

$$s_j(0) = \bar{s}_j, \qquad\qquad\qquad\qquad\qquad j = 1, 2,$$

$$\bar{s}_1 = \bar{s}_2.$$

Then the following equations define a Nash equilibrium:

$$c_{11}(t) = c_{11}(0) \exp(-\rho t/(1 - \gamma)), \qquad c_{11}(0) = \tfrac{1}{4}\rho\bar{s}_1/(1 - \gamma),$$

$$c_{21}(t) = c_{21}(0) \exp(-\rho t/(1 - \gamma)), \qquad c_{21}(0) = \tfrac{3}{4}\rho\bar{s}_1/(1 - \gamma),$$

$$c_{12}(t) = c_{12}(0) \exp(-\rho t/(1 - \gamma)), \qquad c_{12}(0) = \tfrac{3}{4}\rho\bar{s}_2/(1 - \gamma),$$

$$c_{22}(t) = c_{22}(0) \exp(-\rho t/(1 - \gamma)), \qquad c_{22}(0) = \tfrac{1}{4}\rho\bar{s}_2/(1 - \gamma),$$

$$\lambda_1^{(1)}(0) = \gamma^2\left[\frac{\tfrac{1}{4}\rho\bar{s}_1}{1 - \gamma}\right]^{\gamma-1}, \qquad \lambda_2^{(1)}(0) = \gamma^2\left[\frac{\tfrac{3}{4}\rho\bar{s}_2}{1 - \gamma}\right]^{\gamma-1},$$

$$\lambda_1^{(2)}(0) = \gamma^2\left[\frac{\tfrac{3}{4}\rho\bar{s}_1}{1 - \gamma}\right]^{\gamma-1}, \qquad \lambda_2^{(2)}(0) = \gamma^2\left[\frac{\tfrac{1}{4}\rho\bar{s}_2}{1 - \gamma}\right]^{\gamma-1},$$

$$\lambda_j^{(k)}(t) = \lambda_j^{(k)}(0) \exp(\rho t).$$

The "pay-off" to the first country is:

$$V^{(1)} = \gamma\left(\frac{1 - \gamma}{\rho}\right)\left\{\left[\frac{\tfrac{1}{4}\rho\bar{s}_1}{1 - \gamma}\right]^{\gamma} + \left[\frac{\tfrac{3}{4}\rho\bar{s}_2}{1 - \gamma}\right]^{\gamma}\right\},$$

and to the second country is:

$$V^{(2)} = \gamma\left(\frac{1 - \gamma}{\rho}\right)\left\{\left[\frac{\tfrac{3}{4}\rho\bar{s}_1}{1 - \gamma}\right]^{\gamma} + \left[\frac{\tfrac{1}{4}\rho\bar{s}_2}{1 - \gamma}\right]^{\gamma}\right\}.$$

Since $\bar{s}_1 = \bar{s}_2$, $V^{(1)} = V^{(2)}$.

However, the above equilibrium is suboptimal. It is dominated by the solution to (J) obtained by everywhere replacing $\tfrac{1}{4}$ and $\tfrac{3}{4}$ by $\tfrac{1}{2}$. The new pay-off is:

$$V^{(1)*} = V^{(2)*} = \gamma\left(\frac{1 - \gamma}{\rho}\right)\left(\frac{\rho}{1 - \gamma}\right)^{\gamma}\bar{s}^{\gamma}[(\tfrac{1}{2})^{\gamma} + (\tfrac{1}{2})^{\gamma}].$$

This is greater than $V^{(1)} = V^{(2)}$ because

$$(\tfrac{1}{2})^\gamma + (\tfrac{1}{2})^\gamma > (\tfrac{1}{4})^\gamma + (\tfrac{3}{4})^\gamma \qquad (0 < \gamma < 1).$$

References

Khalatbari, F. (1977), Market imperfections and the optimum rate of depletion of natural resources, Economica 44, 409–414.

Kemp, M. C. and N. V. Long (1980), Exhaustible Resources, Optimality, and Trade (North-Holland Publishing Company, Amsterdam).

Levhari, D. and L. J. Mirman (1980), The great fish war: An example using a dynamic Nash–Cournot solution, Bell Journal of Economics 11, 322–334.

Reinganum, J. F. and N. L. Stokey (1981), Oligopolistic extraction of a non-renewable, common-property resource: The importance of the period of commitment in dynamic games, Northwestern University.

Weinstein, M. C. and R. J. Zeckhauser (1975), The optimal consumption of depletable natural resources, Quarterly Journal of Economics 89, 371–392.

Oligopolistic extraction of a common-property resource: Dynamic equilibria

JOHN McMILLAN and HANS-WERNER SINN*

1. Introduction

The speed with which firms choose to extract a natural resource depends crucially on the value the firms attach to the unextracted resource. Under well-defined property rights, abstracting from imperfections in the final market for the firms' outputs, the firms will extract at the socially optimal rate. When the resource is owned in common and entry into the industry is free, the firms have no incentive to conserve the resource because they know that newcomers to the industry will extract immediately any unit of the resource that can be extracted with immediate profits. This case has been thoroughly analysed in the literature.[1] When the resource is owned in common but the number of firms is fixed (perhaps because each extracting firm must have a lease to the property from which the resource is extracted), the firms have some incentive to conserve the resource: they know that immediate profitability does not necessarily result in immediate extraction by rivals. It does not follow, however, that this incentive to conserve the resource is strong enough to generate a socially optimal extraction rate. Each unit of the resource which a firm chooses not to extract today may in part be extracted by a rival film tomorrow; thus, even without free entry, the firms' valuation of the unextracted

*This research was intiated when McMillan was visiting the University of Mannheim. We thank John Chilton, Peter Howitt, and Murray Kemp for comments. An earlier version of this paper was circulated as Research Report No. 8204, University of Western Ontario, February 1982.

[1]See, for example, Berck (1979). Dasgupta and Heal (1979, ch. 3), Gordon (1954), Hoel (1978), and Weitzman (1974).

Essays in the Economics of Exhaustible Resources, edited by M. C. Kemp and N. V. Long
© *Elsevier Science Publishers B.V., 1984*

resource may be too low and the firms may extract the resource too quickly. (The belief that common-property resources are extracted too quickly has motivated much of the regulation of the petroleum industry: see McDonald (1971, chs. 1–3) and Watkins (1977).)

This essay investigates dynamic equilibria for an oligopolistic industry with a given number of firms exploiting a common-property non-renewable resource. It excludes the problem of market imperfections through the assumption of a constant-elasticity demand curve[2] and thus concentrates on the distortions due to the common-pool aspect.

Several recent studies have examined the dynamics of the exploitation of non-renewable common-property resources by an oligopolistic industry. Bolle (1980) considered the case of a common stock of a resource to which several countries have access. Dasgupta and Heal (1979, ch. 12), Kemp and Long (1980), Khalatbari (1977), and Sinn (1983) analysed the problem of oil-well owners who have the right to extract the oil located under their own properties: the oil is in a single pool underground, and seeps from one holding to another at a speed dependent on the relative sizes of the stocks currently under each property.

In modelling dynamic oligopoly, some choice of equilibrium concept must be made. A natural candidate is a dynamic analogue of the static equilibrium concept introduced by Cournot: each firm makes its decisions under the assumption that its rivals' actions are not affected by its own actions. Unfortunately, for dynamic common-property problems the meaning of Cournot-type behaviour is ambiguous. One possible Cournot-type assumption (adopted by Bolle (1980) and Kemp and Long (1980)) is that each agent believes its rivals will follow a particular time path of rates of extraction, regardless of its own actions. An alternative Cournot-type assumption (used by Sinn (1983)) is that each firm believes that, regardless of its own actions, its rivals will extract in such a way as to generate a particular time path of the stock of the resource. A third possibility (Khalatbari (1977), Dasgupta and Heal (1979)) is that each firm believes that its rivals both maintain a given time path of sales and maintain a given time path of the stock of the resource. The qualitative predictions of the models are sensitive to the choice of equilibrium concept: the models of Dasgupta and Heal, Khalatbari, and Sinn predict over-exploitation of the resource, while the Bolle and Kemp–Long models predict Pareto-optimal extraction rates. Thus, the decision as to

---

[2]Isoelastic demand ensures that there is no distortion due to oligopoly power when the commodity is sold on the market; see Stiglitz (1976) and Weinstein and Zeckhauser (1975). On the oligopolistic distortions with non-constant elasticity in a model with no common-property aspect, see Lewis and Schmalensee (1980).

whether or not there is a role for government intervention in common-property markets is dependent upon which equilibrium concept is thought to be appropriate.

In section 2 we examine a more general concept of equilibrium for the dynamic common-property problem by allowing firms to have arbitrary conjectures about their rivals' reactions. Then many equilibria are possible, including in particular the three Cournot-type equilibria.

Fellner (1949) criticized Cournot's equilibrium concept because it required firms' actions to be "right for the wrong reasons": at equilibrium, the firms act consistently but under incorrect assumptions about their rivals' reactions. In a formally static model such as Cournot's, this concept of equilibrium is not unreasonable; if the game is only played once, the incorrectness of conjectures may not be revealed. In an explicitly dynamic model, Fellner's criticism has more force. In a dynamic context, it seems likely that, if conjectures are incorrect, this incorrectness will be revealed, either during the initial adjustments on the approach to equilibrium, or by occasional accidental or experimental deviations after equilibrium has been reached. As an alternative to a dynamic Cournot-type equilibrium, in section 3 we define a rational-expectations equilibrium to be an equilibrium in which firms' conjectures are locally correct.

The model is developed for the case of a common pool of a resource, to the whole of which each firm in the industry has access. The results will be compared with results already reported in the literature. Since many of these existing results refer to the different but related problem of oil in a reservoir seeping from one individually owned property to another, it is necessary to show that the two problems are indeed comparable; this is done in section 4. Section 5 offers concluding comments.

2. Conjectural equilibria

An industry consisting of n firms ($n \geq 2$) exploits a common pool of a non-renewable resource. There is no entry into or exit from the industry. Each firm knows the industry's instantaneous demand function $P(R)$, $P' < 0$, where $R(t) = \sum_{i=1}^{n} R_i(t)$ is the total amount extracted and sold at time t and $R_i(t)$ is the amount extracted and sold by firm i. Assume, moreover, that the demand function is isoelastic, so that $\eta \equiv -P/(RP') > 0$ is constant. Each firm knows the size of the stock of the resource, $S(t)$.

As is standard in such models, extraction is assumed to be costless.[3] Firm *i* chooses an extraction plan seeking to maximize the discounted value of its stream of future profits. Since the market price, and therefore firm *i*'s profit, at time *t* depends upon all the other firms' extraction rates, without some prediction of its rivals' actions firm *i*'s optimization problem is not well defined. Denote firm *i*'s conjecture about the total extraction rate of the other firms by $R^c_{-i}(t)$. Assume firm *i*'s conjectures are of the form:

$$R^c_{-i}(t) = \alpha(t) + \beta S(t), \tag{1}$$

where β is constant, $0 \le \beta < \infty$, and $\alpha(t) + \beta S(t) \ge 0$. The term $\alpha(t)$ in firm *i*'s conjectures indicates that firm *i* believes that, in part, its rivals' extraction rate is autonomous. The term $\beta S(t)$ reflects firm *i*'s belief that a change in the size of the resource stock will cause a change in the rivals' extraction rate; β will be called the "conjectural parameter".

Thus, firm *i* believes that the resource stock will change at the rate

$$\dot{S}^c(t) = -R^c(t)$$
$$= -(R_i(t) + R^c_{-i}(t))$$
$$= -(R_i(t) + \alpha(t) + \beta S(t)). \tag{2}$$

Given $S(0) = S_0 > 0$, firm *i*'s objective is to choose, subject to (2), an extraction plan $R_i(t)$ with $R_i(t) \ge 0$, to maximize

$$\int_0^\infty P(R^c(t)) R_i(t) e^{-rt} dt, \tag{3}$$

where $r > 0$ is the market rate of interest.

The Hamiltonian is:

$$\mathcal{H}_i = \exp(-rt)[P(R^c)R_i - \lambda_i R^c]. \tag{4}$$

Under the assumption of an interior solution, necessary conditions are, from $\partial \mathcal{H}_i / \partial R_i = 0$;

$$\lambda_i = P(R^c)\left(1 - \frac{R_i}{\eta R^c}\right), \tag{5}$$

where

$$\eta > R_i / R^c. \tag{6}$$

[3]The assumption of costless extraction is not essential. The analysis remains valid if there is a constant average cost of extraction k and if η is redefined as $\eta \equiv -(P-k)/P'R$, where η is constant.

Also, from $\partial(\exp(-rt)\lambda_i)/\partial t = -\partial\mathcal{H}_i/\partial S$, and from (1):

$$\dot{\lambda}_i - r\lambda_i = -\beta[P'(R^c)R_i - \lambda_i]. \tag{7}$$

Let $\hat{x}$ denote $\dot{x}/x$. Then, by the use of (5), (7) becomes:

$$\hat{\lambda}_i = r + \beta\left[1 + \frac{1}{\eta R^c/R_i - 1}\right] \tag{8}$$

The transversality condition is:

$$\lim_{t\to\infty} \exp(-rt)\lambda_i(t)S(t) = 0, \tag{9}$$

which requires, because of $\hat{\lambda}_i \geq r$ (from $\beta \geq 0$, (6), and (8)):[4]

$$\lim_{t\to\infty} S(t) = 0. \tag{10}$$

Conditions (2), (5), (7), and (10) determine firm i's extraction path, $R_i(t)$.

Each firm is assumed to make its decision about $R_i(t)$ in this way. In a conjectural equilibrium, firm i's conjecture about the total of its rivals' extraction paths, $R^c_{-i}(t)$, must be equal to the rivals' actual total extraction path found as the solution to such maximization problems: $R_{-i}(t) = \sum_{j\neq i} R_j(t)$. Thus, in equilibrium $R^c_{-i}(t) = R_{-i}(t)$ for all $t \in (0, \infty)$.

We consider only symmetric equilibria, so that in equilibrium $R/R_i = n$. Condition (6) therefore becomes:

$$\eta n > 1. \tag{11}$$

Clearly, $R/R_i = n$ implies that $(1 - 1/(\eta R/R_i))$ is constant; hence in equilibrium, (5) and (8) imply:

$$-\hat{R}/\eta = \hat{\lambda}_i, \tag{12}$$

so that:

$$\hat{R} = -\rho, \tag{13}$$

where

$$\rho \equiv \eta\left[r + \beta\left(1 + \frac{1}{\eta n - 1}\right)\right]. \tag{14}$$

---

[4]This is the point at which it is necessary to assume $\beta \geq 0$ (that is, each firm believes that part of every unit of the resource it leaves unextracted will be extracted by its rivals). If β could be negative, (10) would not follow from (9).

Since (2) and (10) imply that $S(t) = \int_t^\infty R(\tau)\,d\tau$ and since, because of (13), $\int_t^\infty R(\tau)\,d\tau = R(t)/\rho$ we find that:

$$\hat{S} = -R/S = -\rho. \tag{15}$$

This equation also implies that $\rho/n = R_i/S$ for all i, i.e. that ρ/n is the single firm's actual rate of extraction per unit of stock.

In an equilibrium, the transversality condition (9) becomes:

$$\lim_{t\to\infty} \exp(-rt)\lambda_i(0)\exp(t\rho/\eta)S(0)\exp(-\rho t) = 0, \tag{16}$$

when use is made of (12), (13), and (15). Inserting ρ from (14), and after some manipulations, we can write this as:

$$\eta r + (\eta - 1)\beta\left(1 + \frac{1}{n\eta - 1}\right) > 0. \tag{17}$$

Given, from (6), $\eta n > 1$, and given $\beta \geq 0$, (17) is satisfied if and only if either

$$\eta \geq 1 \tag{18a}$$

or

$$\frac{1}{n} < \eta < 1 \quad \text{and} \quad \beta < \frac{\eta r}{(1 - \eta)\left(1 + \dfrac{1}{n\eta - 1}\right)}. \tag{18b}$$

The crucial result of this model is contained in eq. (14); the right-hand side of this will be called the extraction function. Rewrite (14) as:

$$\rho = a + b\beta, \tag{19}$$

where

$$a \equiv \eta r > 0; \qquad b \equiv \eta\left(1 + \frac{1}{\eta n - 1}\right) > 0.$$

Thus, in equilibrium, the unit rate of extraction chosen by all firms, ρ, is a linear, increasing function of β, the conjectural parameter. The faster the firms expect their rivals to extract the resource, the faster they will choose to extract the resource themselves. As will be shown, this self-fulfilling-prophecy aspect can generate instability in common-property markets.

How does the oligopolistic industry's extraction rate compare with the socially optimal extraction rate? The Hotelling rule states that, for Pareto-optimal allocation in the absence of extraction costs and uncertainty, the price of the resource should increase at the rate of interest; that is $\hat{P} = r$. With constant price elasticity of demand, this implies

$$\hat{S} = -\eta r. \tag{20}$$

The conjectural parameter β determines whether or not the market outcome is optimal. Suppose $\beta = 0$. Then, from (20) and (15), the equilibrium rate of extraction is the socially optimal rate. The intuition is that, with this particular value of β, the optimizing firm behaves as if it had well-defined property rights. It believes its rivals maintain a given extraction path independently of its own actions. In effect there is a given quantity of the resource available for it to extract; there is no need to speed up its extraction process in order to prelude extraction by its rivals. The results of Bolle and Kemp and Long correspond to this case.

Suppose $\beta > 0$; this means that the firm believes that, of every unit of the resource it leaves unextracted, part will be extracted by its rivals. Then, because $b > 0$, the extraction function (19) shows that $\rho > \eta r$, and hence $\hat{S} < -\eta r$. There is over-extraction (as predicted by Khalatbari and Sinn for a special case in which β is a technologically-determined positive constant). The larger is the conjectural parameter β, the greater is the degree of over-extraction.

3. Rational-expectations equilibrium

In the previous section it was shown that, corresponding to the infinity of possible conjectures about rivals' reactions, there are infinitely many dynamic equilibria. In this section it is asked whether adopting a stronger equilibrium definition, requiring conjectures to be rational in a sense about to be made precise, reduces the number of possible equilibria.

In a conjectural equilibrium, conjectures are correct at a point, in that the actual rate at which any firm sees its rivals extracting the resource, $S(t)\rho(n-1)/n$, is the same as the rate it conjectured for them, $\alpha(t) + \beta S(t)$. A stronger notion of equilibrium requires that conjectures be correct not only at the equilibrium point but also for some range around it. Suppose the size of the resource stock changes by some small amount ΔS (perhaps because new information becomes available). Then, given the conjectures β, a new conjectural equilibrium will be established where each firm observes its rivals' rate of extraction to increase by

$\Delta S\rho(n-1)/n$. Hence $\rho(n-1)/n$ is the actual marginal rate of extraction on the part of i's rivals. Now define a rational-expectations equilibrium to be such that $\rho(n-1)/n = \beta$, or equivalently:

$$\rho = \frac{n}{(n-1)}\beta. \tag{21}$$

Thus, at a rational-expectations equilibrium the actual marginal rate of extraction is equal to the conjectural marginal rate of extraction. Eq. (21)

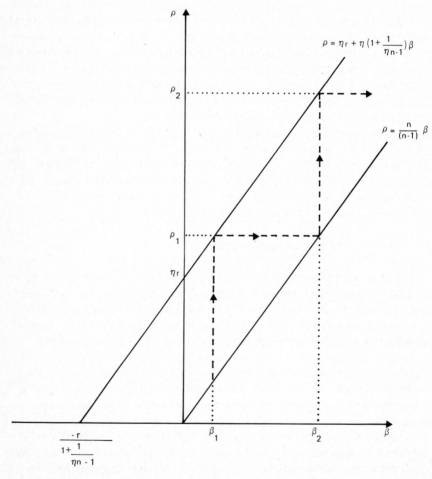

Fig. 11.1   The extraction function and the process of revising the conjectural parameter.

is represented in fig. 11. 1, which also shows the graph of the extraction function (19). If a rational-expectations equilibrium exists, it must be characterized by the point of intersection of the two lines. The location and the existence of this intersection point depend upon the elasticity of the market demand curve. Elementary manipulations show:

$$\eta \gtreqqless 1 \Leftrightarrow b \gtreqqless \frac{n}{n-1} \tag{22}$$

where $b \equiv \eta[1 + 1/(\eta n - 1)]$ is the slope of the extraction function as given by (19).

Consider first the case $\eta \geq 1$. Here, according to (22), the line depicting the extraction function (19) is at least as steep as the line given by (21). Since, from (19), the extraction function has a strictly positive intercept, this implies that the two lines cannot intersect for finite values of ρ and β in the range where $\rho > 0$, that is, where the total extraction per unit of stock is positive. The latter, however, is required by the transversality condition (9) in connection with eq. (15).

Suppose, instead, that $1/n < \eta < 1$. For this case, (22) clearly ensures that there is a point of intersection with $\rho > 0$. But again this point does not satisfy the transversality condition. To see this, note from (18b) that in the case of $\eta < 1$ the transversality condition requires $\beta < \eta r/\{[1-\eta][1 + 1/(n\eta - 1)]\}$. Eqs. (19) and (21), on the other hand, imply that the point of intersection is characterized by:

$$\beta = \frac{\eta r}{n/(n-1) - \eta(1 + 1/(n\eta - 1))}. \tag{23}$$

Elementary algebra shows that (18b) and (23) are incompatible.

Thus, any outcome in which the conjectural marginal extraction rate β and the actual marginal extraction rate $\rho(n-1)/n$ coincide does not satisfy the transversality condition of the individual firm. No rational-expectations equilibrium with finite extraction rates exists.

A rational-expectations equilibrium is a natural end-point for a disequilibrium adjustment process in which firms adjust their conjectures in the light of their observations of their rivals' actual behaviour. To demonstrate the implications of the non-existence of such an equilibrium, consider the firm's reactions to new information. If the system is in an equilibrium, then in the absence of exogenous disturbances the divergence between the actual marginal rate of extraction, $\rho(n-1)/n$, and the conjectural parameter β is not revealed. Suppose, however, there is new (public) information which causes the estimate of the size of the resource stock to be revised by some small amount. Now, given the conjectures, a new equilibrium path will be established and each firm will learn that[5] $\rho(n-1)/n > \beta$; i.e. that its conjecture about the rivals' marginal extraction rate was too conservative. This new information will cause it in some way to revise upwards its conjectural parameter β. According to the extraction function (19) a new equilibrium with a higher rate of extraction ρ per unit of stock is achieved. From (19) and (22):

$$\frac{d}{d\beta}\left[\frac{(n-1)}{n}\rho\right] = \frac{(n-1)}{n}b \gtreqless 1 \Leftrightarrow \eta \gtreqless 1. \tag{24}$$

This means that any change in the conjectural marginal rate of extraction translates into a larger, equal, or smaller change in the actual marginal rate of extraction as the absolute elasticity of demand is larger than, equal to, or smaller than unity, respectively. If $\eta < 1$, then, with a sequence of exogenous disturbances, both rates approach each other. However, as shown above, before they coincide the conjectural equilibrium ceases to exist. If $\eta \geq 1$, new information always causes there to be an equal or increased discrepancy between conjectured and actual marginal extraction rates; new information results in ever faster extraction.

In fig. 11. 1 the arrows depict this process for the particular case in which firms conjecture that their rivals' reactions to extra stock will be the same as their actual reaction at the last observation (with $\eta = 1$).

The non-existence of a rational-expectations equilibrium with finite extraction rates means that every possible equilibrium corresponding to conjectures of the form (1) is unstable in the sense that it is based on misapprehensions by firms about their rivals' behaviour: new information will cause firms to revise upwards their conjectures about their rivals' rates of extraction. This is true in particular of the equilibrium in which extraction occurs at the socially optimal rate (the $\beta = 0$ case).

4. Relationship to seepage models

The model developed above describes a common-property problem in which each firm has access to the whole pool of the resource. Comparisons were made with the results of the problem of Kemp and Long

---

[5]From the discussion in the preceding paragraphs, it is clear that the firm will never observe $\rho(n-1)/n < \beta$.

(1980), Khalatbari (1977), and Sinn (1983) in which the firms own separate oil wells between which there is seepage. It remains to show that the two problems are indeed comparable.

Suppose there are n symmetrically-placed oligopolists owning resource stocks of sizes $S_1, \ldots, S_n$, from which they extract at the rates $R_1, \ldots, R_n$. Let

$$S = \sum_{j=1}^{n} S_j, \qquad R = \sum_{j=1}^{n} R_j, \qquad S_{-i} = \sum_{\substack{j=1 \\ j \neq i}}^{n} S_j \qquad R_{-i} = \sum_{\substack{j=1 \\ j \neq i}}^{n} R_j.$$

Oil seeps between the ith well and the others[6] at a rate which is proportional to the difference between the size of the ith stock S_i and the average size of all the other stocks, $S_{-i}/(n-1)$. Then the single firm's decision problem can be formulated as:

$$\max_{R_i} \int_0^\infty P(R^c(t))R_i(t)\exp(-rt)\,\mathrm{d}t \tag{25}$$

subject to

$$\dot{S}_{-i}(t) = -R_i(t) + s\left(\frac{S_{-i}(t)}{n-1} - S_i(t)\right). \tag{26}$$

$$\dot{S}_i(t) = -R_{-i}(t) + s\left(S_i(t) - \frac{S_{-i}(t)}{n-1}\right), \tag{27}$$

$$R^c_{-i}(t) = \varepsilon(t) + \delta\left(S_i(t) - \frac{S_{-i}(t)}{n-1}\right) - \gamma S_{-i}(t). \tag{28}$$

where $S_i(0) = S_{-i}(0)/(n-1) = S_0/n > 0$, $R^c_{-i}(t)$, $R_i(t)$, $S_i(t)$, $S_{-i}(t) \geq 0$. Eqs. (26) and (27) describe the seepage law, where $s > 0$ is the seepage parameter. Eq. (28) expresses firm i's conjectural hypothesis about the extraction plans of its rivals: γ reflects firm i's conjecture that its rivals will extract at a rate dependent on the size of their stocks; and σ represents firm i's conjecture that its rivals will extract immediately a fraction δ/s of the net inflow of oil from the ith firm's holdings to its rivals' holdings. The model (25), (26), (27), and (28) reduces to the Kemp–Long model if $\delta = \gamma = 0$, to the model of Sinn if $\delta = s$, and to that

---

[6]It is not necessary to consider separately the other $(n-1)$ stocks because the ith firm's decision does not depend upon the way the resource is distributed among its rivals; it is thus sufficient to consider the aggregate variables S_{-i}, R_{-i}.

of Khalatbari[7] if $\delta = s$ and in addition $n \to \infty$.

To relate this seepage model to the model studied in this essay, first note that (26), (27), and (28) can be rewritten with S and S_{-i} as state variables, instead of S_i and S_{-i}, because $S_i = S - S_{-i}$:

$$\dot{S}(t) = -R(t), \tag{29}$$

$$\dot{S}_{-i}(t) = -R_{-i}(t) + s[S(t) - S_{-i}(t)n/(n-1)], \tag{30}$$

$$R_{-i}(t) = \varepsilon(t) + \delta S(t) + S_{-i}(t)(\gamma - \delta n/(n-1)). \tag{31}$$

Consider now the Kemp–Long case $\gamma = \delta = 0$. This is the same as problems (1), (2), and (3) with $\beta = 0$, except for the additional differential equation (30). However, the co-state variable of $S_{-i}(t)$ is zero since, given $S(t)$, a change is $S_{-i}(t)$ could not change the present value of firm i's profits. Hence, the marginal conditions for firm i's decision problem are the same, namely (5) and (7). Only if $S_{-i}(t) > S(t)$ (which would imply $S_i(t) < 0$) could $S_{-i}(t)$ affect firm i's decision problem: however, in a symmetric equilibrium, $S_i(t) = S_j(t)$, this possibility need not be considered. Thus, in equilibrium $S_{-i}(t)$ is an irrelevant state variable in firm i's decision problem and hence the Kemp–Long model is a special case of the model considered in sections 2 and 3.

For the model of Sinn (and of Khalatbari when $n \to \infty$), $\delta = s$. From (30) and (31), $\dot{S}_{-i}(t)$ and hence $S_{-i}(t)$ are independent of $S(t)$: the time path of the stocks of the resource under the properties of i's rivals is exogenous to firm i's decision problem. Hence, firm i conjectures its rivals' rates of extraction are $R_{-i}^c(t) = \alpha(t) + \beta S(t)$, where $\beta = \delta$ and $\alpha(t) = \varepsilon(t) + S_{-i}(t)(\gamma - \delta n/(n-1))$. For this case also, the seepage model is a special case of the model of sections 2 and 3.

A third situation in which the seepage model and the common-pool model coincide is when $\gamma = \delta n/(n-1)$. Then (31) reduces to (1) and again $S_{-i}(t)$ is an endogenous but irrelevant state variable in firm i's decision problem. In this case, firm i conjectures that its rivals react only to the size of the total resource stock and not to its distribution over the properties. Given this conjecture, firm i's own decision depends only on the total resource stock; the conjecture is self-confirming.

---

[7]Strictly speaking, this approach is not compatible with Khalatbari's model, since in that model it is implicitly assumed that firm i conjectures that the whole seepage inflow from the ith firm's holding to its rivals' holdings is immediately extracted by its rivals but not sold on the market (see Kemp and Long (1980, pp. 131–132)). This assumption is innocuous only in the limiting case of $n \to \infty$ (Sinn (1984)); henceforth we will interpret Khalatbari's result as describing the case of perfect competition.

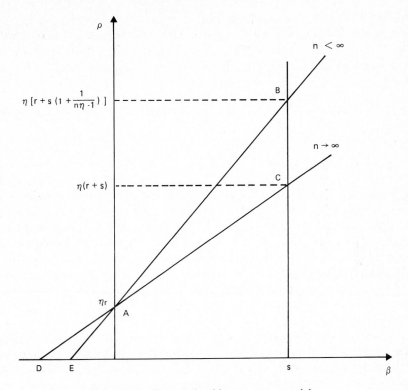

Figure 11.2   The relationship to seepage models.

Figure 11. 2 illustrates the possible equilibria for the seepage model. Possible equilibria lie along the line representing the extraction function (19): line *EAB* for the case of a finite number of firms and line *DAG* for the perfect-competition case. The outcomes described in the literature are special cases of this model: point *A* represents the Kemp–Long solution ($\delta = \beta = \gamma = 0$), point *B* the Sinn solution ($\delta = \beta = s$), and point *C* the Khalatbari solution ($\delta = \beta = s$, $n \to \infty$).

5. Concluding comments

When oligopolists exploiting a common-property resource have non-trivial conjectures about their rivals' actions, infinitely many equilibria are possible, including in particular the Cournot-type equilibria previously analysed in the literature. Conjectures have a self-confirming property: the faster a firm expects its rivals to extract the resource, the faster it will itself extract. There exists no equilibrium with finite extraction rates in which conjectures are locally correct. A consequence of this is that new information about the size of the resource stock will always cause the discrepancy between actual and conjectured reactions to widen; new information will upset any equilibrium and cause the speed of extraction to increase.[8]

The equilibrium concept of this essay was designed to be a direct generalization of the various equilibrium concepts already used in the literature on common-property resources (Bolle (1980), Dasgupta and Heal (1979), Kemp and Long (1980), Khalatbari (1977), and Sinn (1983)). The oligopoly problem described above is an example of a differential game. It therefore should be pointed out that the equilibrium concept used is not one of the concepts usually used in differential-game models; rather, it bears a closer resemblance to the notion of conjectural-variations equilibrium from static oligopoly theory. The closed-loop and open-loop solutions of differential games (see Starr and Ho (1969) for definitions) are both special cases of conjectural equilibria as defined in section 2 above. The open-loop equilibrium involves strategies which do not depend on the current size of the resource stock: it corresponds in this essay to the case $\beta = 0$; i.e. the socially optimal equilibrium. A closed-loop equilibrium would occur in this model when the planned extraction rate is the same as the actual extraction rate at all time points and for all possible sizes of the stock. The rational-expectations equilibrium defined in section 3 is a local approximation to a closed-loop equilibrium; since no rational-expectations equilibrium exists, the analysis of section 3 constitutes a proof that there exists no closed-loop equilibrium in linear strategies with finite extraction rates. Closed-loop equilibria in common-property models have been examined by Reinganum and Stokey (1981) and Eswaren and Lewis (1982). Reinganum and Stokey showed that, for the continuous-time case with elastic demand, there exists a closed-loop equilibrium, involving immediate extraction of the entire stock of the resource. This is consistent with the results above. The proof of the non-existence of a rational-expectations equilibrium in section 3 necessarily assumes that β, and therefore ρ, are finite. Immediate extraction corresponds to infinite values of β and ρ. Clearly, this is consistent with

---

[8]This model, by assuming each firm sells the resource immediately it extracts it, ignores the possibility that the firm might stockpile the resource after extraction. On the importance of storage in exhaustible-resource models, see Hartwick (1981).

eqs. (19) and (21) being satisfied simultaneously; immediate extraction is therefore a rational-expectations equilibrium provided the transversality condition is satisfied. The analysis shows why elastic demand must be assumed in order to generate a closed-loop equilibrium: the transversality condition (18) is not satisfied when there is inelastic demand and infinite β. Furthermore, the adjustment dynamics sketched in section 3 provide some intuitive understanding of why the only closed-loop equilibrium involves immediate extraction.[9]

The model suggests that there is a presumption that a common-property resource will be inefficiently extracted and therefore that there is scope for government intervention. However, with finite extraction rates there are infinitely many equilibria – none a rational-expectations equilibrium – most resulting in over-extraction, but one resulting in socially optimal extraction. The size of the distortion is unpredictable; thus no rectifying system of taxes can be calculated. In contrast to economists' usual prescriptions, quantitative controls seem in this case to be superior to taxes and subsidies. For example, prorationing (fixing a maximum permissible rate of extraction by individual firms) or compulsory or voluntary unitization (operating the whole pool under a single decision-maker and then distributing the profits among the individual firms: that is, collusion among the firms) in effect make β zero and thus ensure that extraction takes place at the socially optimal rate. These are, in fact, methods used in regulating the petroleum industry: see Khoury (1969), McDonald (1971), chs. 9, 10), and Watkins (1970, 1977).

References

Berck, P. (1979), Open access and extinction, Econometrica 47, 877–882.
Bolle, F. (1980), The efficient use of a non-renewable common-pool resource is possible but unlikely, Zeitschrift für Nationalökonomie 40, 391–397.
Dasgupta, P. S. and G. M. Heal (1979), Economic Theory and Exhaustible Resources (Cambridge University Press, Cambridge).
Eswaren, M. and T. Lewis (1982), Appropriability and the extraction of a common-property resource, Discussion Paper No. 82–20, University of British Columbia.
Fellner, W. J. (1949), Competition Among the Few (Knopf, New York).
Gordon, H. S. (1954), Economic theory of a common-property resource: The fishery, Journal of Political Economy 62, 124–142.
Hartwick, J. M. (1981), Learning about and exploiting exhaustible resource deposits of uncertain size, Queen's University, mimeo.

[9]Closed-loop and open-loop equilibria in the common-property problem are further discussed in McMillan (1984).

Hoel, M. (1978), Extermination of self-reproducible natural resources under competitive conditions, Econometrica 46, 219–224.

Kemp, M. C. and N. V. Long (1980), Resource extraction under conditions of common access, in: M. C. Kemp and N. V. Long, eds., Exhaustible Resources, Optimality, and Trade (North-Holland, Amsterdam).

Khalatbari, F. (1977), Market imperfections and the optimum rate of depletion of natural resources, Economica 44, 409–414.

Khoury, N. T. (1969), Prorationing and the economic efficiency of crude oil production, Canadian Journal of Economics 2, 443–447.

Lewis, T. R. and R. Schmalensee (1980), On oligopolistic markets for nonrenewable natural resources, Quarterly Journal of Economics 95, 475–491.

McDonald, S. L. (1971), Petroleum Conservation in the United States: An Economic Analysis (Johns Hopkins Press, Baltimore).

McMillan, J. (1984), Game Theory in International Economics (Paris, Harwood).

Reinganum, J. F. and N. L. Stokey (1981), Oligopolistic extraction of a nonrenewable, common-property resource: The importance of the period of commitment in dynamic games, Discussion Paper No. 508, Northwestern University.

Sinn, H.-W. (1984), Common property resources, storage facilities and ownership structures: A Cournot model of the oil market, Economica, to appear.

Starr, A. W. and Y. C. Ho (1969), Further properties of nonzero-sum differential games, Journal of Optimization Theory and Applications 3, 207–219.

Stiglitz, J. E. (1976), Monopoly and the rate of extraction of exhaustible resources, American Economic Review 66, 655–661.

Watkins, G. C. (1970), Prorationing and the economic efficiency of crude oil production: Comment, Canadian Journal of Economics 3, 511–514.

Watkins, G. C. (1977), Conservation and economic efficiency: Alberta oil proration, Journal of Environmental Economics and Management 4, 40–56.

Weinstein, M. C. and R. J. Zeckhauser (1975), The optimal consumption of depletable natural resources, Quarterly Journal of Economics 89, 371–392.

Weitzman, M. L. (1974), Free access vs private ownership as alternative systems for managing common property, Journal of Economic Theory 8, 255–334.

PART V

EXHAUSTIBLE RESOURCES AND WELFARE ECONOMICS

The efficiency of competitive markets in a context of exhaustible resources

MURRAY C. KEMP and NGO VAN LONG*

1. Introduction

In recent years there has been an avalanche of theoretical analyses of economies based on exhaustible resources. For the most part, attention has been focused on the descriptive modelling of market economies. However, interwoven with ostensibly descriptive analysis there have been many obiter dicta concerning the efficiency of market outcomes; and, very recently, there have appeared several specialized studies of that subject. The picture emerging from the literature is extremely confusing. Some authors seem to take it for granted that, even in a competitive market economy, resources will be extracted in an inefficient fashion; others take it for granted that extraction will be efficient only if competition is perfect and there are enough futures markets (or, sometimes, if foresight is perfect). Nor have the more specialized studies achieved anything approaching a consensus, even under conditions of certainty. Thus, Weinstein and Zeckhauser (1975) have argued that, under competitive conditions with perfect foresight, extraction is necessarily efficient; but Heal (1980) has denied it. Similarly, Weinstein and Zeckhauser (1975), Heal (1975), and Hoel (1978, 1980) have argued that if particular kinds of uncertainty are present and if firms are averse to risk, then, under competitive conditions, the resource-stock will be extracted in an inefficient way; but Kemp and Long (1977a) have insisted that, given enough markets, competitive extraction is efficient.

*We gratefully acknowledge the helpful comments of Michael Hoel, Richard Manning, Hans-Werner Sinn, and Leslie Young. This essay first appeared in W. Eichhorn et al., eds., *Economic Theory of Natural Resources* (Physica-Verlag, Würzburg, 1982) pp. 205–211.

Essays in the Economics of Exhaustible Resources, edited by M. C. Kemp and N. V. Long

In the present essay we report on the debate as it has unfolded to this point. In particular, we seek to appraise the arguments advanced by Heal, Hoel, and Weinstein and Zeckhauser to the effect that the competitive outcome may be inefficient.

Throughout the essay it is taken for granted that the market outcome may be inefficient if any markets are infected by elements of monopoly, if there is a recognized risk of expropriation with inadequate compensation, if expectations of future spot prices are unreliable, if access to a resource-deposit is common to several firms, if technical production externalities intrude, if there is an inescapable moral hazard, or if the supplies of public goods (like information concerning the extent and location of resource-deposits and like public debt in a context of overlapping generations) are inadequate (because, for example, they are under private control).[1] To allow us to focus on more controversial matters, all of these phenomena are assumed away at the outset. It also is recalled, from Malinvaud (1953), that in a developing economy with an infinite horizon saving may be excessive, even under conditions of perfect short-run or myopic foresight. For an exhaustible resource is simply a special kind of capital good and excessive saving may take the form of incomplete exhaustion of the resource. Again to allow us to concentrate on contentious issues, this possibility is ignored throughout.[2]

Following Kemp and Long (1977a, 1978), it will be argued, in sections 3 and 4, that if there are enough competitive markets, then the market outcome is necessarily efficient, but that if agents are sufficiently farsighted and if resource-stocks are of unknown extent, then markets cannot be competitive. These conclusions conflict with those of Heal (1980), on the one hand, and of Weinstein and Zeckhauser, Heal (1975) and Hoel, on the other. We therefore begin with an examination of the arguments advanced by those authors. Heal's (1980) argument is discussed in section 2, the arguments of Weinstein and Zeckhauser, Heal (1975), and Hoel in section 3.

2. Heal on the possible non-convexity of the attainable set

Heal (1980) has argued that, even in the absence of all uncertainty and

---

[1]There are special hairline cases in which extraction is efficient even when a monopolist controls the resource-stock (see Weinstein and Zeckhauser for the case of a non-renewable resource and Kemp and Long (1977c) for the case of a renewable resource), and even when access to the resource-stock is in common (see Kemp and Long (1977b)).

with markets of any degree of completeness, the competitive outcome may be inefficient.

The fundamental theorem of welfare economics asserts that, under the appropriate assumptions, ... a competitive equilibrium, if it exists, is Pareto efficient. In such a model, the vector of initial endowments, which will include the economy's endowment of exhaustible resources, is taken as exogenous and independent of all economic forces and activities. In fact this seems an unreasonable assumption, especially for endowments of resources. There is not a given endowment of oil, independent of market forces: rather, ... the amount available depends on the price of oil. Geologists typically give figures for oil reserves, and reserves of most other minerals, as a function of price, describing in effect a supply curve for the resource ... In such a case, the vector of initial endowments of the economy is best seen not as a given constant vector, say w, but as a price-dependent vector $w(p)$. In

[2]For detailed analysis of the efficiency-implications of these phenomena in a context of exhaustible resources, the reader may refer to Kemp and Long (1977b) on common access, to Long (1975) on the risk of expropriation, to Kay and Mirrlees (1975) on unreliable price expectations, and to Sweeney (1977) on monopoly. Numerical examples of "Malinvaud inefficiency" in a context of exhaustible resources have been provided by Kemp and Long (1979) and by Mitra (1978). Kemp and Long have shown also that the inefficiency can be removed by the provision of public debt, properly timed and in sufficient quantity. In technical terms, the issue of debt forces the economy to behave in a manner consistent with the transversality conditions of the relevant optimal-control problem. In this connection, and in passing, we mention the interesting recent contribution of Pazner and Razin (1980). Following Samuelson (1958), the authors develop a model with an infinite horizon but overlapping generations, each generation living for just two periods of time. However, their model has several distinctive features. Each generation derives utility from the utility of the next generation and therefore has an incentive to raise children and make bequests to them. Moreover, on one interpretation of their model, there is a single commodity, a durable but exhaustible resource stock ("cake") which in each period must be divided between consumption and bequests. Thus, in each period the old must choose both the rate of population growth and the division of the cake between consumption (the consumption of the young and of the old) and bequests. Pazner and Razin show that the outcome of the sequence of decisions by the old is Pareto optimal. They contrast their findings with that of Samuelson, ascribing the disappearance of inefficiency to their assumption that population growth is a matter of choice. But in this they appear to be mistaken: given their other assumptions, inefficiency disappears even if population growth is exogenous. In fact, the treatment of population growth by Pazner and Razin is unsatisfactory. For implicit in their model is the assumption that each child has only one parent. By means of this assumption the optimality-*destroying* public-goods nature of families (each family has two pairs of grandparents) is pushed out of sight. If each child had been allowed a full quota of parents, suboptimality (of an earlier-Samuelson type) would have reappeared. Thus, in summary, the modification of Samuelson's model to accommodate "overlapping" utility functions and resource-durability suffices to restore efficiency, but the further modification of the model to (properly) accommodate choice of population growth causes inefficiency to reappear.

such a situation, the quantity of endowments becomes endogenous: a world with a high price of oil has larger economically relevant reserves than one with a low price.

Now . . . , if endowments are price-dependent, then a competitive equilibrium need no longer be efficient . . . [This] result depends on the fact that the set of allocations – consumption and production plans – which is in principle attainable by an economy, depends . . . on the initial endowment. So if the endowment changes with price, so does the attainable set. So for each price the economy has an attainable set which, under the usual assumptions, is convex. The overall attainable set for the economy is the *union* of the sets attainable at each price, and the union of convex sets need not be convex . . . .

From this we see that the question "Will the competitive market allocate exhaustible resources efficiently?" may have a negative answer for reasons quite distinct from the normal causes of market failure (Heal (1980); see also Chichilnisky and Heal (1979)).

Now in fact "the fundamental theorem of welfare economics" does not require for its validity that the attainable set of the economy be convex. Thus, Heal's conclusion is a non sequitur.

Nor has Heal produced an example of competitive inefficiency. Heal's "supply curve for the resource" could be understood to relate extracted resource to the price of extracted resource. However, extracted resource is not a primary factor; it is the outcome of a productive process and is in parity with any other produced commodity. Heal's supply curve therefore must be understood as relating unextracted resource to the price of unextracted resource. (An example provided by Heal is consistent with this interpretation.)[3] Now the amount of unextracted resource (of a particular quality, or in the aggregate) is a constant, independent of price. If then the supply of the resource depends on price, that can be so only because the resource has alternative uses in the consumption plans of its owners (one thinks of private parkland and leisure). Thus, one can imagine a linear transformation curve linking the amount offered to the factor market $w(p)$ to the amount withheld for private consumption, $\bar{w} - w(p)$. But the amount privately consumed appears neither in Heal's set of allocations nor in his utility functions. If it had done so, the standard arguments of Arrow and Debreu, or of Weinstein and Zeckhauser, would have sufficed to establish efficiency.

[3]For a detailed and critical examination of Heal's example, see Breyer and Reiss (1982).

3. Hoel on the possibility of competitive inefficiency in the face of uncertainty

Whereas Heal's (1980) case for competitive inefficiency was developed in the context of an uncertainty-free economy, his (1975) case, as well as those of Weinstein and Zeckhauser and of Hoel, rests squarely on the presence of a particular kind or source of uncertainty. We begin with Hoel's argument since it has been presented most explicitly and in greatest detail.

It is supposed by Hoel (1978) that after some known future date it will be possible to produce a resource-substitute but that the cost of producing the substitute is known now only in terms of an agreed-upon subjective probability distribution.

Hoel shows that if resource-extracting firms are risk averse, then they will over-extract at all points of time before the substitute becomes available.

However, Hoel's argument rests on the implicit assumption that the resource-extracting firms seek to maximize the present value of expected utility, where utility is a strictly concave function of the proceeds of sale of the resource, in terms of a third, numeraire commodity. No justification for such an assumption is provided. In fact, the assumption fits uncomfortably with two other of Hoel's assumptions: (i) that the community is sufficiently homogeneous to warrant the use of a cardinal social utility function; and (ii) that the social utility function is concave in the combined consumption of the resource and its substitute but linear in the consumption of the numeraire. If (i) is justified by the common supposition that all individuals are alike, both in preferences and in asset-holdings, then one would expect that, in their capacity as shareholders, they would impose on the resource-extracting firms their own utility functions. But then the competitive outcome would be optimal, for each firm would be a small-scale replica of the economy as a whole.

Moreover, it is assumed by Hoel that all commodity markets are spot. If, instead, he had introduced a complete set of contingent futures markets, so that firms are led to seek maximum profits, then again he would have found that competitive equilibrium is socially optimal.

In his later work (1980, especially ch. 3), Hoel considered the implications for efficiency of uncertainty about the date of arrival of the new technology, with the cost of production of the substitute known in advance. Again he was able to show that if resource-extracting firms are risk averse then they will over-extract before the substitute becomes available, and again the argument rests on inconsistent assumptions.

We turn briefly to the arguments for competitive inefficiency developed by Weinstein and Zeckhauser and by Heal (1975). Weinstein and Zeckhauser consider the possibility that the demand for an exhaustible resource is random, while Heal introduces a kind of supply uncertainty distinct from that studied by Hoel. In each case it is shown that competitive extraction is inefficient (excessive) if the extracting firms are averse to risk. However, while the contexts of the Weinstein-Zeckhauser and Heal cases for competitive inefficiency are quite distinct from the context of Hoel's case, the three arguments are subject to the same objections. For in all three arguments one finds precisely the same set of mutually inconsistent assumptions concerning the utility functions of the extracting firms and of the eventual consumers.

We conclude that uncertainty of any of the kinds introduced by Weinstein and Zeckhauser, Heal (1975), and Hoel is harmless in the sense that, by itself, it fails to destroy the efficiency of competitive outcomes.[4]

However that kind of uncertainty is of a special kind. In the world envisaged by Hoel et al., the probabilities attached to alternative states of the world are given by Nature, independently of the activities of agents; that is, they are of a type admitted by Arrow and Debreu. It is not surprising therefore that uncertainty of the type studied by Hoel et al. is compatible with competitive efficiency.

It is possible that the probabilities attached to alternative states of the world depend on the planned actions of agents. For example, the capacity of an agent to deliver a commodity at a future date may be uncertain, with the degree of uncertainty depending on what the agent plans to do before the delivery date. In those circumstances, the probability which is attached to the state of the world in which the agent is unable to deliver on the due date is under the control, partial or complete, of the agent. Clearly, the owner of a resource-deposit of unknown extent is such an agent. It follows that the Arrow Debreu proof of competitive optimality is inapplicable when there is uncertainty concerning the extent of the deposit. The question of competitive optimality is re-opened.

It has been shown by Kemp and Long (1977a) that if markets are

---

[4]The counter argument which has been directed to Weinstein and Zeckhauser, Heal (1975), and Hoel can be reformulated and directed to the claim by Batra and Russell (1974) that, for a small trading country facing random world prices, free trade may be suboptimal. See Kemp and Ohyama (1978).

sufficiently numerous and of the right kind, then, even when the state-of-the-world probabilities depend on the choices of agents, the competitive outcome is optimal.[5] We therefore seem to be justified in concluding that, whatever the source of uncertainty, the competitive outcome will be efficient if only there are enough markets.

4. The implausibility of the assumption of competition

But is it plausible to assume that markets are competitive? Or is there an underlying incompatibility between the assumption of universal competition and the assumption that the economy is based on exhaustible resources? In this brief final section we oppose the drift of earlier parts of the essay by arguing that the answers to these questions should be No and Yes, respectively.

Suppose that the extent of the deposits of some exhaustible resource is unknown. Then, however numerous the extracting firms may be, provided only that they are sufficiently far-sighted, each firm will formulate its plan of extraction in the light of the possibility that, some day, it will be the only firm left with a positive stock of the resource and thus will enjoy monopolistic power. In other words, the required degree of foresight is incompatible with pure price-taking by the extracting firms.

If competition must be abandoned, so must the efficiency of competitive allocations. It is intuitively clear that a firm will extract less rapidly when it recognizes the possibility of eventual monopoly than when it fails to recognize the possibility. (For a formal proof, based on the assumption of perfectly foreseen spot prices,[6] see Kemp and Long (1978).) Since the outcome is efficient when the possibility of eventual monopoly is ignored, the outcome will generally be inefficient when the possibility is recognized.

---

[5]Loury (1978) has obtained a similar result. The proofs provided by Kemp, Long, and Loury relate to a pure-exchange economy but can be extended to allow for production.

[6]A proof based on the alternative assumption of a complete set of conditional commodity markets can be constructed.

References

Batra, R. N. and W. R. Russell (1974), Gains from trade under uncertainty, American Economic Review 64, 1040–1048.

Breyer, F. and W. Reiss (1982), Variable resource endowments and the convexity of the attainable consumption set, in: W. Eichhorn et al., eds., Economic Theory of Natural Resources (Physica-Verlag, Würzburg).

Chichilnisky, G. and G. Heal (1979), Welfare economics of competitive general equilibrium with variable endowments, Columbia University Working Paper.

Heal, G. (1975), Economic aspects of natural resource depletion, in: D. W. Pearce, ed., The Economics of Natural Resource Depletion (Macmillan, London) pp. 118–139.

Heal, G. (1980), Intertemporal allocation and intergenerational equity, in H. Siebert, ed., Erschöpfbare Ressourcen (Arbeitstagung des Vereins für Socialpolitik, Mannheim 1979). (Duncker and Humblot, Berlin).

Hoel, M. (1978), Resource extraction when a future substitute has an uncertain cost, Review of Economic Studies 45, 637–644.

Hoel, M. (1980), Extraction of an Exhaustible Resource under Uncertainty, Volume 51 of W. Eichhorn and R. Henn, managing editors, Mathematical Systems in Economics (Verlag Anton Hain, Meisenheim am Glan).

Kay, J. A. and J. A. Mirrlees (1975), The desirability of natural resource depletion, in: D. W. Pearce, ed., The Economics of Natural Resource Depletion (Macmillan, London) pp. 130–176.

Kemp, M. C. and N. V. Long (1977a), Eating a cake of unknown size: Pure competition versus social planning, Australian National University Working Paper; reprinted in: M. C. Kemp and N. V. Long, eds., Exhaustible Resources, Optimality, and Trade (North-Holland, Amsterdam, 1980) essay 5.

Kemp, M. C. and N. V. Long (1977b), Resource extraction under conditions of common access, University of New South Wales Working Paper; reprinted in: M. C. Kemp and N. V. Long, eds., Exhaustible Resources, Optimality, and Trade (North-Holland, Amsterdam, 1980) essay 10.

Kemp, M. C. and N. V. Long (1977c), The management of a renewable resource: Monopoly versus competition, University of New South Wales Working Paper; reprinted in: M. C. Kemp and N. V. Long, eds., Exhaustible Resources, Optimality, and Trade (North-Holland, Amsterdam, 1980) essay 6.

Kemp, M. C. and N. V. Long (1978), The optimal consumption of depletable natural resources: Comment, Quarterly Journal of Economics 92, 345–353; reprinted in: M. C. Kemp and N. V. Long, eds., Exhaustible Resources, Optimality, and Trade (North-Holland, Amsterdam, 1980) essay 4.

Kemp, M. C. and N. V. Long (1979), The underexploitation of natural resources: A model with overlapping generations, Economic Record 55, 214–221; reprinted in: M. C. Kemp and N. V. Long, eds., Exhaustible Resources, Optimality, and Trade (North-Holland, Amsterdam, 1980) essay 9.

Kemp, M. C. and M. Ohyama (1978), The gain from free trade under conditions of uncertainty, Journal of International Economics 8, 139–141.

Long, N. V. (1975), The pattern of resource extraction under uncertainty about possible nationalization, Journal of Economic Theory 10, 42–53.

Loury, G. C. (1978), The optimal exploitation of an unknown reserve, Review of Economic Studies 45, 621–636.

Malinvaud, E. (1953), Capital accumulation and efficient allocation of resources, Econometrica 21, 233–268.

Mitra, T. (1978), Efficient growth with exhaustible resources in a neoclassical model, Journal of Economic Theory 17, 114–129.

Pazner, E. A. and A. Razin (1980), Competitive efficiency in an overlapping-generation model with endogenous population, Journal of Public Economics 13, 249–258.

Samuelson, P. A. (1958), An exact consumption-load model of interest with or without the social contrivance of money, Journal of Political Economy 66, 467–482.

Sweeney, J. L. (1977), Economics of depletable resources: Market forces and intertemporal bias, Review of Economic Studies 44, 125–141.

Weinstein, M. C. and R. J. Zeckhauser (1975), Optimal consumption of depletable natural resources, Quarterly Journal of Economics 89, 371–392.

Essay 13

Optimal taxation and economic depreciation: A general equilibrium model with capital and an exhaustible resource

NGO VAN LONG and HANS-WERNER SINN*

1. Introduction

The study of the taxation of natural resources has typically been of a partial equilibrium nature. Exceptions to this general observation include Kemp and Long (1980, essay 17) and Sinn (1980) which serve as a basis on which the present paper is built.

The main objectives of this essay are to demonstrate that some received results in the partial equilibrium normative theory of resource taxation are incorrect, and to explore the effects of various taxes in a general equilibrium model which encompasses earlier models as special cases.

Economists have long debated about the efficient taxation of natural resources and capital goods, but so far little agreement has been reached on the matter. The following quotation from Auerbach (1982, p. 355) describes not unfairly the state of the art:

There are few problems in tax analysis which have generated as much study and discussion among economists as the question of how to formulate "neutral" tax incentives for investment. This concentration

*We would like to thank Murray Kemp for helpful comments. Previous versions of this paper have been presented to seminars at Vienna University of Technology, CORE (where Ngo Van Long was a visiting research associate), and University of Mannheim. We wish to thank the participants at these seminars for their useful suggestions. Financial support of the Sonderforschungsbereich 5, Deutsche Forschungsgemeinschaft, is gratefully acknowledged.

Essays in the Economics of Exhaustible Resources, edited by M. C. Kemp and N. V. Long
© *Elsevier Science Publishers B.V., 1984.*

of research effort may be traced to the importance and relevance to policy design of the issues under investigation. In this light, it is especially distressing to the economist and government planner alike that no consensus has been reached concerning the proper approach to take when adjusting taxes. On the contrary, authors continue to analyze the problem of investment incentives using distinct criteria, each calling markedly different tax schemes neutral. In each case, satisfaction of the neutrality criterion is argued to lead to an efficient allocation of capital, but this cannot be simultaneously true for different criteria.

The main reason for diverging results in taxation theory is that authors typically do not fully specify the underlying model in a general equilibrium framework, and therefore their claims that their proposed tax rules would bring about an efficient allocation of resources often cannot be easily assessed.

In this essay we are concerned with the problem of optimal taxation in the resource sector given that capital income in other sectors is taxed according to predetermined, immutable rules. In most Western economies these rules are essentially those of Schanz, Haig and Simons (see Goode (1977) for details), which require that interest income from financial investment and the returns from real investment be taxed where, concerning the latter, debt interest and economic depreciation have to be tax deductible.

The problem we pose is a second-best problem of taxation. This is not a new problem. It has been studied by various authors, but no concensus has been reached. A major problem in the existing literature has been the failure to define production efficiency in an intertemporal framework. Authors often equate their definitions of neutrality with efficiency, or postulate neutrality as a "principle". (See Auerbach (1982) for further discussion.) In the context of an economy with natural resources, Garnaut and Clunies Ross (1979) and Swan (1976) both argue in favour of neutrality, even though they disagree concerning the neutrality of certain proposed tax rules. Swan (1976) upholds the "principle of neutrality" based on economic depreciation, and argues that economic depreciation in the mineral industry should be tax deductible in the same way as in other industries. Dasgupta, Heal and Stiglitz (1980) and Dasgupta and Heal (1979) claim that economic depreciation (defined as the "decrease in the value of the oil field") should be subtracted from the value of the gross returns to the oil company:

This "depletion allowance" would be equivalent to what has been called *true economic depreciation* in the context of durable capital goods. It would provide an appropriate measure of net income and would, at the same time, be non-distortionary, provided that interest income is taxed (Dasgupta, Heal and Stiglitz (1980, p. 159)).

The idea of taxing the resource sector according to the Schanz–Haig–Simons rules (as summarized above) might seem at first appealing in the light of the theorem on economic depreciation independently formulated by Johansson (1961, esp. pp. 148n, 211n; 1969) and Samuelson (1964), for this theorem says that with true economic depreciation and with a given market rate of interest the values of the mines, as well as the value of all investment projects in other sectors, are independent of the tax rate, thus ensuring that the so-called "intersectoral efficiency condition" in taxation theory is satisfied. However, while "intersectoral efficiency" is certainly desirable in a first-best world with no other distortions, it is completely unclear whether it is a desirable goal in a world where the taxation of interest income distorts the consumption-saving decisions on the part of households.

In the present essay we show that, indeed, this is not generally the case. We demonstrate that, under certain conditions, it is not desirable to allow the mining firm to deduct economic depreciation (defined as the decrease in the value of the mine), and we identify the source of the error made by those who advance the general claim that "there is no bias in extraction pattern" if the tax allowance is "on the true economic depreciation of the deposit" (Dasgupta and Heal, p. 371).

True economic depreciation is in some sense the negative of "true capital gains". We shall try to clarify the precise relationship between these two concepts and show the implications of our results for the desirability (or undesirability) of capital gains taxation.

In addition to the economic depreciation issue we also briefly consider other forms of efficient taxation, such as a tax on a dividend payout and a specially designed production-based royalty.

2. Second-best taxation and the undesirability of the economic depreciation rule

In this section we construct a simple model which contradicts the assertion made by Dasgupta and Heal (1979), Dasgupta, Heal and

Stiglitz (1980), and others, concerning the supposedly efficient tax rule based on true economic depreciation. We also propose a second-best tax rule, which will be formulated in proposition 2.2.

Since our model is a general equilibrium one, with consumers and producers solving intertemporal maximization problems, our argument will be long and, in places, tedious. Readers who are mainly interested in our findings and not so much inclined to follow the technical steps may find it more useful to read proposition 2.1 and the ensuing discussion at the end of section 2, where a common sense account of the findings will be given.

2.1. *The structure of the economy*

For simplicity, we consider an economy consisting of three interrelated sectors. The first sector, called the Ricardian sector, uses labour (L_R) to produce a Ricardian good which can be consumed or invested. The second sector is the "manufacturing sector", producing manufactured consumption goods by means of capital (K) and labour (L_M), the capital good being produced by the Ricardian sector. The last sector is called the "extractive sector". It uses labour (L_E) to extract natural resources which are directly consumed. We assume for simplicity that the first and third sectors draw labour from a common pool, while the manufacturing sector uses specialized labour, so that, in equilbrium,

$$L_R + L_E = \bar{L}_C; \qquad L_M = \bar{L}_M,$$

where $\bar{L}_C$ and $\bar{L}_M$ are fixed supplies of the two types of labour. Thus, the three consumption goods compete for resources either directly or indirectly (in the case of the manufacturing sector, via its demand for capital goods which are produced by labour in the Ricardian sector).

The production function in the manufacturing sector is given by:

$$Q_M = F(K, L_M),$$

where F is homogeneous of degree one and has all the usual neoclassical properties.

The output of the extractive sector is given by:

$$Q_E = (1/b)L_E,$$

so that the cost of extracting one unit of the extractive good is b units of the Ricardian good. The output of the Ricardian good is:

$$Q_R = \bar{L}_C - L_E = \bar{L}_C - bQ_E.$$

We assume that the economy is competitively organized. For each sector there is one representative firm. All three firms are owned by a representative household which, in addition to the wage income, receives dividends and interest income. All agents are endowed with perfect foresight and take the price paths as exogenously given in their individual optimization problems.

Money in this economy is simply a unit of account, there is no stock of real balances. Nominal prices are denoted by $q_i(t)$ ($i = R$, M, E) and nominal wages by $W_i(t)$ ($i = R$, M, E). We will write $W_C \equiv W_R = W_E$.

There is a uniform capital income tax at the rate γ which is applied to the interest income received by households, and to company income (whether retained or distributed). In other words, the personal and the company tax systems are fully integrated. (In section 3 the effect of an additional tax on dividends is considered.)

The Ricardian sector and the manufacturing sector are taxed according to the Schanz–Haig–Simons rules which require the deductibility of debt interest and economic depreciation. The tax treatment of the extractive sector is the subject of our discussion. Labour income is not taxed.

By its very definition the Ricardian firm has no intertemporal optimization problem to solve and hence does not require a formal analysis. Obviously, it neither generates profits nor a tax revenue. The problem of the household, the manufacturing firm, and the extractive firm, however, need explicit consideration.

2.2. *The problem of the household*

Households hold assets in the form of bonds or shares. It is assumed that each bond is a promise to pay a stream of interest $\langle r(t) \rangle$, where $r(t)$ is the market rate of interest at time t. Thus, the price of a bond is unity, and there are neither capital gains nor losses in bond holding.

Each individual maximizes the discounted stream of utility,

$$(\text{P1}) \quad \int_0^\infty [U_M(C_M) + U_E(C_E) + U_R(C_R)] \exp(-\rho t)\, dt,$$

subject to the constraint that the value of his consumption plus the value of his asset accumulation equals his after-tax income:

$$\sum q_i C_i^d + \dot{B} + \sum Z_j \dot{S}_j = (1 - \gamma)rB + \sum D_j S_j + W_C \bar{L}_C + W_M \bar{L}_M, \tag{1}$$

where

C_i^d = planned purchase of the ith good, i = E, R, M,
B = the quantity of bonds the individual plans to own,
Z_j = price of a share of the jth firm,
S_j = number of shares of the jth firm the individual plans to own,
r = the rate of interest,
γ = the tax rate on interest income,
D_j = dividend per share of the jth firm (net of income tax),
W_i = nominal wage rate (i = C,M),
ρ = the rate of utility discount ($\rho > 0$),
q_i = price of the ith good.

In addition to constraint (1), we also impose the following non-negativity constraints:

$$S_j(t) \geq 0, \tag{2}$$

and

$$\sum S_j(t) Z_j(t) + B(t) \geq 0. \tag{3}$$

In words, the individual is not allowed to hold negative quantities of shares (shortselling is ruled out), and his net borrowing cannot exceed the value of his shares.

Assuming that (P1) has an interior solution (a solution with $C_i^d(t) > 0$, i = E, M, and strict inequality holding for (2) and (3)), the consumer's optimal paths of consumption and asset accumulation must satisfy the following conditions:

$$(\dot{Z}_j + D_j)/Z_j = (1 - \gamma)r, \tag{4}$$

$$U_R'(C_R(t))/q_R(t) = U_E'(C_E(t))/q_E(t) = U_M'(C_M(t))/q_M(t) \tag{5}$$

and

$$U_i'(C_i(t)) \exp(-\rho t)/U_i'(C_i(0)) = q_i(t) \exp[-(1 - \gamma)rt]/q_i(0). \tag{6}$$

Condition (4) is the usual arbitrage condition: the capital gain plus dividend per share is equated to the opportunity cost of holding shares (the after-tax return on bond holding). Condition (5) is the static efficiency condition, that the marginal utility per dollar spent on the ith good at time t be equated to the marginal utility per dollar spent on the jth good at time t. Condition (6) is the intertemporal counterpart of condition (5): that the marginal rate of substitution between dated goods be equated to their relative costs. Defining

$$\lambda(t) = U_i'(C_i(t))/q_i(t),$$

we can write (6) in the alternative form:

$$\dot{\lambda}/\lambda = \rho - (1-\gamma)r,$$

or

$$[C_i U_i''/ U_i'](C_i/C_i) = \rho - (1-\gamma)r + (\dot{q}_i/q_i). \tag{7}$$

Equation (4) can be integrated to yield:

$$Z_j(s) = \int_s^\infty D_j(t)\exp\{-(1-\gamma)[R(t)-R(s)]\}\,dt, \tag{8}$$

where

$$R(t) \equiv \int_0^t r(t')\,dt'. \tag{9}$$

In obtaining (8), we have assumed that share prices do not explode to infinity, or, more precisely, that:

$$\lim_{t\to\infty} Z_j(t)\exp[-(1-\gamma)R(t)] = 0. \tag{10}$$

2.3. *The problem of the manufacturing firm*

We now turn our attention to the problems of the firms. In line with Fisher's separation theorem, it seems reasonable to assume that each firm seeks to maximize $Z_j(0)$, the wealth of existing shareholders.

At this stage, it is convenient to choose the Ricardian good as the numeraire; thus:

$$q_R(t) = 1. \tag{11}$$

Assume that the tax laws define the income or profit of the manufacturing firm as:

$$Y_M = q_M(t)F(K, L_M) - W_M L_M - rB_M - \delta q_R K, \tag{12}$$

where B_M is the firm's nominal stock of debt (which is the same as the real stock of debt in terms of the Ricardian good), and δ is the rate of physical depreciation.

Let

T_M = tax payments,
$\dot{B}_M$ = additional finance obtained from the sale of new bonds,
$Z_M \dot{S}_M$ = additional finance obtained from the sale of new shares.

Total dividend payments are given by:

$$D_M(t)S_M(t) = q_M F(K, L_M) - W_M L_M - rB_M - T_M$$
$$+ \dot{B}_M + Z_M \dot{S}_M - q_R I, \tag{13}$$

where $I(t)$ is the firm's purchases of investment goods. We assume that the tax laws require that $D_M S_M$ be non-negative and not greater than Y_M if the latter is positive.

For simplicity, in this section we assume that the company tax rate is the same as the tax rate on interest income received by individuals, and that there are no other taxes, so that

$$T_M = \gamma Y_M. \tag{14}$$

It is well known that under this assumption firms will be indifferent between debt financing and equity financing. Thus, we may set:

$$\dot{S}_M = 0; \qquad S_M(t) = S_M(0). \tag{15}$$

Using (11)–(15), the firm's objective can be written as:

$$\text{(P2)} \quad \underset{L_M, \dot{B}_M, I}{\text{Max}} \int_0^\infty [(1 - \gamma)(q_M F(K, L_M) - W_M L_M - rB_M)$$
$$+ \gamma \delta K - I + \dot{B}_M]\alpha(t)\,dt,$$

where

$$\alpha(t) \equiv \exp[-(1-\gamma)R(t)]. \tag{16}$$

The maximization is subject to:

$$\dot{K} = I - \delta K, \tag{17a}$$

$$K(0) = K_0 \text{ given}, \qquad B_M(0) \text{ given}, \tag{17b}$$

and

$$\lim_{t \to \infty} B_M(t)\alpha(t) = 0. \tag{18}$$

Condition (18) states that the firm cannot indefinitely service its debt by contracting more debt. Condition (18) is implied by the requirement that dividend payout be not greater than income.

Now from (9) and (16):

$$\int_0^t [\dot{B}_M - (1-\gamma)rB_M]\alpha(t')\,dt' = B_M(t)\alpha(t) - B_M(0). \tag{19}$$

Using (18) and (19), problem (P2) can be re-written as:

(P2') $\displaystyle\max_{I,L_M} \int_0^\infty [(1 - \gamma)(q_M F(K, L_M) - W_M L_M) + \gamma\delta K - I]\alpha(t)\,dt$

subject to (17a). The Hamiltonian of (P2') is:

$$H = \alpha(t)[(1-\gamma)(q_M F(K, L_M) - W_M L_M) + \gamma\delta K - I] + \psi(I-\delta K).$$

Along an interior solution, it is necessary that:

$$\alpha(t) = \psi(t), \tag{20}$$

$$q_M F_L = W_M, \tag{21}$$

and

$$\dot{\psi}_M = \delta\psi_M - \alpha(t)[(1-\gamma)q_M F_K + \gamma\delta]. \tag{22}$$

From (20) and (22):

$$(1-\gamma)r(t) = -\dot{\psi}_M/\psi_M = (1-\gamma)(q_M F_K - \delta), \tag{23}$$

which is basically the Johansson–Samuelson neutrality result.

2.4. *Taxing the extractive sector: A second-best problem*

Let us pause here and study the steady state of our economy under the assumption that there are no natural resource deposits. We assume for simplicity that the government uses the tax revenue to purchase manufacturing goods and distributes them to individuals. (One may think of "free books" distributed to school children.) This assumption is made because it is not our purpose to study the problem of optimal provision of public goods. Another simplifying assumption that will be adopted is that $U_M(C_M)$ and $U_E(C_E)$ are strictly concave and increasing functions, and that $U_R(C_R)$ is linear in C_R, so that by a suitable choice of units:

$$U'_R(C_R) = 1. \tag{24}$$

Using (7), (24), and the normalization given by (11), we obtain the condition determining the rate of interest:

$$r(t) = \rho/(1-\gamma), \quad \text{all } t, \tag{25}$$

provided that $C_R > 0$.

The steady-state equilibrium can be characterized by the following equations:

$$q_M^* = U_M'(C_M^*), \tag{26a}$$

$$C_M^* = F(K^*, \bar{L}_M), \tag{26b}$$

$$q_M^* F_K(K_M^*, \bar{L}_M) - \delta = r = \rho/(1-\gamma), \tag{26c}$$

$$C_R^* = \bar{L}_C - I^* = \bar{L}_C - \delta K^*. \tag{26d}$$

Assume that the economy is initially in a steady-state equilibrium, and that suddenly S resource deposits are found. Given that the rate of capital income tax γ is an immutable feature of the economy, the question we want to ask is whether, on efficiency grounds, the "true economic depreciation" of deposits should be allowed as a tax deduction.

At first sight, one might be tempted to answer the above question in the affirmative, as did Dasgupta and Heal (1979), Dasgupta, Heal and Stiglitz (1980), and many others who advocate "inter-sectoral neutrality". The argument for "inter-sectoral neutrality" typically runs as follows. In the absence of taxation, at each point of time the intertemporal rates of transformation are equated, i.e. the rates of return on all assets are equalized, so that

$$q_M F_K(K_M, L_M) - \delta = r = (\dot{q}_E - b\dot{W}_E)/(q_E - bW_E), \tag{27}$$

where the right-hand side of (27) is the rate of return from leaving the resource underground. In the presence of capital income taxation, since the first equality in condition (27) remains satisfied (see eq. (23)), it is argued that efficiency requires that the second equality in (27) be satisfied also.

The above argument rests on the presumption that the theorem on second best does not apply in this case. A close inspection of the properties of the present model suggests that the argument for inter-sectoral neutrality may be faulty. For the consumer's marginal intertemporal rate of substitution is no longer equated to the producers' marginal intertemporal rates of transformation when there is capital income taxation. This is reflected in the consumer's equilibrium condition (25).

We now set out to prove that in the context of our model, given that the presence of the tax rate γ is an immutable feature of the economy, it is better not to allow extractive firms to deduct economic depreciation from their taxable incomes.

Assume that the true economic depreciation is tax deductible in the extractive sector. The tax liability of the extractive firm is:

$$T_E = \gamma[(q_E - b)Q_E(t) - A(t) - rB_E(t)], \tag{28}$$

where $A(t)$ is the firm's true economic depreciation and B_E is its stock of debt. Since the value of the firm is

$$V(X(t), t) = (q_E(t) - b)X(t) \tag{29}$$

(where $X(t)$ is remaining stock at time t), the true economic depreciation is

$$A(t) = -\mathrm{d}V/\mathrm{d}t = -\dot{X}(q_E - b) - \dot{q}_E X \tag{30}$$

$$= Q_E(t)(q_E - b) - \dot{q}_E X. \tag{31}$$

The extractive firm's stream of dividend pay-out is:

$$D_E(t) = (q_E - b)Q_E - T_E - rB_E + \dot{B}_E. \tag{32}$$

Using (28), (31), and (32):

$$D_E(t) = (q_E - b)Q_E - \gamma \dot{q}_E X - r(1 - \gamma)B_E + \dot{B}_E. \tag{33}$$

By the same reasoning which led from (P2) to (P2′), the last two terms in (33) can be omitted and hence the firm's maximization problem can be written as

$$\text{(P3)} \quad \max_{Q_E} \int_0^\infty [(q_E - b)Q_E - \gamma \dot{q}_E X]\, \alpha(t)\, \mathrm{d}t,$$

where $\alpha(t)$ is given by (16) and where

$$\int_0^\infty Q_E(t)\, \mathrm{d}t \leq X_0, \qquad Q_E(t) \geq 0. \tag{34}$$

Transforming the integral constraint in (34) into the differential form,

$$\dot{X}(t) = -Q_E(t), \qquad X(0) = X_0,$$

$$\lim_{t \to \infty} X(t) \geq 0, \qquad Q_E(t) \geq 0, \tag{35}$$

we obtain the Hamiltonian:

$$H(t) = \alpha(t)[(q_E - b)Q_E - \gamma \dot{q}_E X] - \mu(t)Q_E. \tag{36}$$

The necessary conditions are:

$$(q_E - b)\alpha(t) - \mu(t) \leq 0 \quad (= 0, \quad \text{if } Q_E(t) > 0), \tag{37}$$

$$\dot{\mu} = -\partial H/\partial X = \gamma\alpha(t)\dot{q}_E. \tag{38}$$

Along a positive extraction path, condition (37) yields:

$$\dot{q}_E/(q_E - b) = (\dot{\mu}/\mu) - (\dot{\alpha}/\alpha). \tag{39}$$

Using (37), (38), and (39), we obtain:

$$\dot{q}_E/(q_E - b) = r(t). \tag{40}$$

Thus, if the true economic depreciation is an allowable tax deduction, the inter-sectoral neutrality condition (27) will hold (recall that $W_E(t) = q_R(t) = 1$). The path of consumption of the extractive good can be obtained using (40), (5), (24), and (25):

$$U_E''(Q_E)\dot{Q}_E/(U_E' - b) = \rho/(1 - \gamma). \tag{41}$$

Given our simplifying assumptions, it is clear that the manufacturing sector remains in its steady state described by (26a)–(26d).

We now show that the time path of consumption of the extractive good, as given by (41), is inferior to the outcome of the alternative tax regime which does not allow extractive firms to deduct true economic depreciation from the taxable incomes. Under this alternative tax regime, the stream of dividend payout by the representative extractive firm is:

$$D_E(t) = (1 - \gamma)(q_E - b)Q_E(t) - r(1 - \gamma)B_E + \dot{B}_E, \tag{42}$$

so that the firm's problem is:

$$(P4) \quad \max_{Q_E} \int_0^\infty (1 - \gamma)(q_E - b)Q_E(t)\alpha(t)\,dt,$$

subject to (35).

In this case, along a positive extraction path (with $Q_E(t) > 0$ for all t), it is necessary that rent rise at the net rate of interest:

$$\dot{q}_E/(q_E - b) = -\dot{\alpha}/\alpha = (1 - \gamma)r(t). \tag{43}$$

Since $U_E = q_E$, the consumption path is given by:

$$U_E''(Q_E)\dot{Q}_E/(U_E' - b) = (1 - \gamma)r(t) = \rho. \tag{44}$$

It remains to show that the consumption path given by (44) is superior to that given by (41). Since in both cases the paths of consumption of the manufacturing goods are identical, it suffices to show that (44) is the solution of the following centralized maximization problem:

(P5)   max $\int\limits_{0}^{\infty} [U_E(Q_E) + U_R(Q_R)] \exp(-\rho t)\, dt$

subject to (35) and

$$Q_R = \bar{L}_C - \delta K^* - bQ_E. \tag{45}$$

It is a routine matter to see that (P5) yields condition (44).

To summarize our result, we state the following proposition:

Proposition 2.1.   Under the assumptions of the model, it is suboptimal to allow extractive firms to deduct the economic depreciation from their taxable incomes, although capital income in the rest of the economy is taxed according to the Schanz–Haig–Simons rules.

The economic common sense behind our result is that since consumers equate the marginal rate of time preference to the net rate of interest, $(1-\gamma)r(t)$, while the allowance of economic depreciation in the manufacturing sector makes producers equate the net marginal product of capital with the gross rate of interest, $r(t)$, it is not necessarily desirable to achieve inter-sectoral neutrality. To allow true economic depreciation allowance in the extractive sector would induce that sector to choose an extraction path which equates the rate of return on holding the resource with the gross rate of interest, $r(t)$. This would result in too rapid an extraction path, since $r(t)$ is greater than the equilibrium rate of time preference, $(1-\gamma)r(t)$.

The assertion that "economic efficiency requires that some depletion allowance be provided" (see Dasgupta, Heal and Stiglitz (1980, p. 160)), is, in general, incorrect. More generally, "inter-sectoral neutrality", which is advocated by many authors, should not be accepted – without qualification – as a desirable criterion for judging tax rules.

Our model relies on the separability of the utility function and the partial separability of the production structure. Perhaps in a model where these restrictions are removed, there would be a trade-off between intersectoral neutrality on the one hand, and the equality between the rate of time preference and the rate of increase of rent on the other hand.

It is clear from our model that an efficient second-best taxation is a tax on the real cash flow of the mining firm, which at the same time allows the tax deductibility of the interest the mining firm pays to its creditors. Note that this tax is not the same as the Brown tax which is the optimal first-best tax in the absence of taxes on other sources of capital income, and which requires that debt interest be non-deductible from the tax base (see Brown (1948) and Garnaut and Clunies Ross (1979)). Thus we can state:

Proposition 2.2.   An efficient second-best tax on the extractive firm is a tax on real cash flow where the tax rate equals that on interest income and interest is tax deductible.

3. The effect of other taxes

In this section we examine the effects of some other forms of taxation, using the model developed in the preceding section.

3.1. *A tax on capital gains in the extractive sector*

True economic depreciation allowance is in fact a form of capital gains tax, if capital gains are defined as the negative of the true economic depreciation. Another form of capital gains tax is a tax at the rate $\gamma > 0$ on the increase in the value of the existing stock, ignoring the fact that the stock is being depleted at the rate $Q_E(t)$. This form of taxation is considered in Sinn (1980, sections 4.5 and 4.6). If it is assumed that debt interest is deductible to ensure an interior financial equilibrium of the firm, the representative extractive firm's tax liability is:

$$T_E(t) = \gamma(\dot{q}_E X - rB_E). \tag{46}$$

Inserting (46) into (32) again gives eq. (33) for the dividend payout. As a result, this form of taxation is equivalent to a tax on profit with true economic depreciation.

The economic reason for this equivalence is that true economic depreciation is equivalent to the taxation of unrealized capital gains, $\dot{q}_E X - Q_E(q_E - b)$, and that the increase in the value of the existing stock, $\dot{q}_E X$, is the sum of unrealized and realized capital gains, where the latter equals the net revenue from current extraction, $Q_E(q_E - b)$.

From proposition 2.1 it follows that, given the assumptions of the present model, it is suboptimal to supplement a Schanz–Haig–Simons tax applied to capital income in general by a tax on realized and unrealized capital gains in the resource sector.

3.2. *An additional tax on dividends*

It has been shown that a tax on the real cash flow of the mining firm (with debt interest being tax deductible) is efficient in the second-best sense. But this is not the only efficient form of taxation.

Another tax with this property is a tax on the dividend payout by the mining firm. Such a tax has been suggested by the Meade Committee (1978) for corporations in general and has been studied by King (1974), Auerbach (1979), Bradford (1981), and Sinn (1982) in various contexts. Assume that the efficient profit tax considered in section 2.4 is levied and let γ^* denote the additional tax for corporate distributions. Then, instead of (42), the dividend payout of the mining firm is:

$$D_E(t) = (1-\gamma^*)[(1-\gamma)(q_E-b)Q_E - r(1-\gamma)B_E + \dot{B}_E], \tag{47}$$

and the firm's maximization problem becomes

$$(P6) \quad \max_{Q_E, \dot{B}_E} \int_0^\infty (1-\gamma^*)[1-\gamma)(q_E-b)Q_E - r(1-\gamma)B_E + \dot{B}_E]\alpha(t)\,dt$$

subject to (35) and

$$\lim_{t\to\infty} B_E(t)\alpha(t) = 0. \tag{48}$$

Since the term $(1-\gamma^*)$ is a constant it obviously does not affect the solution of the optimization problem. Moreover, because of (19) and (48), the value of the integral does not depend on the time path of debt. Thus, the firm is indifferent between paying dividends and reducing its stock of debt. Hence the solution of (P6) is identical to that of (P4). It follows that the tax on the distributions of the mining firm is efficient, given the structure of our model and given an immutable Schanz–Haig–Simons tax on other sources of capital income.

3.3 *The effects of a sales tax and/or a production-based royalty on the extractive firms*

Production-based royalities and sales taxes are of great practical importance. We therefore study the question of how such taxes should be designed from the point of view of second-best efficiency.

Assume that extractive firms have to pay $\mu_E(t)$ dollars per unit of extraction, and that the royalty payments $\mu_E(t)Q_E(t)$ can be offset against income tax. Then the firm's dividend payout is:

$$D_E(t) = (1 - \gamma)(q_E - b)Q_E - r(1 - \gamma)B_E + \dot{B}_E - (1 - \gamma)\mu_E(t)Q_E. \quad (49)$$

Clearly, $\mu_E(t)$ can also be interpreted as a per-unit sales tax, in which case $q_E(t)$ is the price gross of tax and $q_E(t) - \mu_E(t)$ is the price net of tax. Alternatively, define

$$P_E(t) = q_E(t) - \mu_E(t), \quad (50)$$

and define $\theta(t)$ by

$$q_E(t) = [1 + \theta(t)]P_E(t), \quad (51)$$

then

$$\mu_E(t) = [\theta(t)/(1+\theta(t)]q_E(t), \quad (52)$$

so that any equilibrium gross price path $q_E(t)$ which results from the imposition of a per-unit sales tax path $\mu_E(t)$ can also be obtained by imposing an ad valorem sales tax at rate $\theta(t)$, where $\theta(t)$ is suitably chosen so that (52) is satisfied.

Under the assumption of zero extraction cost, Kemp and Long (1980, essay 17, pp. 207–208), and Sinn (1980, section 4.2) have shown that a constant ad valorem tax rate $\theta \leq 1$ has no effect on the extraction path and hence no effect on the gross price path $q_E(t)$. In that special case, $\mu_E(t)$ rises at the net rate of interest:

$$\dot{\mu}_E/\mu_E = -\dot{\alpha}/\alpha = (1-\gamma)r(t). \quad (53)$$

Condition (53) is also necessary and sufficient for the neutrality of the per-unit sales tax path $\mu_E(t)$ in the more general case where extraction cost is non-zero, and in fact even when the average extraction cost b is dependent on the remaining stock $X(t)$. If b is stock-independent, the proof of this proposition is simple (see Dasgupta and Heal (1979, p. 364), for an arbitrage type of argument). We now offer a more general proof which allows for the possibility that $b = b(X(t))$.

In the absence of the tax $\mu_E(t)$, the Hamiltonian of the firm's maximization problem is:

$$H_0 = \alpha(t)(1-\gamma)[q_E(t) - b(X)]Q_E(t) - \mu_0(t)Q_E(t), \quad (54)$$

where $\mu_0(t)$ is the shadow price of the resource deposit. If $Q_E^*(t) > 0$ until the exhaustion date T_0, then the optimal path is characterized by the conditions:

$$\alpha(t)(1-\gamma)[q_E(t) - b(X)] = \mu_0(t), \tag{55}$$

$$\dot{\mu}_0(t) = \alpha(t)(1-\gamma)b'(X)Q_E, \tag{56}$$

and

$$\mu_0(T_0) \geq 0, \qquad X(T_0) \geq 0, \qquad \mu_0(T_0)X(T_0) = 0. \tag{57}$$

In the presence of the sales tax path $\mu_E(t) \neq 0$, the Hamiltonian is:

$$H_1(t) = \alpha(t)(1-\gamma)[q_E(t) - b(X) - \mu_E(t)]Q_E(t) - \mu_1(t)Q_E(t), \tag{54'}$$

and the counterparts of (55)–(57) are:

$$\alpha(t)(1-\gamma)[q_E(t) - b(X) - \mu_E(t)] = \mu_1(t), \tag{55'}$$

$$\dot{\mu}_1(t) = \alpha(t)(1-\gamma)b'(X)Q_E, \tag{56'}$$

and

$$\mu_1(T_1) \geq 0, \qquad X(T_1) \geq 0, \qquad \mu_1(T_1)X(T_1) = 0. \tag{57'}$$

Clearly, the necessary and sufficient conditions for the time paths $q_E(t)$ and $b(X(t))$ to be the same in both cases are:

$$\alpha(t)\mu_E(t) = \text{constant} = \alpha(0)\mu_E(0), \tag{58}$$

$$0 \leq \mu_1(t) = \mu_0(t) - \alpha(t)\mu_E(t)(1-\gamma). \tag{59}$$

In other words, if the sales tax path $\mu_E(t)$ is such that

$$\mu_0(T_0) - \alpha(T_0)\mu_E(T_0)(1 - \gamma) \geq 0,$$

and if $\mu_E(t)$ rises at the rate $(1 - \gamma)r(t)(\equiv -\dot{\alpha}(t)/\alpha(t))$, then the sales tax is only a tax on pure rent. In the special case where the deposit is not exhausted, $\mu_0(T_0) = 0$ and hence $\mu_E(t) = 0$ for all t.

From (52) and (58), an ad valorem sales tax is neutral only if the proportional rate of change of $\theta(t)/[1+\theta(t)]$ equals

$$\chi(t) \equiv (1-\gamma)r(t) - (\dot{q}_E/q_E),$$

which is different from zero if extraction cost is positive.

4. Concluding remarks

The basic point of this essay, which goes far beyond the natural resource problem, is to raise doubt on the applicability of the fundamental Johansson–Samuelson theorem of taxation theory. Too much has been claimed by some authors when referring to this theorem.

The false interpretation seems to originate from Samuelson himself, for he claimed that his theorem implied the desirability of economic depreciation and the taxation of all kinds of capital gains. This claim is justified in a very limited sense only. It is certainly true that economic depreciation ensures the inter-sectoral neutrality of a general income tax. However, inter-sectoral neutrality is only desirable in a first-best world where the consumer's saving decision is not distorted, i.e. where the right volume of the overall stock of resources is transferred to the future. In the presence of an interest income tax, which is a crucial assumption underlying the Johansson–Samuelson theorem, this condition is not met because the interest income tax clearly distorts saving decisions.

The second-best taxation problem which is studied in this essay and to which the Johansson–Samuelson theorem is often applied is whether saving in the form of natural resources should be penalized, given that the penalization of saving in the form of capital goods is an immutable fact. Most authors implicitly suggest that the solution to this problem is to penalize saving in the form of natural resources, too. This amounts to telling the farmer to kill his cow when his sheep has died. The present approach, instead, recommends to keep the cow alive, i.e. not to discourage the preservation of natural resources through true economic depreciation allowances or the taxation of capital gains, even though too few capital goods of other kinds are left to future generations.

We do not deny that our recommendation rests on the special assumption of a separable utility function. However, this assumption, albeit special, is not at the extremes, but is rather somewhere in the middle of the spectrum of possibilities. If cows and sheep are complements, then one may conjecture that the optimal policy for the farmer is to kill the cow (i.e. a tax system that discourages the conservation of resources may be appropriate). If, on the other hand, cows and sheep are substitutes, there is an even stronger reason for prolonging the life of the cow, and resource conservation should be encouraged. Perhaps, rather than deducting economic depreciation from the tax base, it might be better to add it to the tax base in this case.

The analysis in this essay was conducted without imposing a government revenue constraint. We assumed that the tax revenue is used to buy manufactured goods for distribution to private consumers, but we did not require that the taxation of the resource sector bring about a given present value of tax revenue. The reason is that we wanted to study the problem in the way it was posed by Dasgupta, Heal and Stiglitz, in order to check the validity of their findings. Our basic result, that true economic depreciation allowance is suboptimal, stays unchanged if such a revenue constraint is imposed. For, by a suitable choice of the dividend tax rate γ^*, as studied in section 3.2, we can attain the target revenue without changing the extraction path, provided of course that the tax burden is sufficiently low to be compatible with positive share prices of mining firms.

All of this shows how little is known about the structure of dynamically efficient tax systems. There has been a decade of intensive work in the static theory of optimal taxation, but it seems obvious to us that basic results achieved are not directly transferrable to dynamic economies by a mere reinterpretation of variables. Interest income, depreciation allowances, capital gains taxation and the like are aspects to which there are no counterparts in static models. Hopefully, the next decade will be devoted to a discussion of the numerous problems in dynamic taxation theory that are yet to be solved.

References

Auerbach, A. J. (1979), Wealth maximization and the cost of capital, Quarterly Journal of Economics 93, 433–466.

Auerbach. A. J. (1982), Tax neutrality and the social discount rate, Journal of Public Economics 17, 355–372.

Bradford, D. F. (1981), The incidence and allocative effect of a tax on corporate distributions, Journal of Public Economics 15, 1–22.

Brown, E. C. (1948), Business income taxation and investment incentives, in: L. A. Metzler et al., eds., Income, Employment, and Public Policy (Norton, New York).

Dasgupta, P. S. and G. M. Heal (1979), Economic Theory and Exhaustible Resources (James Nisbet & Co., Digswell Place, Welwyn).

Dasgupta, P. S., G. M. Heal and J. E. Stiglitz (1980), The taxation of exhaustible resources, in: G. A. Hughes and G. M. Heal, eds. Public Policy and the Tax System (George Allen & Unwin, London).

Fisher, I. and H. W. Fisher (1942), Constructive Income Taxation: A Proposal for Reform (Harper, New York).

Garnaut, R. and A. Clunies Ross, (1979), The neutrality of resource rent tax, Economic Record 55, 193–201.

Goode, R. (1977), The economic definition of income, in: J. A. Pechman, ed., Comprehensive Income Taxation (Brookings Institute, Washington).

Institute for Fiscal Studies (1978), The Structure and Reform of Direct Taxation; Report of a Committee chaired by Professor J. E. Meade (Allen & Unwin, London).

Johansson, S. E. (1961), Skatt – investering – värdering (Stockholm).

Johansson, S. E. (1969), Income taxes and investment decisions, The Swedish Journal of Economics 71, 104–110.

Kaldor, N. (1959), An Expenditure Tax (Allen & Unwin, London).

Kay, J. A. and M. A. King (1978), The British Tax System (Oxford University Press, Oxford).

King, M. A. (1974), Dividend behaviour and the theory of the firm, Economica, 41, 25–34.

Kemp, M. C. and N. V. Long (1980), Exhaustible Resources, Optimality, and Trade (North-Holland Publishing Company, Amsterdam).

Samuelson, P. A. (1964), Tax deductibility of economic depreciation to insure invariant valuations, Journal of Political Economy 72, 604–606.

Sinn, H.-W. (1980), Besteuerung, Wachstum and Ressourcenabbau: Ein allgemeiner Gleichgewichtsansatz, in: H. Siebert, ed., Erschöpfbare Ressourcen (Duncker and Humblot, Berlin). English translation: Taxation, growth and resource extraction. A general equilibrium approach, European Economic Review 19 (1982) 357–386.

Sinn, H.-W. (1982), Besteuerung, Wachstum und Kapitalstruktur, habilitation thesis, University of Mannheim (forthcoming: Mohr, Tubingen).

Swan, P. L. (1976), Income taxes, profit taxes and neutrality of optimizing decision, Economic Record 52, 166–181.

Author Index

248

Ohlin, B.   165
Ohyama, M.   222
Okuguchi, K.   27, 189

Pazner, E. A.   219
Preinreich, G.   165

Ray, D.   27
Razin, A.   219
Reinganum, J. F.   189, 212
Reiss, W.   220
Robson, A.   6
Ross, A. C.   228, 240
Russell, W. R.   222

Samuelson, P. A.   163, 165, 186, 219, 229,
    235, 243, 244
Schanz, G.   228, 229, 231, 239, 241
Schmalensee, R.   200
Scott, A.   3
Shimomura, K.   13, 29, 40, 75
Siebert, H.   4
Simons, H.   228, 229, 231, 239, 241
Sinn, H.-W.   105, 189, 199, 200, 205, 209,
    210, 212, 217, 227, 240, 241, 242

Solow, R. M.   4, 5, 6, 13, 14, 17, 32, 57, 75
Starr, A. W.   212
Stiglitz, J. E.   6, 138, 200, 228, 229, 230,
    236, 239, 244
Stokey, N. L.   189, 212
Suzuki, H.   5, 6, 13, 25
Swan, P. L.   228
Sweeney, J. L.   219

Tawada, M.   27

Ulph, A.   105

Wan, F. Y.   6, 57, 75
Wan, H. Y.   163, 165
Watkins, G. C.   200, 213
Weinstein, M. C.   7, 196, 200, 217, 218,
    220, 221, 222
Weitzman, M. L.   199
Wicksell, K.   163, 166, 174

Young, L.   217

Zeckhauser, R. J.   7, 196, 200, 217, 218,
    220, 221, 222

Subject Index